the
Effective Practice
of MINISTRY

the
Effective Practice
of MINISTRY

ESSAYS IN MEMORY OF
CHARLES SIBURT

Tim Sensing, editor

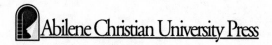
Abilene Christian University Press

The Effective Practice of Ministry

Essays in Memory of Charles Siburt

Tim Sensing, editor

ACU
PRESS

Copyright © 2013 by Abilene Christian University Press

ISBN 978-0-89112-328-6
LCCN 2013010040

Scripture quotations marked NIV are taken from The Holy Bible, New International Version®, NIV®
Copyright © 1973, 1978, 1984, 2011 by Biblica, Inc.™ Used by permission. All rights reserved
worldwide.

Scripture quotations marked NIV1984 are taken from The Holy Bible, New International Version®,
NIV® Copyright © 1973, 1978, 1984 by Biblica, Inc.™ Used by permission. All rights reserved
worldwide.

Scripture quotations marked NRSV are taken from the New Revised Standard Version Bible,
copyright © 1989 the Division of Christian Education of the National Council of the Churches of
Christ in the United States of America. Used by permission. All rights reserved.

Scripture quotations marked RSV are taken from the Revised Standard Version of the Bible, copyright © 1946, 1952, and 1971 the Division of Christian Education of the National Council of the
Churches of Christ in the United States of America. Used by permission. All rights reserved.

LIBRARY OF CONGRESS CATALOGING-IN-PUBLICATION DATA
The effective practice of ministry : essays in memory of Charles Siburt / editor, Tim Sensing.
       pages cm
   Includes bibliographical references and index.
   ISBN 978-0-89112-328-6 (alk. paper)
   1. Pastoral theology. 2. Church work. I. Sensing, Tim. (Timothy R.), 1959-
   BV4011.3.E39 2013
   253--dc23

2013010040

Printed in the United States of America

Cover design by Sandy Armstrong
Interior text design by Becky Hawley Design

For information contact:
Abilene Christian University Press
1626 Campus Court
Abilene, Texas 79601

1-877-816-4455 toll free
www.abilenechristianuniversitypress.com

In Memory of Charles Siburt

The contributors to this volume esteem Charles
as their trusted friend, mentor, and teacher.

Contents

Foreword

ROYCE MONEY

Dr. Charles A. Siburt was an extraordinary Christian man. Minister, scholar, mentor, friend, innovative leader, and peacemaker are only a few of the descriptors of my friend. We saw him live among us, and we saw the spirit of Jesus in every dimension of his life. And we saw him battle a rare form of cancer for nearly three years, facing the dreaded disease with courage, determination, and faith. Charlie was a great storyteller. And his own story is one filled with insights that inspire us to grow in the likeness of Jesus.

Upbringing and Calling

Charlie was born November 27, 1946, in Denison, Texas. He grew up as a preacher's kid: his father served as minister to churches across Texas and New Mexico. The youngest of three children and the only son of Austin and Imogene Siburt, Charlie made a decision to follow in his father's footsteps. After graduating from Midland High School in 1964, Charlie attended Lubbock Christian University, earning an associate's degree in 1966.

It was there that he met Judy Bailey of San Diego, California, who is an important part of our story. They were married December 28, 1967. Charlie and Judy transferred to Abilene Christian University, and they graduated in 1968. He began his graduate work at ACU and earned the MDiv in 1971 and later a DMin degree from Austin Presbyterian Theological Seminary in 1978. Driven by his love for people and his desire to assist them in crisis, Charlie also did advanced work in counseling and in conflict resolution.

After graduating in 1971, Charlie and Judy began their full-time ministry, just as Charlie's father had done. They served various churches in Texas and Colorado, and were involved in a successful ministry at the Glenwood Church of Christ in Tyler when my "formal" contact with them began. I was chairman of the Graduate Bible Department at ACU, the precursor to the Graduate School of

Theology. I had followed Charlie and Judy and their career in ministry and was certain that Charlie needed to be on the faculty at ACU because of his remarkable gifts for ministry. So I went to Tyler and tried my best to lure Charlie and Judy to ACU, but to no avail.

Not one for giving up on a good idea, I renewed the conversation and the offer two years later in 1988. To my surprise, Charlie was receptive and after a short time accepted our offer to come to ACU. We had asked him to serve as a full-time faculty member in the Graduate Bible Department, to teach ministry courses, and head up the brand new Doctor of Ministry program.

Later on, I asked Charles, "What made the difference between your refusal in 1986 and your acceptance in 1988?" He replied:

> My father's funeral. All that time since our initial conversation two years earlier, I thought about what you said, that ACU would represent an opportunity for me to multiply my ministry and influence to many more preachers and other church leaders than if I were in local congregational ministry. Then I thought of my father. He had spent his life ministering faithfully to smaller congregations, and that was a good thing. But here [at ACU] was a rare opportunity for me to be a minister, teacher, and mentor to many young ministers, church leaders, and those in full-time ministry. The platform of influence is much bigger. And at my father's funeral, I saw that insight and decided that if I still had the opportunity at ACU, I would take it.

It was easy for Charlie and Judy and for several of us at ACU to see the hand of God in all these deliberations. At the time, however, it was not as easy for the good people of the Glenwood Church of Christ in Tyler, Texas to see it. In fact, it took a while for them to forgive me for "stealing" the Siburt family. Charlie even advised me to stay out of Tyler for a time until things settled down. I have been back since and was warmly received by the Glenwood folks. They too saw that they were a part of God's larger plan for Charlie, Judy, John, and Ben. Charlie and Judy and their family were greatly loved. Yet, we would all now agree that in this transition from the Glenwood church to ACU, Charlie and Judy came once again to understand God's clear call for them, apart from all others. I am grateful to the elders of the Glenwood Church of Christ for underwriting the publication of this tribute volume.

And so the Siburt family moved to ACU in 1988, and things have never been the same. I soon found out that the best way for Charlie to work was to give him a lot of room and let him exercise his gifts. He could be a team player when the occasion called for it, but Charlie was somewhat of a free spirit who needed to soar on the wings of the will of God. And soar he did!

It is difficult to talk of Charlie's so-called handicaps, particularly with his vision problems, because he so masterfully overcame them. We obtained a computer that could essentially read books to him. Charlie was amazing. You see, due to a degenerative eye condition, Charlie was legally blind during his time at ACU. His capacity for memorization and for remembering facts, events, and people is legendary. His sense of humor about his physical limitations was an indication to all that Charlie had decided, as the Apostle Paul did, that these matters were not going to hinder his calling from the Lord. He became an inspiration to students, colleagues, and countless friends with his positive attitude, his keen wit, and his thorough knowledge of his subject matter.

Accomplishments

I recently began a list of the various things in which Charles was involved. In addition to his outstanding teaching career, Charlie focused on things such as: congregational assessments, research on a variety of ministry-related topics, leadership training, conflict management, ministry search consultation, and preaching (one of the best I ever heard). He was a counselor, therapist, confidant to hundreds of ministers and elders, and on and on the list goes. For a short period of time, he directed the ACU Bible Teachers Workshop and was director of the off-campus graduate programs, as well the director of the Doctor of Ministry program.

Then, there was the beginning of ElderLink fifteen years ago, a ministry focused on giving local church elders the necessary tools to be servant leaders. He was also the leader in developing the Ministers' Support Network, an intensive retreat program for ministry couples to encourage them in their calling.

Charlie had advanced counseling and therapy credentials—the highest he could obtain. He did post-doctoral work in conflict resolution, focusing especially on conflict within churches (in the rare event that such a thing should ever occur, Charlie would say). The following is a sample of Dr. Siburt's twenty-four-year career at ACU:[1]

- Charlie was a member of fifteen professional organizations (an *active* member, attending the annual meetings).
- He served on forty-four different committees at ACU, including the Presidential Search Advisory Committee, and as an advisor to the Purpose and Governance Committee of the ACU Board of Trustees— primarily because he knew so many people, and he was full of wisdom.

- He served as Vice President for Church Relations for six years (2004–2010), and during that time was on the senior leadership team of the university.
- Charlie last served ACU as Associate Dean for Ministry Programs and Services.
- Charlie was an active and involved elder during most of the last twenty-four years.
- He served on at least five community boards, including a stint on the Hospice of Abilene board.
- He wrote numerous articles for books and journals and co-authored several books on Christian leadership.
- Charles was instrumental in obtaining a comprehensive health-care plan for full-time ministers—a much-needed service. The organization he helped create to administer the plan is called Christian Leaders Benefits Alliance.
- He published annually a report on ministers' compensation, giving many local congregational leaders a comparison base for appropriate support of their ministry staff.
- He designed and administered numerous survey and assessment instruments involving several aspects of church leadership and congregational life.
- He gave presentations, workshops, and church consultations all over the country (and occasionally beyond), numbering into the hundreds.

By this time you may have guessed that Charlie was a meticulous record keeper, with dates, topics, and locations for all this information. According to American Airlines, Charles logged more than one million miles (a conservative estimate). That is not counting all the other airlines. Sometimes Judy was with him, but many times he went alone. For a number of years, Charlie was gone thirty or more weekends a year, assisting churches and their leaders. In 1998 Charles was awarded the O. L. and Irene Frazer Professorship for Church Enrichment, a position he occupied until his death. During his tenure, Charles received several awards and recognitions from his first alma mater, Lubbock Christian University, and from Abilene Christian, Pepperdine, Herald of Truth Ministries, and several others.

I must mention the thousands of phone calls Charlie would receive from preachers, former students, elders and a variety of other people seeking his advice on a wide range of topics. It was not uncommon for him to receive several of these calls a day. His vast network of friends and associates is nothing short of incredible.

Charlie's "Other" Side

To complete the picture of Charles Siburt, we should perhaps mention one other dimension of his personality of which some may not be aware. Through the years, he developed a nickname that may need a bit of explaining. At times, he was referred to as "Chain-saw Charlie." This kind, gentle man with a booming voice and big smile, whom people *thought* they knew, had another side. He had a unique way of communicating difficult messages to people who needed to hear them. He had a way of jarring certain people into reality.

For example, Charlie was telling me one time about a young minister who called him in a real crisis. The preacher said, "Dr. Siburt, I've just been fired at my church, and I don't understand what happened. What do you think it means?" Charlie replied, "It *means* you don't have a job!" And then Charlie in typical fashion followed up with some advice on what to do next, along with a generous amount of encouragement.

Some of Charlie's pronouncements and sayings were rather vivid, shall we say, but they were often humorous and always insightful, accurate, and full of wisdom. Rest assured that these hard sayings were always couched in redemptive terms. They were designed to jolt people out of denial and confusion into reality so that they could take whatever steps were necessary toward recovery and resolution. With certainty, I can say that these "Charlie-isms" will be repeated among his friends and admirers for a long time.

Charlie and the Golf Cart

One of my all-time favorite stories about Charlie I will call "When Charlie Drove." A few years ago, my wife, Pam, and I were in Hawaii with Charlie and Judy, Tom and Sandra Milholland, and Tony and Barbara Ash—all of us longtime friends. Tom and I decided to play golf one day, so I asked Charlie if he would like to ride along in my cart. He said he would love to do that. When I wheeled up to the first tee box, I said, "Charlie, why don't you just drive the golf cart. There is a nice brown cart path to follow. You simply have to keep the left side of the cart on the edge of the brown path. He looked at me with delight and said, "You would really do that?" I paused a second and said, "Yes." He added, "I can be your ball spotter too." We all laughed.

Charlie could not wait to get started. I resolved to myself that I would do my best not to touch the steering for the entire round. We agreed that I would give Charlie some "coaching" and verbal instructions, in order to keep him posted on what lay ahead. Now this golf course was not flat—it was built on top of some cliffs bordering on the Pacific Ocean. It was an interesting ride!

When we got to about the fifteenth hole, a long way from the clubhouse, up came one of those sudden summer showers that are frequent in Hawaii. Charlie said, "What should we do?" I said, "Drive on. A deal is a deal. We will have to make it back to the clubhouse the best we can, and you are still the driver."

So off we went, getting soaked in the process. Charlie got us there safely, complete with a triumphant smile that he wore the rest of the day. And I never touched the wheel of the golf cart, even though I thought about it a time or two. Upon reflection, that incident no doubt strengthened my belief in guardian angels—either Charlie's or mine!

Disease, Faith, and Faithfulness

In the last year of Charlie's life, we witnessed his determination and his faith up close. We saw his heroic and courageous teaching of his graduate ministry classes in late May and early June, just a few weeks before his death. These stories are already legendary, how Charles would come literally from the hospital and go directly to class. Sometimes he returned to the hospital after class for additional treatments so that he could teach the next day.

His courage and determination to regain his stamina from the onset of his illness, time after time, so that he could teach, consult, and encourage others, is amazing. When I would ask Charlie what he wanted me to pray for, he would always say, "Courage." Well, Charlie, God gave you courage, and a lot more. And as a result of your example, we have courage in us—we are *encouraged* by your example and by your tremendous faith in God.

Finally, I want to pay tribute to Judy. She has been for all these years a true partner in ministry with Charlie, and she has done it with class and with at least an equal amount of conviction of her own calling from the Lord as Charlie had of his. Charlie would say she had more. She was the love and inspiration of his life. She has been courageous and faithful and encouraging in the most trying of circumstances, a true yokefellow in doing God's work. On behalf of all of us who admire and appreciate her and Charlie, I say thank you. We notice, and we are inspired by her love for Charlie and their dedication to kingdom matters.

And to John and Ben, not only Charles's sons in this world, but also sons in the Lord, who are carrying on their father's legacy in such a fine way through lives of ministry. Their father could not have been more proud of them. He told me so many times. The legacy of Dr. Charles Siburt will live on in their lives and in the lives of thousands of people whose lives he has touched in transforming ways.

Doxology

During the last week of Charlie's life, Judy said to me as we were leaving his room in the hospital, "Can you imagine a world without Charles Siburt?" I said, "No." Now I cannot imagine a heaven without him. From John's Revelation: "Then I heard a voice from heaven say, 'Write this: Blessed are the dead who die in the Lord from now on. 'Yes,' says the Spirit, 'they will rest from their labor, for their deeds will follow them.'" (14:13 NIV) Praise be to God for the victory! May God bless the memory of Charles A. Siburt, whose works shall live on for many generations to come.

Eulogy, July 14, 2012

————————————————

[1] See Appendix C.

Preface

TIM SENSING

The Doctor of Ministry (DMin) degree culminates with a final thesis and an oral defense. In the DMin, the final thesis describes and evaluates a participatory action research project.[1] Often referred to as a project thesis, this capstone experience is an application of contextual theology designed to foster the effective practice of ministry. Contextual theology is an ecclesiology shaped by the incarnation of God at a particular place during a specific time.

My own DMin project thesis came into view in my reflexive look at my embedded context.[2] Additionally, I read homiletical literature that molded my theological core identity and method. My prior preaching habits addressed my needs for finding the right sermon form, uncovering the accurate analysis of the text, and performing the script in such a way as to teach, delight, and move the audience for the sake of the gospel. Yet, while churches affirmed my preaching ministry, I saw little transformation in the lives of people. As one church leader informed me, "People will always do what they want to do." The literature claimed that newer approaches to homiletics would increase listener participation in the sermon process and suggested such involvement would impact their faith and change their way of being in the world. Through my engagement in the DMin project, my preaching changed, and so did the congregation's response to my preaching. Through my DMin experience, I became an intentional reflective practitioner.

What distinguishes between an expert and a novice?[3] The literature points to the twin assets of *sapience* and *habitus*. Experts have a shared wisdom and practice that enables others to follow their example. For instance, an expert archaeologist could possibly spend her entire career traveling the well-worn path between library and lecture hall, but I doubt many graduates would emerge under this educational setting alone who would go on to make important discoveries in the field. Rather, lifelong learning happens when the professor takes her class to the desert and points to a distant horizon, exclaiming, "Do you see it? Just over the ridge, north of the ravine, is a tell. Under that mound we will dig." The expert embodies the practice.

Best practices in any field are not simply a set of effective actions, but a comprehensive and coherent set of practices that are steeped in context-specific theory. Best practices in practical theology are the result of intentional reflective actions accomplished by excellent performers that are significant, sustainable, and transferable in the life of the church. Although DMin projects are designed with one particular context in mind, the wider field (the universal church) should be kept in close proximity. The standards for the DMin degree require that projects be public and useable to make a professional contribution to the church.[4]

At the heart of DMin programs is the intent that projects enhance ministerial practice and be applicable to other practitioners in the field. Charles Conniry argues that DMin education enhances the skills of pastors and leaders and serves the church and its leaders in the actualization of the vision of the degree.[5] Likewise, Barbara Horkoff Mutch sees DMin education as a means to professional knowing ("knowing-in-action" and "reflection-in-action").[6] DMin professional knowledge should be shared with the various publics served by DMin programs. The projects selected for this book not only exemplify the intent of the standards, but also, according to their faculty, exceed those standards and display the best practices of effective ministry.

The contributors to *The Effective Practice of Ministry* graduated from Abilene Christian University's Doctor of Ministry program directed by Charles Siburt. These authors took time from their work to honor Charles's memory and practice in both the academy and church. They looked to him as their mentor and friend. In him, they saw God's continuing activity with people.

Effective Practice recounts best practices in congregational life in order to exemplify pragmatic articulations of beliefs about ministry in action. The interventions were chosen because they demonstrated effective practices of incarnational ministry. The qualitative research methods employed by these practitioners verify that these interventions are valid (determined to be methodologically and theoretically sound). Therefore, all of these best practices suggest that these interventions will work or be adaptable in other similar locations.

The projects described here, represent the most common topics in the DMin program at ACU: spiritual formation, leadership development, catechesis, preaching, and missional initiatives in the larger community. For example, in Chapter One John Siburt addresses church leadership development by exploring virtue formation. No chapter in the book exemplifies the heart of Charles's work more than his son's work in helping leaders become more effective in their service. Closely related, in Chapters Two and Three Aaron Walling and John Grant describe ways congregations can enhance the elder-selection process by increasing the opportunities for reflective discernment on the part of candidates.

Chapters Four through Seven describe educational ministries that take catechesis seriously. Carson E. Reed roots catechetical ministries in a clearer understanding of the Bible's relationship to church practices. Bert Reynolds follows in the next chapter in a project designed to help Bible class teachers implement a curriculum of spiritual formation. Chris Smith and Tommy King have similar projects that prepare congregations to address faith formation in children. Smith's chapter describes a parent training class that fosters a better theology of baptism for children. Emerging from a theology of children, King developed a Faith Decisions class designed to assist families as they journey towards discipleship.

With an increasing appreciation for the church's need to address marginalized people groups, Chapters Eight through Ten explore various congregational responses. Jerry Shields leads a team into concrete ways a congregation can practice hospitality to strangers. Dan Bouchelle utilizes the many-faceted ways the Bible presents good news to reach various intercultural groups living in the church's neighborhood. And in a controversial political climate, Stephen Austin finds faithful ways to respond to the needs of undocumented folk in Houston.

The final three chapters also showcase projects that interject new life into the ongoing work of God's people. Jonathan W. Camp addresses the widening gap between the generations at a large church by exploring the theology of God's household. Allen Burris turns the question, "What is the matter with preaching?" to address the responsibility of congregational hearing. Finally, John Knox develops an initiative that enables the local congregation to become a critical response team in times of community crisis. The authors of these DMin project theses aspire to honor God's actions in the world by entering local communities with the gospel for the sake of others. Many other ACU DMin projects could have functioned as representative models of effective practice; these were chosen to inspire your work in God's field.

When I began working on this project, Mark Hamilton, David Fleer, and Royce Money encouraged me with their enthusiasm for the book. Along the way they have served as my advisors. Mark guided me through many of the editorial processes needed for putting an anthology together. David organized the book presentation and luncheon to honor the Siburt Family at the Christian Scholars Conference in 2013. Royce secured outside funding in support of the project. Each joyfully served me in ways that enriched my soul for I knew their service was a dedication of love to Charles, Judy, and their family.

Thoughtful primary advisors, including Jeff Childers, Frederick Aquino, Stephen Johnson, Mark Love, Tom Millholland, Leonard Allen, David Wray, Jack Reese, Charles Siburt, and myself, guided these project theses. Some of them advised me about project selections for this book. Additionally, Shelby Webb, my graduate assistant, worked tirelessly to fine tune the editing of each chapter.

Finally, I want to thank the elders at the Glenwood Church of Christ in Tyler, Texas. Through their support, this project came to fruition and the proceeds from the book will be contributed to the Charles and Judy Siburt Endowed Scholarship.

On the one hand, the following anthology reflects the abundant definitions of ministry that influence seminaries and churches across the country. On the other hand, the practices delineated here reflect an incarnational approach to ministry, a contextual theology embedded in lived experience and in imitation of God's way on earth. My motive for showcasing DMin project theses is rooted in my conviction that good theology makes a difference in the lives of people. Despite the diverse definitions and practices of ministry, DMin projects share the intent to enhance ministerial leadership in the life of the church. DMin graduates represented in *Effective Practice* want to make a difference not only in their local churches, but also for the larger kingdom. I believe your church can implement one or more of the projects. May your congregation be blessed and challenged by these practices that intend to effect change for God's glory and by God's grace.

Tim Sensing

August 26, 2012

---

1. Tim Sensing, *Qualitative Research: A Multi-Methods Approach to Projects for the Doctor of Ministry Thesis* (Eugene, OR: Wipf & Stock, 2011).

2. Tim Sensing, "Testing the Validity of Buttrick's Homiletic: Preaching from Matthew 13" (doctoral thesis, Harding School of Theology, 1994).

3. Hubert L. Dreyfus and Stuart E. Dreyfus, *Mind over Machine: The Power of Human Intuition and Expertise in the Era of the Computer* (New York: Free Press, 1986), describe the process of moving from novice to expert in five stages: novice, advanced beginner, competent, proficient, and expert.

4. Association of Theological Schools, http://www.ats.edu/Accrediting/Pages/ StandardsOfAccreditation.aspx, Section F.

5. Charles J. Conniry, "Reducing the Identity Crisis in Doctor of Ministry Education," Theological Education 40, no. 1 (2004): 147.

6. Barbara Horkoff Mutch, "Assessing a Doctor of Ministry Program," *Theological Education* 39, no. 2 (2003): 87–88.

Contributors

Stephen Austin—Director, Texas International Bible Institute, Houston, Texas, and Instructor of Bible for the College of Biblical Studies, ACU, Abilene, Texas.

Dan Bouchelle—President, Missions Resource Network, Bedford, Texas.

Allen Burris—Preaching Minister,Mitchell Church of Christ, Mitchell, Indiana.

Jonathan Camp—Assistant Professor, Department of Communication, and Director, Master of Science in Organizational and Human Resource Development Program, ACU, Abilene, Texas.

Craig Churchill—Associate Professor of Library Science and Theological Librarian, ACU, Abilene, Texas.

John Grant—Church Administrator, College Hills Church of Christ, Lebanon, Tennessee.

Karissa Herchenroeder—Administrative Coordinator, Doctor of Ministry Program, ACU, Abilene, Texas.

Tommy King—Preaching Minister, Johnson Street Church of Christ, San Angelo, Texas.

John Knox—Preaching Minister, Granbury Church of Christ, Granbury, Texas.

Royce Money—Chancellor of Abilene Christian University, Professor of Church History, Executive Director of the Siburt Institute for Christian Ministry, ACU, Abilene, Texas.

Carson Reed—Director, Doctor of Ministry Program, and Assistant Professor of Practical Theology, Graduate School of Theology, ACU, Abilene, Texas.

Bert Reynolds—Preaching Minister, Chenal Valley Church of Christ, Little Rock, Arkansas.

Tim Sensing—Associate Dean and Professor of Ministry and Homiletics, Graduate School of Theology, ACU, Abilene, Texas.

Jerry Shields—Pastor, First Baptist Church, Colorado City, Texas.

John Siburt—Assistant Vice President of Programs, CitySquare, Dallas, Texas.

Chris Smith—Preaching Minister, Harpeth Hills Church of Christ, Brentwood, Tennessee.

Aaron Walling—Preaching Minister, Cinco Ranch Church of Christ, Katy, Texas.

Finding Practical Theology's Location

TIM SENSING

Google Maps and Google Earth open new possibilities for people to explore the planet. If you begin with Google Maps, Figure 1.1 represents the only way to see the entire planet in one frame. You can slide the perspective south to see Antarctica, but not east or west. You will note that Europe is in the center. Western civilization's designations of east and west emerge from understanding Europe in this way. Google Maps does not allow you to opt for a different orientation. There is no way to center Russia in such a way that the country is not split. Google Maps provides you a way of seeing the world that sustains a Western perspective.

Figure 1.1

Google Earth is a different tool altogether. You can turn and maneuver your perspective in any way you want. For example, Figure 1.2 situates Australia in a central position. The perspective is so different that an American might get lost trying to visualize which way is home.

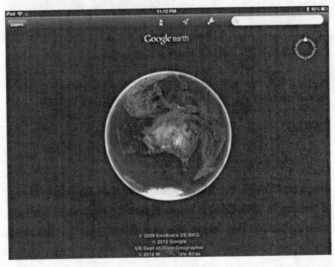

Figure 1.2

Finally, Figure 1.3 disorients people completely. Many students in my classes have a difficult time finding their place, plotting east and west, or naming the landmass on the screen. Soon someone will name it correctly, but the pause before the answer is striking.

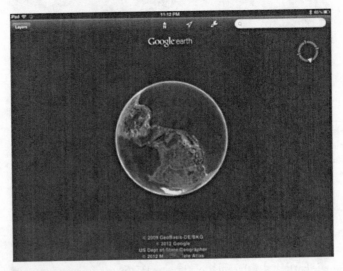

Figure 1.3

The exercise opens students to a conversation about how they see the world from a single social location.[1] The act of looking at maps is contextual. It not only influences how they see the world, it also affects how they live in the world. Likewise, practical theology is contextual to the core. Practical theology is ecclesiology that is embedded in historic places and times. It is an ecclesiology that is embodied by people more so than a dogmatic idealism found in theoretical treatises.

The contextual nature of ministry should not surprise us. The contextual nature of the gospel is grounded in Jesus dwelling in our midst. The same gospel is embodied differently in Jerusalem than it is in Rome. The rural, middle-Tennessee congregation of my grandparents looks and acts differently than the college town of my midwestern roots. The two places exhibit distinctive issues, personalities, and preferences. While they share much in common (tradition, national origin, language, etc.), no one confuses the two. They are more like second cousins than siblings. On any particular Sunday, the conversations in the foyers are not the same. While both talk about the weather, one worries about the crops, the other the game.

Recently, a conversation on a cooking show about the various qualities of olive oil caught my attention. The expert suggested not buying products from Italy or Spain but from California. He noted, "Location makes all the difference in the world for your recipes. Currently, California has the best olive oil." Winemakers would make a similar argument for the importance of location. The science of enology estimates that there are more than ten thousand kinds of grapes used to produce various styles of wine. Today only a fraction of those are available on a commercial scale, with over two hundred varieties commonly used. Enologists, viticulturists, and winemakers are versed in how to best grow and season grapes to produce wine with character, elegance, and strength.[2] Winemakers often discuss how *terroir* denotes the numerous environmental factors (such as region, soil quality, drainage, air temperature, humidity levels, etc.) that effect the flavor qualities of the final product. *Terroir* can be very loosely translated as "a sense of place," which is embodied in certain characteristic qualities of the ecosystem, the sum of the effects that the local environment has had on the production of the product.[3] While some large-scale producers blend wines in order to achieve uniformity and consistency year to year, wines defined by their locality celebrate and affirm their *terroir*.

The movie *All in This Tea* also demonstrates the notion of *terroir*. Tea importer David Lee Hoffman travels through China in search of premium teas. The film notes how different growers carefully handpick and dry their teas to achieve a unique smell, taste, and color. The growing of the finest tea depends not only on the region and soil, but also on the practices of the grower.[4] Any farmer knows that the same variety of fruit or vegetable might taste completely different depending on the pH, moisture, temperature, and other environmental factors of the place the seed is planted. Even the next valley over can change not only the taste but also the marketability of the product. Farming is always contextual.

The contextual nature of theology saturates the pages of *The Effective Practice of Ministry* and defines not only the chapters but also the life and ministry of Charles Siburt, who affected each of the authors in powerful ways. Charles's life and ministry embodied the definition of contextual theology. Anyone who looks at his life would be quite surprised by any suggestion of tension between theory and practice. He lived a symbiotic life between his academic pursuits and service to the church. Yet that tension between theory and practice has controlled the academic conversations about practical theology for a long time.

Practical Theology as a Practice

Is "practical theology" an oxymoron? The debate often states that theology deals with "theory" while practice deals with "real" life. Subsequently, practical theology gets a bad rap—sometimes referred to as "hints and tricks" of the trade or orthopedic shoes for the minister, merely methods, techniques, and strategies. And many practical theologians carry an inferiority complex whenever they enter academic conversations. Miroslav Volf addresses the origins of the tension:

> It lies in the distinction between the theoretical and the practical sciences that goes all the way back to Aristotle and his disciples. According to this distinction, the goal of the theoretical sciences is truth, and the goal of the practical sciences is action. Aristotle considered the theoretical sciences, in which knowledge is pursued for knowledge's sake, a higher wisdom than the practical sciences, which are pursued for their usefulness. It has long been debated how theology fits into this Aristotelian scheme. . . . Obviously, if theology is a theoretical science, then it only secondarily has something to do with practices; one has to make separate inquiry into practical implications of knowledge pursued for its own sake. But if theology is a practical science, then practices are from the start included within the purview of its concerns.[5]

Practice has emerged as a fundamental lens to view ministry. Dorothy C. Bass defines a Christian practice as a formative activity that "Christian people do together over time in response to and in the light of God's active presence for the life of the world in Christ Jesus."[6] In other words, "a way of life" or the patterns of people's lived experience. Bass lists four key components:

> First, as meaningful clusters of human activity (including the activity of thinking) that require and engender knowledge on the part of practitioners, practices resist the separation of thinking from acting, and thus of Christian doctrine from Christian life. Second, practices are social, belonging to groups of people across generations—a feature that undergirds the communal quality of the Christian life. Third, practices are rooted in the past but are also constantly adapting to changing circumstances, including new cultural settings. Fourth, practices articulate wisdom that is in keeping of practitioners who do not think of themselves as theologians.[7]

And this is how Charles Siburt saw the effective *practice* of ministry. Ministry is not just a set of skills but a way of seeing the world and a way of being in the world. Charles was a *bricoleur*, an artisan, or a kind of professional do-it-yourself person who used tools and skills from multiple sources to produce a *bricolage*, that is, a pieced-together, close-knit set of practices that provide solutions to a problem in a concrete situation. The *bricolage* changes and takes new forms as different tools, methods, and techniques are added to the puzzle. He was like a general contractor who refurbishes older homes. There is no telling what one will find when you look between the studs, above the ceiling, or under the floorboards. Yet the general contractor will be able to diagnose and prescribe a beautiful and workable remodeled home. Charles was often called the "Church Doctor." He drew upon a vast array of specialties in order to cure, prevent, and promote health within a particular congregation. He was like a virtuous Gregory House of Fox TV fame, who specialized as a virtuoso diagnostician. While Charles saw more ugliness in the church than one should, he loved the church. When others were tempted to give up, Charles saw the church as a glorious place of God's activity partnering with saints. As an academic in the seminary, Charles applied theory to practice every day for the sake of the church. He refused to treat congregations as places to be reduced to a template or stereotype. He declined to talk about theology in the classroom without a case study, example, best practice, or lived experience. But his integrative perspective was not always so prevalent in the academy.

The Life and Times of Practical Theology

The split between theory and practice is not new nor is the dispute easily solved. As Volf notes above, the argument goes back to the beginning of time, or at least to Aristotle's *Metaphysics*.[8] That story affects practical theology in a profound way during the opening decades of the nineteenth century. Many historians ironically look to Fredrick Schleiermacher (1768–1834) as the father of modern practical theology and also the initiator of its demise as a discipline.[9] The question of how theology justified itself as an independent discipline dominated the discussion. Because the University of Berlin was deliberately designed as a research university, it was questioned whether a theological faculty belonged. Therefore, queries arose like, "What is theology's place in the university?" And, "What is theology's status as a science?" Schleiermacher intended to establish theology as *Wissenschaft* (the disciplined critical research of a field of study as a science as opposed to professional education of ministers). Therefore, the first theological faculty at Berlin had to emphasize the doctorate. Schleiermacher justified theology on the same ground that other state-authorized faculties rationalized their existence. He mediated the debate by siding with the tradition that theology is not a pure science that deals with universal truths but a positive science with specific historical and cultural components. Human culture contains certain identifiable areas of practice that pertain to fundamental human needs. Within the university there existed other positive sciences like philosophy, medicine, and law. Positive faculties originate in the need to give cognitive and theoretical foundations to an indispensable and social practice. These areas of practice call for a specially trained leadership, and that leadership in turn requires "knowledge" pertinent to that area of practice.[10] Theology, he argued, should be included as a recognized domain on the same basis.

According to Schleiermacher, theology has to do with a specific religious community with its distinctive mode of faith, tradition, and piety, and not with religion in general. The knowledge which theology accumulates is the knowledge (theory) needed by the leadership operative in the social ordering and survival of that specific religious community. Theology, then, is the discovered knowledge for clerical tasks and responsibilities.

Prior to Schleiermacher, theology had evolved into a four-fold classification scheme. The field of theology was divided into four sciences: Bible, church history, dogmatics, and practical theology. However, he reasoned, if theology has become dispersed into various independent disciplines, how can there be any single subject matter of those disciplines or criteria to which they are bound?

Schleiermacher argued for the unified nature of theology. Unity is based upon the purpose of theology and the educational requirements of church leadership. He argued that the core of theology's purpose focused on an elaborate definition of Christianity. He used the term *Christianity* in its broadest sense as the criteria of what is healthy faith for the community. Christianity is understood by historical and philosophical theology.

As a response to the traditional four sciences, he proposed a three-fold pattern of inquiry represented by a tree. My adaptation (Figure 1.4) of the tree image includes a contemporary listing of the various subdisciplines.

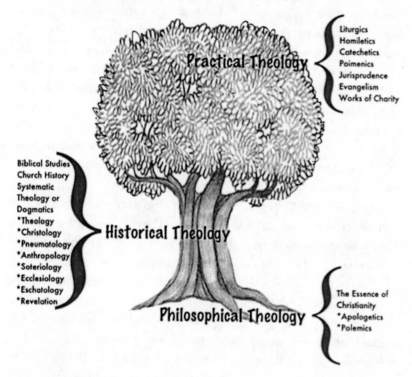

Schleiermacher's Tree

Brief Outline of the Study of Theology, 1811, 1832

Adapted by Tim Sensing (May 2012)

Figure 1.4

Philosophical theology was the *root* system of the tree. It answers the question, "What is essentially Christian?" The roots hold the practical and historical disciplines together and include the subjects of apologetics and polemics. The *trunk* of the tree represents historical theology that studies the faith community in the past and present. The use of the historical method is what binds the areas of biblical studies, church history, and systematic theology together. Finally, the *crown* of the tree symbolizes practical theology. Practical theology served the clergy as a means by which the faith community might preserve its integrity and supply normative rules for carrying out the tasks of Christian ministry. Additionally, practical theology is able to assess the activities, procedures, and operations of the church's ministry. Finally, practical theology provided the theory related to the praxis of the church's leadership and conducive to the health of the faith community. Schleiermacher understood practical theology to be the theoretical undertaking of the tasks involved more so than the specific actions necessary to carry out those functions. He wanted to increase theological formation more than skills. For Schleiermacher, practical theology is not a cluster of proficiency courses or whatever is trendy in the churches, but an analysis of theological activity in the church in order to increase Christian faithfulness. His call was for greater accountability, not to skills, but to a theology of faithfulness of practice. The second edition of *A Brief Outline of the Study of Theology* in 1830 dropped the tree image because Schleiermacher wanted to emphasize the unity of the disciplines and not leave the impression that practical theology, the crown or glory of the tree, took precedence over the other two areas.

Yet, in the immediate years following Schleiermacher's proposal, a split occurred between theory and practice yet again. Theology became a science that moved towards specialization of the discrete parts. Practical theology became the outworking rather than the source of theological understanding of practice. Much of the dissension was due to practical theology being too narrowly defined by the church of his day delimiting the subject to preaching the word and administering the sacraments. Through continued evolution, practical theology became divorced from the new movements of systematics and biblical studies. An example of that evolution affected me when I applied for a PhD at a prestigious university. In an interview with the dean, I was asked my area of interest. I responded, "Homiletics." She replied, "We do not do practical theology here but only the traditional disciplines."

The fault of the division does not rest in one camp or the other. Both share culpability. Practical theology did not develop into its own domain (a field of study with a body of knowledge). It turned to the domains of social science for a source of knowledge. Practical theology allowed the social sciences to form rather than inform theology, thus increasing the study and acquisition of techniques. Homiletics turned to communication theory; Poimenics to psychology;

catechetics to education theory, and so forth. The resulting split occurred between the domain of the professor (Scripture, doctrine, and history) and the domain of the clergy (practical theology). Over time, the separation between theory and practice hardened because the huge increase in knowledge related to skills increased exponentially and no one person could claim expertise.

As the nineteenth century unfolded, a single core identity that connected church practice with Christianity (as defined by Schleiermacher) no longer provided unity for practical theology as a field of study.[11] The ascertaining of how the nature of Christianity itself sets forth requirements, principles, and rules that preside over the church's activities was lost. Practical theology broke apart into subdisciplines representing the discrete tasks of ministry. And at various times and in diverse ways, each of these subdisciplines lost their way in their reliance upon assorted and related social sciences. In the most recent past, practical theology became a synonym for pastoral theology or more precisely, pastoral care and counseling. The only choice for a doctoral student was to pursue a degree in one of the discrete subdisciplines. But even then, seminaries would often hire as professors to teach in these fields someone with a correlative degree in the social sciences. If a doctoral student wanted to concentrate on a holistic understanding of practical theology, the only degree possible was pastoral care. While some schools advertised leadership as the key component in such emphases, the control of the social sciences in leadership studies exemplified the worst-case scenario.

However, in the past few decades, the recovery of a holistic understanding of practical theology has returned to the seminary, literature, and by extension, the church.[12] Today, practical theology unites the traditional five subdisciplines of Catechetics, Homiletics, Liturgics, Poimenics (pastoral care and counseling), and Jurisprudence (leadership) with four additional fields of Halieutics (missions and evangelism), Mystical Theology (spiritual formation and spirituality), Congregational Studies, and Works of Charity (ministries of justice and mercy or social ethics). Practical theology is now a term that defines the aggregate of separate disciplines, each one with its specialists and auxiliary sciences. Currently, practical theology is informed by the social sciences but resists being formed by those disciplines. The organizing principles needed for integration among the collective subdisciplines revolve around theological core identity and method.[13] While diverse interpretations and proposals are prevalent and healthy, it behooves faculties, students, and ministers to seek clear and concise articulations of their specific theological methods and core identities.

Theological Core Identity

Charles Siburt saw the harmony between theory and practice. He did not see the "either/or" side of the polarities but the "both/and" landscape that resides within congregations. Theology is not merely the pursuit of an intellectual vision but a compelling account of a way of life in God. Beliefs and practices are intertwining functions. Volf talks about all this in terms of "belief-shaped practices" and "practice-shaping beliefs."[14] To separate the two, if possible at all, is to do a disservice to both. Theology is something to be known, lived, and experienced by a particular community. For Charles, his academic career was profoundly interconnected in the local life of the church. He found his theological core identity and theological method there.

Miller-McLemore describes the recent trend for seeking a holistic definition for practical theology. Different constituencies use the term in various ways. To cover the diverse yet interdependent uses, she defines practical theology using four categories: (1) the activity of faith; (2) an approach or method to theology and religious faith; (3) a curricular area with a variety of subdisciplines that focus on ministerial practice; and (4) an academic discipline that pursues the substantiation of the above three enterprises. While my training falls into category three, my definition below seeks to unify the field as a discipline using the rubric of theological core identity and method (category four).[15]

To find the coherence between theory and practice, I take my cues from Charles by articulating here my own understandings of practical theology. Theologians must make their intentional practices explicit. My theological identity revolves around the notion that the primary activity of a practical theologian is communal, critical, transformative, and public.[16] *A practical theologian applies theology in all its forms in contemporary contexts in order to transform the community of God into the image of Jesus.* I modify this definition when I examine a particular subdiscipline. My area of expertise is homiletics. My question becomes, "What is the theological activity of homiletics?" Therefore, *preaching is the proclaiming of theology in contemporary contexts in order to transform the community of God into the image of Jesus.* Although each of these phrases may engender debate, let me unpack my perspective.

Proclaiming: Metaphors abound that describe the preaching event. The Bible allows for a rich diversity of options, such as herald, witness, watchman, ambassador, vessel, storyteller, pastor, aroma, prophet, and others. To be bound by one metaphor delimits preaching in ways that exclude rather than include. Of all the words in my definition, this is the most difficult to choose. The herald metaphor is routinely associated with the activity of proclaiming. Yet the herald metaphor often implies that a person is a mouthpiece or conduit for the very words of God. It accords with the Second Helvetic Confession, "the preached word of God is the Word of God" for the people of God.[17] While not intended, the herald metaphor often relegates the preacher to a secondary role or even worse deletes the minister from the equation altogether. The word "witness" is attractive. The activity of a witness is testifying. When I preach, I desire to share with the congregation my personal experience with God and God's Good News. I want to tell anyone who will listen what I have seen and heard in the text and in my experience with God. But I want to do more than just offer evidence. I want to announce, confess, profess, and proclaim in order to persuade. The preached word of God becomes the Word of God only when listeners respond, participate, and become performers of the Word; the Word incarnate and embodied in the people of God for the sake of the world.

As a believer, I have a stake in the game, a vested interest. The thin line between words like *persuade* and *sell*, *testify* and *manipulate*, and *convince* and *indoctrinate* has been easily and frequently crossed. But in the marketplace of ideas, I do not want a timid voice that merely offers the Gospel as one viable option among a host of other selections. If the ship has been lost for days at sea, the lookout cries out, "I see land!" If my neighbor attended the inauguration of the President, I want to see her pictures and hear her say, "You should have been there! It was the best day of my life." When my doctor comes with a diagnosis, I want her to confidently state the prognosis. Preachers should speak with confidence and boldness about what they have seen and heard. The preacher's proclamation focuses the eyes and ears of the audience so that they too can behold, witness, declare, and act. So I intensify the activity of a witness from testifying to proclaiming.

Theology: Theology is a big word. It is a big enough word to carry weight. Some definitions in the literature narrow the conversation so tightly that they stifle the variety needed in congregations. For instance, Augustine's desire to use the Great Commandments as a lens for interpretation and homiletics will enhance preaching. If I applied the litmus test of loving God and loving my neighbor to my sermons, my preaching would improve. What if every sermon in the land submitted itself to the scrutiny of Augustine's assessment? The world would certainly be healthier. Likewise, the word *gospel* has been suggested as the screening tool for sermons. It is advocated that every sermon be a gospel sermon. Every sermon must be deemed "good" news. Again, I am convinced that the profession of preaching and the influence of the church would inherently boost the credibility and the efficacy of preaching if "good news" was adopted as the judicative criteria. Yet, although not necessarily so, some topics and texts might be diluted of their meaning and power if the vise of such a lens squeezed too much of their life from their veins.[18] For example, the imprecatory psalms might not only be watered down but also excised altogether. Some narratives that have troubled lectionary compilers for centuries and exegetes even longer would certainly be deleted from the canon if they could only be discussed as "good news" or through the lens of the Great Commandments. Consequently, I use the word *theology*. Theology is the big word. Theology allows for the range of options needed by congregations for the whole work and word of God and God's people.

Furthermore, I am committed to listening to congregational lived experience as one source for my theological understandings. I do not see the application of theology as an unpacking of a pristine jewel that God delivers via the UPS store. All theology is contextual, as I noted above. From God's story intersecting the church's story, theology emerges from below, as well as from above. As a resident theologian, I want to employ various resources available to me, including Scripture, tradition, history, and experience. Preachers can do great harm when they come to congregations with their own theological agendas and impose them on trusting people who hired them to lead the church into the ways of God. Alister McGrath agrees when he says:

> Respect for place signals a willingness to work with the local situation, rather than trying to convert it into another place. Clergy who arrive in a new parish often bring with them the working assumptions and methods of their previous parish, often failing to realize how these practices and assumptions are embedded in the particularities of another place, and fail to connect adequately with their new situation.[19]

Instead, I recommend preachers listen to the congregation so that through time the story of how God is calling that body into God's will is heard. The preacher will investigate the local community in order to see how the church has in the past and can in the future be a neighbor. Ethnography becomes a pastoral practice and an informant to the local theology.

Theology is a big word. The arms of theology are open wide enough to include rather than exclude.

In the Contemporary Context: What other option do I have? So much of the preaching I hear as I travel around the country falls into the category of history. Preachers are explaining what happened and what was said in the past.

Somehow, the misconception has emerged that declares that all churches need to do is understand the facts of archaeology, history, exegesis, etc., and the bridge to the contemporary world will be easily traversed. My seminary training concentrated on how to unpack and explain the Bible. Once the "truth" was uncovered, my earliest lessons in preaching taught me to explain it, apply it, and illustrate it. The ancient debate between Plato and the Sophists, that recurred between the Old Homiletic and the New Homiletic, was one-sided. For me, this generated a host of past-tense sermons that downloaded data. It took a while for me to figure out that I did not live back then nor had anyone sitting in front of me. I live in the here and now. I choose to live today. My homiletic has a *terroir*, a located activity in time and space. The folks coming to worship God on any given Sunday come full of joys, sorrows, pains, anxieties, hopes, dreams, and fears. They have forces that are tearing up their days in awful and gut-wrenching ways. They have blessings that are enriching their lives bountifully. They come with expectations to hear a word from God that speaks to them in their context. This is why it is important to make a turn toward the listeners and to take their context seriously.

In Order to Transform: Texts accomplish a variety of functions. They teach, affirm, remind, warn, urge, comfort, exhort, encourage, call, claim, challenge, correct, delight, rebuke—the list is endless. But the primary purpose of God in the world is to call people to be in relationship. God's story begins in the fellowship of a Trinitarian relationship. The eschaton begins a new chapter of God's story where all who are reconciled are called to live continuously in fellowship with God. In between the prologue and the epilogue is an amazing story of God's love reuniting humanity to God's creative intent. Nowhere is that articulated better than by Paul in 2 Corinthians 3:18 when he says, "And all of us, with unveiled faces, seeing the glory of the Lord as though reflected in a mirror, are being transformed into the same image from one degree of glory to another; for this comes from the Lord, the Spirit" (NRSV).

In my definition of preaching, the phrase *in order to transform* addresses intent. More specifically, "What is the purpose of preaching?" While some transformations are instantaneous and dramatic, normally communal change develops over time—a process of becoming. In my preaching classes, I press students to write clear and concise function statements that have strong active verbs that call for affective and behavioral changes. The Bible does inform, but the authors of the biblical texts do not write in order to download truths to their audiences. On the contrary, the authors write because the occasion demands a word from God that addresses problems and issues that are tearing up their days. Through the eternal truths of God's identity and God's story, God desires us to respond, to be transformed, to change our habits and practices, so that we can be in fellowship with God's Self and God's people for the sake of the world.

The Community of God: We live between the times, between the advents of Jesus' incarnation into our world and Jesus' inauguration of a new age to come. The life God gives us between these advents has meaning. God is not just doing time. In between the times, God calls humanity to participate in God's life through the process of continuing God's reconciling work. Preaching addresses the present tense because God desires to bless humanity in the life provided now. Preaching addresses the future tense (in a proleptic sense) because God's story is heading somewhere. And God's primary vehicle in history has been and still is embodied in community. Beginning with Abraham, God called Israel to be a people set apart from others so that all nations might have hope. In Jesus, God continues to set apart a community so that all peoples of the earth could be blessed. So often preaching addresses the individual in ways that make church a self-help therapy club rather than the life-giving fellowship. Scripture addresses community. Preaching must restore that emphasis.

Into the Image of Jesus: The telos of preaching has many possible theological ends and diverse theological motifs are found throughout Scripture.[20] For instance, one such end occurs in the intersection of anthropology and ecclesiology in the incarnation of Jesus, in whom God exhibits the fullness of divinity. Jesus reveals the intent God desired for all humanity in creation (Gen. 1:27; 5:1–2; 9:6). Through recreation of God's image, the community of God's people receives the fullness of God (Col. 2:9–10). The Gospels tell the story of Jesus so that we can not only behold his identity but also follow in his steps. Luke writes Acts to record the witness of the people continuing Jesus' work as a community. The letters call churches back to the "mind of Christ" so that they will continue faithfully their life of imitation. Therefore, *preaching proclaims theology in the present tense in order to transform the community of God into the image of Jesus.*

Theological Method

My theological core identity forms and informs my theological method. If the purpose of theology is to generate an understanding of faith that transforms communities into the image of Jesus, then my theological method should function in a coherent way leading to such transformation. As people live out their faith, theological reflection enables them to engage in practices and godly lives that honor God. My understanding thus corresponds with Elaine Graham's proposals about theological reflection. "First, theology informs the processes that enable the *formation of character*. Second, theology assists in building and maintaining the *community of faith*. Third, theology enables the relating of the faith-community's own communal identity to the surrounding culture, and the *communication of the faith* to the wider world."[21]

People, whether they know it or not, do theology. My theological reflection method motivates me to assist congregations to intentionally think theologically. At the convergence of what people believe and how people live exists an assortment of inconsistencies. Theological reflection focuses on the junction of inconsistency in order to enable people to discover God's presence and movement in their lives. Theological reflection seeks congruity and integration between belief and practice. Theological reflection on practice increases the capacity of congregations to renew themselves as communities of faith in service to their neighborhood, community, and world. Therefore, I advocate that ministers train congregations to utilize practical skills of observing, articulating, deciding, and acting, based on a process of spiritual discernment. In time, the congregation becomes a collective theologian in residence.

Most theological reflective methods rely upon some form of an action-reflection model.[22] A consistent pastoral practice of action-reflection that leads to further intentional action will transform people over time into a community that engages the life of God for the sake of the world. Ministers become proactive learners and risk takers by moving into the center of the learning situation. Expertise is reflexive, problem-based, intuitive, and synthetic. It is always contextual to and contingent on a particular situation. Becoming a reflective practitioner is a strenuous and ongoing journey, but that process can become a natural part of everyday thinking, deciding, and acting. Over time, the twin assets of sapience and habitus emerge.

What are the various elements of a theological reflection model? Patrick Keifert lists them as follows: "This act of spiritual discernment grows out of attending to three sources for spiritually relevant knowledge for spiritual discernment: (a) tradition, especially Scripture, (b) culture and society, and (c) the experience of the faithful, both personal and communal. In each of these moments, the basic questions remain the same: 'What is God up to here?' and 'What is the Word of God for us in this place and time?'"[23] These three sources, or angles of interpretation, are key ingredients for my model (see Figure 1.5).[24]

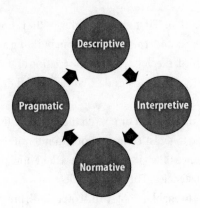

Figure 1.5

I begin with Keifert's third source, lived experience (both communal and individual). Where else can a person start? If I begin with one of the theological resources like Scripture, I can only begin with it from my experience of Scripture. I was first introduced to Scripture through the witness of my parents and home church. I went to Bible class on Sunday mornings and Wednesday evenings. Many teachers told me the grand stories of faith. Long before any formal training, I read the text for many hours in private devotion. I passed Bible exams in order to move from fourth to sixth grades. My father is an engineer. My mother is a bookkeeper. I have an undergraduate degree in environmental science. All these experiences shape the way I read texts. Eventually, even my formal training in critical methods was shaped by a tradition rooted in Lockean epistemology and Common Sense Realism.[25] Everyone starts with experience. What other option is there?

Terry Veling agrees, "Practical theology necessarily attends to the conditions of human life. It is concerned with the unique, the particular, the concrete—this people, this community, this place, this moment, this neighbor, this question, this need, this concern."[26] And elsewhere he states, "This is how practical theology typically begins . . . with a situation, a concern, a question, an experience, an issue, an event—something, at least, that claims attention."[27]

My preunderstandings and my perceptions of reality are determined by my lived experiences. My lived experiences need attending to as I reflect on the meaning of those experiences. Reflexivity is essential. I must understand my stance, role, preunderstandings, motives, and influence in the process. Experiences include: personal relationships, community relationships, religious traditions, politics, work, education, leisure time, and feelings. I will be attentive to the experiences of others, including gender, ethnicities, socio-economics, and other ways people experience their lives. As I consider my lived experiences and the perspectives of others, a dialogical process ensues. Conversation allows for inter-ruption, disagreement, and surprise. I must listen, not debate. I must be attentive, intelligent, responsible, loving, and able to change. Conversation is not a sharing of ignorance but a journey to find my voice and to hear others' voices.

And as I engage in the dialogical process, I will facilitate the voice of others, become comfortable with silence, and not insist on having the last word. Conversation is a communal act that allows for differences and fosters respect. Examining communal experiences is sometimes described as "exegeting people" or following the path of interpreting experience. Hermeneutics is not something humans do, it is ontologically who we are. Humans are interpretive beings and the church excels in the arts of theologically informed hermeneutics.

In order to examine experience, I will need detailed access to primary data that allows for examination. Verbatim accounts, critical incident reports, case studies, journal entries, field notes, and other qualitative data provide ample evidence for consideration. Critical reflexivity sees the polyvalent aspects of motives, outcomes, influences, interpretations, etc. Examining the layers, sharp corners, and textures will bring to light aspects that are often marginalized or rationalized by simplistic thinking or hegemonic motives. Faith and its practices are not objects to be examined, but are embodied. Practical theology reflects on faith as a performative and embodied act, that the gospel is not simply something to be believed but also something to be lived. Human experience is a place where the gospel is grounded, embodied, interpreted, and lived out. The beginning point for reflection is lived experience.

The second angle or source for theological reflection is the particular context or location where I live or the church dwells. As noted above, practical theology is contextual theology. Context includes examining the diverse intercultural settings that reside around us. Culture is like the atmosphere we breathe, permeating via capillaries throughout all our human cells. The conversation between my experiences and the culture are hard to differentiate. I am silently and thoroughly formed by culture. The classic definition of culture comes from Clifford Geertz in *The Interpretation of Cultures* when he says culture is "webs of significance" that humanity has spun. According to Geertz, culture "denotes an historically transmitted pattern of meanings embodied in symbols, a system of inherited conceptions expressed in symbolic forms by means of which [people] communicate, perpetuate, and develop their knowledge about and attitudes toward life."[28] Another classic definition comes from Richard Niebuhr in *Christ and Culture*. He states culture is " that total process of human activity and that total result of such activity to which now the name *culture*, now the name *civilization*, is applied in common speech . . . It comprises language, habits, ideas, beliefs, customs, social organization, inherited artifacts, technical processes, and values."[29] Cultural elements include: convictions, values, assumptions, biases, formative symbols, ongoing interpretations, social roles, systemic forces, political structures, philosophies, sciences, and the social sciences. And all these cultural phenomena are connected to various uses of power. The second angle is context that is culturally understood and assessed in its plurality of forms.

The third angle or source for theological reflection involves various theological resources. Scripture, church history, ecclesial traditions, and personal faith not only inform my discernment but also transform how I interpret my experiences and the culture around me. Ministers spend most of their academic career examining the complex nature of the theological resources in seminary. It is the one angle that often dominates the discussion and overtly takes control. My dialogical method requires that these resources be aware and respectful of the other two angles. Nevertheless, my theological convictions call me to respect this angle as an invitation to see God more clearly. The theological resources provide a vision for the future that is based upon the ongoing story of God's working in the world. This angle has both a pastoral and a prophetic edge. It offers God's grace and challenge. It is from the theological resources that the church is called to engage the world.

The critical correlation or triangulation of the three angles of interpretation emerges as the key aspect of how my theological reflection model works. The three angles enter into a dialog with one another. Richard Osmer gives a credible way to engage in that conversation with four simple questions—What is going on? Why is this going on? What ought to be going on? How might we respond?—and from them describes the four tasks of practical theology: the descriptive, the interpretive, the normative, and the pragmatic.[30]

Figure 1.6

One angle is not more spiritual than another. God resides in all three. Congregational discernment begins with the communal experiences. Often these experiences are described as the practices or actions that people participate in together as they live out their faith. Next, those experiences engage in a conversation with the theological resources and the larger culture. Finally, through decision and action, the process completes one rotation of an ongoing reflection cycle (or spiral).

Figure 1.7 is a depiction of how I understand my model. Picture the process as a spiral that rotates forward from one moment of reflection to the next.

Figure 1.7

After the dialog with experience, context, and theology, a person makes a decision that leads to action. I define action as beliefs, habits, and practices. These actions will lead to new lived experiences. And the cycle continues. Over time this becomes a way of seeing and way of being in the world. Throughout the process, I keep my theological core identity present: *a practical theologian applies theology in all its forms in contemporary contexts in order to transform the community of God into the image of Jesus.* Effective ministers will have a theological method that engages in a triadic reflection that leads to action that establish practices for the sake of the world. And in time and location, God's glory is revealed.

The local community can engage in the same "action to reflection to change" model that I have described for an individual. Communal theological reflection that is intentional will move the congregation to the telos of being transformed into the image of Jesus. In other places, Paul would describe the process as sanctification. Eventually, the intersections of inconsistencies between beliefs and practices will be transformed into highways that lead to lives that honor God and churches that are glorious to behold.

Conclusion

A few years ago, my family and I were traveling in the Southeast on vacation. Late Saturday night, a storm covered the entire area with a sheet of ice. Power lines and branches lay scattered throughout the region. Nevertheless, being proud Hoosiers who knew no fear of snow, we went to church. We arrived with six other brave souls. The song leader was conscious of the situation. He traversed two hymns, a prayer, communion, and announcements in ten minutes. Even then, our eyes watered from the fumes of a kerosene heater. After the invitation song was announced, a guest speaker began his forty-five-minute dissertation. His subject was . . . can you guess? Of course, "church attendance." What is more relevant to those who braved the harsh elements in order to attend? These are moments that define the phrase, "preaching to the choir." And these are the moments that cause us to laugh because they are sad and too typical. Sometimes church is discouraging. Sometimes we all lose heart. Sometimes we just want to quit. Where is the glory?

Much of contemporary church life does not appear glorious. Preachers and teachers disappoint us. Infighting, sectarianism, meanness, and selfishness become our identifying marks. Sometimes the mire is public for all to see. The indecent exposure by the volunteer at the youth retreat is broadcast by the local news. The man who converted my father committed adultery with an elder's spouse. The deacon curses in the foyer at the nursery attendant for being late. But mostly, the bitterness and bickering of folk are hidden corrosives that gnaw and bedevil. Insinuations and whispers occur in the corner more often than on Twitter. Sometimes we just want to quit. Where is the glory?

At ACU, I hear story after story of churches picking apart young ministers who leave school with such high hopes and confidence, only to return with disappointment and despair. Church can be discouraging. Such disappointments undermine our own confidence that God is at work in the context of the church. It is enough to cause us all to lose heart. Even the mundane and the boring are better than what is seemingly our lot. The church is in disrepair. Where is the glory?

If only we could see the kind of glory that is described in the mountaintop experience of Sinai! Now Moses had a glorious ministry (Exod. 34:29–35). Imagine the scene where the ministry is so glorious that the minister's face glows with God's presence. Images of Charlton Heston fill our minds. Wow! What a ministry! Moses leads his people from bondage to freedom. Moses gives his people Torah, a way to walk in the paths of God. Who wouldn't want to be compared to Moses? If only Paul's ministry had glory like Moses's.

And Paul agrees (2 Cor. 3:7–18). He states that the old covenant "came in glory." Paul knows the misgivings of some about his local ministry. And that is when Paul changes the conversation. The Israelites could not even bear to look at Moses's face (3:7). The central issue with Moses's shining face was not its glow, but its fade. Moses's glory was passing. The central focus of 3:7–11 is not the denial of the glory of the law, but the comparison of the Sinai covenant with Paul's own ministry of the new covenant. Indeed, Paul refers to the two covenants as two ministries. Moses's ministry was glorious. But Paul says he knows about an even greater glory, a glory that will not pass away.

Despite the appearances, Paul's ministry is even more glorious than that of Moses. Moses veiled his face to hide its fading glory. He placed a veil over his face to keep the Israelites from seeing the end of the glory. As Paul changes the conversation from Moses' glorious ministry, he does not set himself up as the point of comparison but speaks instead about the local church at Corinth. Paul allows the church to shine with an unveiled face as evidence of God's glorious ministry. "We all" refers, not only to Paul himself, but to all who have "turned to the Lord." This community of faith, as Paul's letter of recommendation (2 Cor. 3:2), beholds the glory of the Lord (cf. Exod. 16:7, 10), just as Moses did. However, unlike Israel, the Christian community beholds the glory of the Lord "with unveiled faces." As we turn to the Lord we are "being transformed into the same image from one degree of glory to another" (2 Cor. 3:18 NRSV). Despite the appearances of ineffectiveness, the testimony to our ministry is the transformation of the church into God's divine image. By the message of the cross, we are transformed into the image of Christ. It is the church that stands as God's letter of recommendation, the fact that you have believed, you have responded, you have become people of God.

Despite the appearances, we have seen God's glorious ministries in the face of Jesus. We see transformation taking place wherever we see a cup of water given in his name, a people who sacrifice themselves for the poor, a people who care for the bereaved, and a people who show hospitality to a stranger. God's glorious ministry is an effective practice when God's ministers partner with God to apply theology in all its forms in contemporary contexts in order to transform the community of God into the image of Jesus. God's glorious ministry is seen at a church of all places when the people actively practice theology as a way of life for the sake of the world.

I don't know your stories. Nonetheless, let me venture to guess. If your church conducted an evening service with an open microphone where various congregants were asked to come and share stories of times when they experienced the loving face of Jesus shining in the face of one of their brothers and sisters, then all in attendance would behold the glory of the Lord. *The Effective Practice of Ministry* shares several stories of glorious ministries. This book is a microphone for storytellers of God's kingdom to share what God is doing among other faithful people. Elders are appointed in God-honoring ways. Leaders are trained to serve with integrity and grace. Teachers are prepared to open new eyes of faith. Parents are guided to raise their children in the Lord. Strangers are welcomed with the peace of Christ. And pew sitters are prepared to hear the gospel with new ears. Whenever we see people abandoning themselves for the sake of others, we see the transformation of lives from one degree of glory to another (2 Cor. 3:18). Because of God's glory, we do not lose heart (4:1–6). Because it's God's glory, we plunge in with both feet and eyes wide open—and that's the call of the gospel.

---

1. My thanks to Dr. Emily Click, Harvard Divinity School, who used the Google Map and Google Earth exercise at the Association for Theological Field Education 31st Biennial Consultation, San Juan, Puerto Rico, January 19–22, 2011.

2. http://www.oenologist.com/index_grape-varietals.htm.

3. http://tablascreek.typepad.com/tablas/2008/10/terroir-then-an.html; http://www.wineanorak.com/terroir2.htm.

4. Movie review by Chuleenan Svetvilas at http://fest07.sffs.org/films/film_details.php?id=6.

5. Miroslav Volf, "Theology for a Way of Life," in *Practicing Theology: Beliefs and Practices in Christian Life*, eds. Miroslav Volf and Dorothy C. Bass (Grand Rapids: Eerdmans, 2002), 246.

6. Craig Dykstra and Dorothy C. Bass, "Times of Yearning, Practices of Faith," in *Practicing Our Faith: A Way of Life for a Searching People*, ed. Dorothy C. Bass (San Francisco: Jossey-Bass, 1997), 5. See also L. Gregory Jones and Kevin R. Armstrong, *Resurrecting Excellence: Shaping Faithful Christian Ministry* (Grand Rapids: Eerdmans, 2006), 54.

7. Bass, "Introduction," in *Practicing Theology*, 6.

8. Aristotle, *Metaphysics*, trans. Hippocrates G. Apostle (Des Moines, IA: Peripatetic Press, 1966), 993b, Book. 20.

9. Friedrich Schleiermacher, *Brief Outline of Theology as a Field of Study: Revised Translation of the 1811 and 1830 Editions*, trans. Terrence N. Tice (Louisville: Westminster John Knox, 2011). John E. Paver, *Theological Reflection and Education for Ministry*, (Hamshire, Eng: Ashgate, 2006), informs many of my thoughts on Schleiermacher. See also, Edward Farley's *Theologia: The Fragmentation and Unity of Theological Education*. (Eugene, OR: Wipf & Stock, 2001), and Gordon S. Mikoski, "Mainline Protestantism," in *The Wiley-Blackwell Companion to Practical Theology*, ed. Bonnie J. Miller-McLemore (West Sussex, UK: Blackwell, 2012), 557–566.

10. Farley, *Theologia*, 86.

11. Richard R. Osmer, "The United States," in Miller-McLemore, *Wiley-Blackwell Companion*, 495–504.

12. Miller-McLemore, *Wiley-Blackwell Companion*, 2.

13. My articulation of organizing principles for practical theology is a response to the ongoing challenges faced by the discipline. Mikoski, "Mainline Protestantism," 562–564, describes those challenges as 1) the difficulty of definition, 2) the failure to delineate internal boundaries, 3) the struggle over the principles of integration among the various subdisciplines, 4) the lack of negotiation of a relationship with field education, 5) the search for the appropriate method, 6) the search for appropriate pedagogies, and 7) the challenge of institutional survival while maintaining services to the church.

14. Volf, "Way of Life," in *Practicing Theology*, 250–254.

15. Bonnie J. Miller-McLemore, *Christian Theology in Practice: Discovering a Discipline* (Grand Rapids: Eerdmans, 2012), 100–110. See also: Kathleen A. Cahalan and James R. Nieman, "Mapping the Field of Practical Theology," in *For Life Abundant: Practical Theology, Theological Education, and Christian Ministry*, eds. Dorothy C. Bass and Craig Dykstra (Grand Rapids: Eerdmans, 2008), 62–85; and Miller-McLemore, *Wiley-Blackwell Companion*, 5, 13.

16. Sensing, *Qualitative Research*, xviii-xxxiii.

17. "The Second Helvetic Confession," *The Book of Confessions, The Constitution of the Presbyterian Church (USA)*, Part I (Louisville: The Office of the General Assembly, 1996), 5.004, 55.

18. Likewise, the narrowing of the subject occurs with Gerhard von Rad's "salvation history," Rudolf Bultmann's "authentic existence," and Karl Barth's "Christology."

19. Alister E. McGrath, "The Cultivation of Theological Vision: Theological Attentiveness and the Practice of Ministry," in *Perspectives on Ecclesiology and Ethnography*, ed. Pete Ward (Grand Rapids: Eerdmans, 2012), 121.

20. For example, the *Sophia* tradition found in the Wisdom tradition.

21. Elaine Graham, Heather Walton, and Frances Ward. *Theological Reflection: Methods*, vol.1 (Norwich, UK: SCM Press, 2005), 10.

22. Donald A. Schön, *The Reflective Practitioner: How Professionals Think in Action* (Burlington, VT: Ashgate, 1995).

23. Patrick Keifert, "The Return of the Congregation to Theological Convention," in *Testing the Spirits: How Theology Informs the Study of Congregations*, ed. Patrick Keifert (Grand Rapids: Eerdmans, 2009), 21.

24. Figure 5 is the first cycle of a larger process depicted in Figure 7.

25. Tim Sensing, "Baconian Influences on Preaching," *Stone Campbell Journal* 4 (Fall 2001): 163–185.

26. Terry Veling, *Practical Theology: On Earth as It is in Heaven* (Maryknoll, NY: Orbis, 2005), 16.

27. Ibid., 217.

28. Clifford Geertz, *The Interpretation of Cultures* (New York: Basic Books, 1973), 89.

29. Richard Niebuhr, *Christ and Culture* (New York: HarperCollins, 2001), 32.

30. Richard R. Osmer, *Practical Theology: An Introduction* (Grand Rapids: Eerdmans, 2008), 4. Osmer's model is just one example of a common cyclic pattern found throughout the literature. For example, Thomas Groome, *Sharing Faith: A Comprehensive Approach to Religious Education and Pastoral Ministry* (San Francisco: HarperSanFrancisco, 1991), 155--283, describes five movements for shared praxis: (1) description or naming the present action; (2) critical reflection or interpretation; (3) making explicit the Christian story; (4) a dialectical hermeneutic; and (5) discernment for future action.

CHAPTER 1

Crossing the Threshold

JOHN SIBURT[1]

"Crossing the Threshold" describes a strategic planning project initiated by the Richardson East Church of Christ. The purpose of the project was to formulate a process through which the Richardson East elders discerned and articulated relevant Christian virtues within the communal life of the church. The articulation of these Christian virtues contributed to the congregation's cultivation of a theological identity that included participation in certain habits, attitudes, and practices.

The problem addressed by this project was the lack of an intentional process of catechetical instruction through which congregants cultivate virtues. Richardson East primarily functioned as a conglomerate of ministry programs, activities, and small groups, in which members were invited to "do" ministry, but rarely provided insight into how to be more Christian in what they do. The expectations of church membership were primarily articulated in terms of attendance at events such as worship and Bible class, and the contribution to ministry in some fashion, but they were not generally defined as the personification of the Christian life through participation in Christian virtues.

Historically, Christianity has acknowledged a connection between truth and goodness. Christianity stands to benefit from the reclamation of this epistemic understanding of truth as something one loves, participates in, and by which one experiences transformation. Specifically, my project sought to help Richardson East restore the therapeutic power of the Christian faith by intentionally applying knowledge of God to the process of character formation. Richardson East's capacity to apply knowledge of God in the shaping of human character resulted in the articulation and cultivation of Christian virtues within the lives of its members.

Many churches articulate congregational vision in terms of external factors such as worship style, denominational affiliation, or ministry programs. However, Richardson East derived its vision from a robust theology of ecclesial identity rooted in practices, habits, and attitudes that cultivate informed judgment, the ability and desire to appropriately employ knowledge of God to particular situations. By intentionally functioning as a community of virtue, Richardson East embodied God's best hopes for human dignity and excellence. As Ellen Charry says: "At a time when many social institutions appear morally endangered, and persons flounder intellectually, morally, and spiritually, the Christian theological tradition, and the Christian community generally hold the promise of being both a guiding and a transforming agent of persons and institutions along the lines of God's highest hopes for creation."[2]

The cultivation of Christian virtue in the lives of contemporary Christians has suffered from the separation of theology and spirituality. Most articulations of the Christian faith operate within a truncated epistemology that defines knowledge as the objective comprehension of facts instead of experiential participation in truth. The result is a deficient self-understanding in which the church views itself as something less than a community of Christian virtue and Christian theology remains irrelevant to the witness of the church and the lives of Christian people. Until contemporary Christianity reclaims the pastoral function of doctrine, it will continue to be critiqued for its inability to develop human excellence, character, and dignity.[3]

Forming the Congregation into a Community of Virtue

Elders Leading Spiritual Formation[4]

A few years ago David and Sherry waited in the Intensive Care Unit of Children's Hospital in Dallas. Their daughter, Tatum, clung to life awaiting a liver transplant. A few days earlier Tatum appeared to be a perfectly healthy seven-year-old girl until a "stomach bug" turned out to be a vile intruder that ravaged her liver. Each day numerous Christians from nearby Richardson East Church of Christ visited David and Sherry. Some would stay for only a moment, while others camped out for hours. One hundred forty-five people made their way to the Children's Hospital ICU to enter into David and Sherry's pain, each one doing their part to care for David and Sherry.

One person ensured food was brought down to the hospital every day. Another person handled phone calls. Some offered prayers of intercession while others held David and Sherry's hands in silence. On the third day someone thought to offer leftovers to another family in the waiting room and from that point on meals originally intended to nourish David and Sherry began feeding every family in the ICU. Around that time one of the elders from Richardson East noticed another family crying in the corner of the waiting room. He went over to the young husband and wife and asked about their child. After twenty minutes of listening to this young couple share their grief and fear, the elder asked if he could pray for them. He spread his arms around the couple and drew them into his embrace, offering prayers of intercession for their infant son.

The actions of this elder deeply impacted these parents and inspired other Christians from Richardson East to initiate conversations with and offer support for families in the ICU. The community gathered around David and Sherry in a moment of crisis became a powerful force of Christian love. At one point during the ordeal a nurse, amazed by the display of support, asked David, "Who are you people?" The experience taught the entire congregation that "who we are" is a community of virtue formed in the image of Jesus Christ.

Unfortunately, the church does not always have such a clear sense of its own identity. The lack of a coherent self-understanding diminishes the church's effectiveness as a witness to the world by diverting its resources away from its true mission. Faithful engagement with an increasingly post-Christian culture requires the church to articulate its distinct identity as a Christlike community of virtue. Who is given the task of ensuring that the church is a community in which Christian virtue is both embodied and cultivated? Elders.

The New Testament portrays elders as examples of Christian virtue "above reproach" (1 Tim. 3:2–3) and "blameless" (Titus 1:7). Elders are charged to "preach with sound doctrine and to refute those who contradict it" (Titus 1:9b NRSV). Elders are to watch over the flock and to shepherd the church by protecting the church from "savage wolves" who come in and distort the truth (Acts 20:28–30). As the church's local theologians, the elders are to interpret the Christian faith in a manner conducive to the cultivation of Christian virtue.

The letters of Paul provide valuable insights into the work of church leadership. Paul consistently portrays spiritual formation as the goal of church leadership. For Paul, ministry is participation in God's work of transforming the community of faith until it is "blameless" at the coming of Christ.[5] He views the church as unfinished business continually in need of leaders to guide it in the process of Christlike transformation.

The Pastoral Epistles describe how the transformation of the church functions as a manifestation of God's grace bringing "salvation to all" while training Christians to live "self-controlled, upright, and godly" lives as a people "zealous for good deeds" (Titus 2:11–14 NRSV). By holding firm to Christian teaching elders enable the community of faith to fulfill its aim, which is "love that comes from a pure heart, a good conscience, and sincere faith" (1 Tim. 1:5 NRSV), and "a quiet and peaceable life in all godliness and dignity" (1 Tim. 2:2 NRSV). In contrast to false teachers who poison people with harmful ideas, elders remain focused on training in godliness (1 Tim. 4:7) by holding firm to the faith and guarding the deposit of faith (2 Tim. 1:13–14).

Elders need not feel overwhelmed by their role as examples and teachers of virtue since they can rely on God's Holy Spirit to be an active participant in Christian character formation. God fuels the life and ministry of the church by pouring out God's Holy Spirit (Acts 2:33) so that the church might participate in the work of God. The Holy Spirit bestows the power to redraft one's character (Gal. 5:16–26), channel one's talents and energies outward for the common good of the church (1 Cor. 12:1–11), and direct the mind toward living a godly life in anticipation of Jesus' return (Rom. 8 and 1 Cor. 2:6–15). God forms the church into "a dwelling in which God lives by his Spirit" (Eph. 2:22 NIV). The indwelling presence of God's Spirit calls the church into a dynamic way of life marked by change, transformation, and revelation.

The cultivation of Christian virtue in the lives of contemporary Christians has suffered from the separation of theology and spirituality. Most articulations of the Christian faith operate within a reduced understanding of knowledge that defines it as the objective comprehension of facts instead of experiential participation in truth. The result is a deficient self-understanding in which the church views itself as something less than a community of Christian virtue and Christian theology remains irrelevant to the witness of the church and the lives of Christian people. Elders must do theology with a focus toward spirituality: the quest for a fulfilled and authentic Christian existence by bringing together fundamental doctrines of Christianity and concrete experiences.

The good news for elders regarding the cultivation of virtue does not have to be imported into the church. The people, practices, and habits already functioning in the life of the faith community are trustworthy resources for virtue formation. Rituals such as baptism, the Lord's Supper, preaching, and the singing of hymns contribute to the formation of Christian character. Likewise, spiritual disciplines such as prayer, confession, contemplation, fasting, and hospitality train the church to know and love God. Exemplary practitioners of the faith serve as sources of wisdom in the process of Christian character formation as well.

The challenge for elders is to create an environment whereby these spiritual resources are intentionally accessed as tools for spiritual formation. The environment most conducive to spiritual formation is one that recognizes the holistic nature of Christian spirituality and makes room for diverse spiritual styles. Too often the community of faith mistakes uniformity for unity and thus robs itself of the opportunity to be exposed to a rich variety of Christian expression. Christian unity, as well as Christian virtue, is cultivated in the midst of diversity. In such an environment, the church is able to muster both deep thoughts and deep feelings about the life of faith while living with both humility in God's mystery and confidence in God's activity.

Corporate worship is a prime location for the formation of Christian virtue. Worship is a dynamic experience in which Christians glorify God and God shapes Christian people. The ultimate goal of Christian worship is not to ensure acts of worship are performed according to some rigid sense of first-century protocol. Rather, the goal of Christian worship is the formation of a Christlike people who glorify God and collaborate with God in bringing about God's intentions in the world.

Imagine the formative power that might be unleashed in a congregation's worship if its elders chose not to evaluate faithful worship based on its adherence to traditional forms or its ability to entertain, but according to its ability to form Christlike virtue in its participants. Songs would be judged not only on their musical style but on the language and message they provide the singer. The prayers of the worshiping community would reflect both its diversity and its relationality. Scripture readings, testimonies, and even sermons would become more interactive and communal. Virtue-forming worship would also reclaim the significance of rites of passage. Births, deaths, weddings, school promotions, seasonal events, and even liturgical seasons would be embraced as experiences of spiritual formation.

Richardson East conducts a baby-dedication ceremony for every newborn in our church family. The ceremony acknowledges the child as a gift from God and charges the parents to be stewards of that gift by raising the child in faith. The church is charged to be a community of support in which the parents and child can grow in faith. The church responds to the charge by reciting a pledge of support to the parents and then an elder prays a blessing over the family. There is great formative power in this kind of communal experience. The ritual sends the message that the spiritual formation of the newborn is the unfinished business of the entire church and that this process of formation will be shepherded by the elders.

Fittingly, the Richardson East elders send the same message to the newly baptized. Baptism, when articulated with theological robustness and practiced with intentionality, is one of the most formative of Christian practices. Baptism is much more than the culminating event of salvation in an individual's life. In order for a church to fully experience the transformative power of baptism, elders need to frame it as a beginning point of spiritual transformation and not the culmination of it. It needs to be reclaimed as a communal experience, one performed in the presence of the believing community and with an understanding that it initiates one into the believing community.

For example, when Miriam decided to be baptized one Thursday night she called Michael, an elder at the church she had been attending. Instead of meeting Miriam at the building to baptize her that night, Michael asked Miriam if she would be willing to wait until Sunday morning so she could be baptized in the presence of the community of faith. Miriam was nervous about being up in front of the large crowd, but Michael convinced her that the experience would have communal impact if she waited until Sunday. On Sunday morning, Michael baptized Miriam in front of the entire church.

The baptism began before the church with Michael's rendition of Miriam's growing involvement with the church. Michael told Miriam how much she and her family meant to his family and then reflected on the power of baptism. He said that baptism not only washes away Miriam's sin but underscored how it will bring to her the power of God's Holy Spirit. He said that God's Spirit would continue to work in her life to form her more fully into the image of Christ. Michael then asked Miriam to look out into the faces gathered for worship and said that baptism initiates her into the body of Christ and that the church, as the body of Christ, will be a source of love and support to as she grows in Christlikeness.

Following Miriam's baptism the church applauded and sang with thanksgiving. Miriam then reentered the auditorium to greetings by numerous members of the congregation welcoming her into the family of faith. Miriam later thanked Michael for convincing her to wait until Sunday, saying, "I did not really know what I was getting myself into." Michael did. And because of his wisdom, Miriam's baptism was a lesson in spiritual formation.

Baptism provides elders a powerful symbol through which they can teach Christian virtue to the community of faith. Paul does this very thing in Colossians 3 when he says: "So if you have been raised with Christ [in baptism], seek the things that are above, where Christ is, seated at the right hand of God. Set your minds on things that are above, not on things that are on earth, for you have died, and your life is hidden with Christ in God" (3:1–3 NRSV). Paul tells the Colossians what vices they need to put to death and get rid of as well as what virtues they are to put on and clothe themselves with. He concludes the charge with an emphasis on community or "one anothering" in which the Christian community is called to bear with, forgive, and love one another.

When Richardson East experienced more than ten baptisms in a six-week span, the elders decided to invite all of the recently baptized persons to an elders meeting. The elders welcomed the newly baptized and their families into the meeting and then took turns talking about baptism and its importance in Christian discipleship. The meeting concluded with the elders praying over each of the newly baptized and their families. As the families left the meeting one remarked how powerful it was to have the elders pray over them. Another said, "I have never been to a meeting like this one." These shepherds sent a powerful message of their role in the congregation's spiritual formation through their invitation, prayers, celebration, and blessings.

The Lord's Supper is another communal experience containing immense formative power for the community of faith. Too often the Supper has morphed into a time of individual meditation or stagnant memorial, when its practice is meant to be both communal and dynamic. Jesus did not intend for the Supper to be an obligation of obedience but a means of grace through which the Christian community is nourished by God's Spirit as it joins together as participants in the life of Christ. Worshipers need to have the experience of sitting at table with Jesus, who welcomes all people as a loving host. Likewise, the Supper serves an important role in virtue formation by calling on Christians to be reconciled to one another before coming together at table.[6]

Once or twice a year, the Richardson East elders serve communion to the congregation. The elders and their wives stand at tables positioned throughout the auditorium and receive participants as they arrive at the table. They offer the bread and cup to each participant and then offer a word of blessing or encouragement. Participants often comment about how the experience communicates the nature of the elders' love for Richardson East and provides a renewed sense of the communal nature of the Christian faith.

Are there appropriate times to experience the Lord's Supper other than Sunday morning worship? I remember, during college years, sharing in a Lord's Supper meal at the home of an elder. The Supper was part of an actual meal. Instead of rushing through the experience in five or ten minutes, participants were given time to be reflective and share thoughts and feelings with the group.

As the bread and cup were passed from person to person each one offered the emblems to the next saying, "the body of Christ, the blood of Christ given for you." The experience created a natural conduit through which those present began sharing deeper aspects of their life stories with one another.

Speaking of stories, elders are wise to engage a community's narrative self-understanding by identifying and reciting stories that illustrate the best of the Christian life. These narratives shape the character of a community. For example, the elders of the Richardson East Church of Christ tell a powerful story about a time in the 1980s when, despite the abundance of fear and limited knowledge about AIDS, Richardson East ministered to a group of people dying from AIDS. The church earned a reputation as a caring church because it chose to care for people living on the margins of society.

Testimony is a powerful resource for spiritual formation. A few years ago when Richardson East installed new elders, each one was asked to give a testimony about his faith journey. The testimonies provided the congregation insight into how the church's life formed the elders into credible church leaders. Recently, one of the elders facilitated a Wednesday night experience in which people shared testimonies about being faithful in the midst of adversity. The genius of the format was how the church discovered that its spiritual formation could be nurtured by its own experiences.

Testimony also encourages the church by illustrating ways the church's life impacts people. Sarah, my wife, and I experienced God's work through the life of the church. In a hospital room one spring morning a doctor told us our five-month-old daughter, Katie, had a seizure disorder that if left untreated would debilitate her for the rest of her life. The news sucked all of the oxygen out of the room. We stood there in stunned silence, feeling the full weight of the doctor's words.

When the doctor left the room Sarah and I were too devastated to speak. We just held each other tightly and cried. For months we had been keenly aware of the goodness of God. We had experienced firsthand God's love and creativity through the conception and birth of our daughter. We viewed Katie as an affirmation that God is a God of life, light, and love. Now we were not so sure. Where was God in this horrible news? Where was God when Katie's brain was being wired together? Days later, Sarah cried out to God, "Where are you?"

About that time, two of Sarah's friends from our church's small group came and put their arms around her. Sarah received those friends as God's answer to her prayer. It was as if God was saying to her, "Here I am. I am 'Emmanuel,' I am with you." Throughout Katie's health crisis it was the church that served as "God with us." It was the church that embodied the power of God at work in us and literally served us as the hands and feet of Christ. Church people cared for our basic needs, listened to our pain and anger, shared in our hope, and rejoiced with us over the brain surgery that ended Katie's seizures and offered her the chance to grow into the healthy little girl she is today. Sarah and I still do not know where God was when Katie's brain was being wired together but we sure know where God was while we dealt with Katie's diagnosis and treatment. God was with us through the body of Christ, the church.

Stories like ours remind the community of faith about the power of God at work in daily rituals of care, hospitality, and community. Elders not only lead by participating in these rituals but by emphasizing their power to the church. The same is true for the numerous disciplines that nurture spiritual formation outside of the church's worship life. Spiritual disciplines such as study, prayer, fasting, silence, solitude, and Sabbath work to shape Christians into the image of God. Such disciplines do not get expressed in the life of a church through *programs*. Rather, they are *culturally infused*.

Elders infuse such practices into church culture by *modeling* their practice. In addition to practicing the disciplines individually, elders incorporate them into the routines of congregational life. For example, some elder groups are moving away from a business-model approach to elders' meetings and are introducing spiritual practices into the meetings. In the new format, elders are spending more time together in study, *lectio divina* ("holy reading" or prayerful meditation), and other devotional readings of Scripture while delegating business matters to other gifted people in the church. Meetings are becoming venues for elder groups to pray over church members and actively offer them pastoral care and support.

Elders are also recognizing ways to *implement* spiritual practices into church processes such as minister searches, leader selections, and various congregational events. The elder selection process is a significant opportunity for instructing the church about the nature of the Christian life. To encourage thoughtful discernment within the congregation regarding the nature of church leadership, some churches are engaging fresh readings of Scripture that provide a broader picture of virtue in the life of the Christian leader.

For example, the lists of elder qualifications contained in the Pastoral Epistles are not intended to function as a uniform set of qualifications. Rather, they function to stir the imagination of the local congregation as it engages in discernment about what habits, attitudes, and experiences make one credible as a leader and representative of the body of Christ. Too often a rigid reading of these texts disqualifies virtuous leaders from serving as elders because of adverse experiences in their lives (divorce, rebellious child, or inability to have children). However, Christians can be credible examples of virtue precisely *because* of how they faithfully deal with adversity.

Perhaps the church will be best equipped to live into its identity as a community of Christian virtue if it considers an understanding of virtue that is broad enough to include both those who have avoided public adversity and those who have faithfully lived through it. Perhaps the diversity of experience will broaden the leadership's influence as a source of hope and love. The community of faith draws strength both from leaders who embody certain ideals and leaders who endure certain realities.

The question for elders to ponder is how much they are willing to trust God's Spirit to work through the discernment of the community in calling credible leaders from both backgrounds. The discernment process would require dialogue with a rich diversity of Scripture as well as focused communal participation in communal spiritual practices. The process will likely be complicated and cause anxiety for those uncomfortable with ambiguity. However, the community of faith will learn a great deal about what it means to be the people of God if it is forced to discern what it means to be a credible leader of the people of God.

Once the congregation selects elders, the new elder group can educate the church on the nature of virtue by how it chooses to function as leadership. In the same way that division and viciousness within an eldership can destroy a church, unity and virtue among the elders can nurture a church toward spiritual formation. Imagine the powerful transformation that can occur in the life of a church when its elders intentionally articulate expectations about how power is handled and shared. Consider what kind of impact an eldership can have on a congregation if it models healthy attitudes and practices regarding decision making and conflict.

A helpful practice in this regard is the creation of an elder covenant whereby an eldership articulates its expectations for its members. A covenant communicates an eldership's expectations of itself to the entire congregation and provides the eldership with a platform of credibility from which it can call others to lives of Christian virtue. For example, one elder group made a decision-making covenant stating that each decision would be made only after prayer and discussion that honored the group's diverse opinions. Once a decision was made it would be communicated as one voice by the leadership. Another elder covenant promised that elders would share God's love with one another by being open, engaging, transparent, and kind to one another.

It is appropriate for elders to hold the entire congregation accountable to the same basic values. Christian virtue needs to be articulated as an expectation for the community of faith. Perhaps your elder group might consider crafting a covenant for the entire church. Some churches are developing membership covenants to present as part of a new member orientation process. The covenant is not intended to be enforced in an authoritarian or overbearing manner, but is intended to create a sense of direction and accountability for each person's participation in the habits, practices, and attitudes of the Christian life.

Scripture provides helpful imagery for articulating expectations about the virtuous nature of the Christian life. One such image portrays the gospel as medicine for the soul. Healing was a core component in Jesus' ministry. When he entered a village, the sick became well. The good news of Jesus still heals sickness today. Thus, it is appropriate for elders to expect the community of faith to participate in a way of life that promotes health. Imagine how healing language could illustrate how the practices, attitudes, and habits of the Christian life function as gospel medicine.

The covenant could articulate expectations of health and wellness for church members. It could describe manners in which the love of Christ treats sin, sickness, and death in order to make us whole, healthy, and alive. Included in the covenant could be recommended practices and processes leading to spiritual fitness. The covenant could identify types of sickness and spiritual disease. Included in the covenant would be processes by which Christians deal together with sin, disagreement, and division.

Perhaps your elder group could craft a covenant based on the imagery of abundant life described in John 10. In a culture that touts various portrayals of "the good life," it is helpful for elders to articulate a vision of abundant life as participation in the ways of Jesus Christ. What if elders created a covenant in which abundant life is found through participation in Christian virtues? The covenant might draw on descriptions of virtue like the fruits of God's Spirit listed in Galatians 5 or on Paul's description of the good life in Philippians 2 as having the same mind as Christ Jesus.

The benefit of this type of covenant statement is that it makes implicit behavioral expectations explicit. Churches already function according to certain informal behavioral expectations. For example, most churches expect members to give generously of both their time and money. Churches expect participants to attend worship services, engage in ministry, and form relationships with other Christians, but rarely are such expectations proactively articulated. The community of faith may not engage generosity, worship, or ministry with intentionality if its leaders do not provide a clear understanding about how these behaviors form Christian people.

There is immense spiritual power in articulating such expectations publicly. For example, one group of elders consistently expects church members engaged in conflict with one another to deal directly with one another. Any church member who attempts to talk to the elders about a conflict is first asked about what happened when they spoke directly to the other party. If the person has not communicated with the other party, the elders ask them to first try to resolve it. The expectation applies to conflict with ministry staff as well. If anyone comes to the elders with a complaint about a minister, the elders ask, "What happened when you talked with him/her about it?" If the person has not directly communicated with the staff person, the elders refrain from action until the direct conversation occurs.

By creating an explicit expectation about how conflicts are handled within the community of faith elders provide a strong public lesson to the congregation about how to engage in difficult conversations, receive criticism, and yet remain united with people who do not share their opinions. Not surprisingly, the church gained a reputation for being a place people come to heal after experiencing elsewhere church-related pain and division. One new member claims, "Anyone who has been through a church split knows the pain it creates. This church does not let that kind of thing happen here." What a striking example of how elders form churches into communities of virtue!

One hazard of church leadership is our exposure to both the best and the worst expressions of the Christian faith. Too much exposure to anemic forms of Christian discipleship can tempt us to lower our expectations for the church. Do not yield to the temptation. God is dreaming big dreams for the church and you can help make those dreams come true. What do you believe God wants your church to be known for? What virtues do you believe your church best embodies? What kind of spiritual formation can you imagine taking place in the life of your congregation over the next ten years?

Elders, you face a high calling in helping the church maintain its ecclesial identity and extend its communal witness. The fundamental mission of the church is to embody and continue the work of Christ as the agent by which God redirects people to their true identity and shapes human character formation. I hope that the suggested practices, processes, and habits contained in this chapter provide you with helpful tools for instructing congregations in the virtuous ways of Jesus Christ. As one whose faith has been shaped by many faithful elders over the years, I will pray in the words of Paul that you "lead a life worthy of the calling to which you have been called."

Statement of Virtues[7]

Christianity is a way of life grounded in the way of the Triune God as manifested in the person of Jesus Christ. For Christians God is the beginning and the end of all things, the ultimate source and goal of the Christian life. As Christians, we draw our identity from God as a people formed by God to live under the Lordship of Jesus Christ, empowered by God's Spirit to fulfill God's intention that the entire world know and love God.

The nature, purpose, and destiny of the Christian life is found in Jesus Christ, who is

> the image of the invisible God, the firstborn of all creation; for in him all things in heaven and on earth were created, things visible and invisible, whether thrones or dominions or rulers or powers—all things have been created through him and for him. He himself is before all things, and in him all things hold together. He is the head of the body, the church; he is the beginning, the firstborn from the dead, so that he might come to have first place in everything. For in him all the fullness of God was pleased to dwell, and through him God was pleased to reconcile to himself all things, whether on earth or in heaven, by making peace through the blood of his cross. (Col. 1:15–20 NRSV)

Those who live the way of Jesus Christ are "new creations" (2 Cor. 5:17 NKJV), recreated by God to be "ministers of reconciliation" and "ambassadors of Christ." God has given humanity

> [a] share in His own Image, that is, in our Lord Jesus Christ, and has made us after the same Image and Likeness. Why? Simply in order that through his gift of God-likeness in us we may be able to perceive the Image Absolute, that is the Word Himself, and through Him to apprehend the Father; which knowledge of our Maker is for us the only real happy and blessed life. (St. Athanasius §11, p. 38)

God restores our divine nature by renewing our minds (Rom. 12:2) until we have the mind of Christ (Phil. 2). The leaders of the Richardson East Church of Christ invite you to cross the threshold into the Christian life as embodied in this faith community. We want to share with you a list of virtues that we believe are relevant in cultivating knowledge and love of God: *love, faith, hope, humility, peacemaking, forgiveness, wisdom, kindness, gentleness,* and *gratitude.*

The Richardson East elders believe that God's primary work of grace in our lives is the cultivation of Christlike virtue in each of us. If one crosses the threshold into the Christian way of life, one experiences the indwelling power of the Holy Spirit as active in the life of the church. Christians collaborate with the Holy Spirit and participate in the life of God through spiritual disciplines and practices that produce virtue. The Richardson East Church of Christ chooses to join God's Spirit at work among us by intentionally cultivating Christian virtue in the following ways:

- Preaching and teaching led by virtuous elders and ministers
- Worship as participation in the transforming work of God
- Fellowship with Christlike examples
- Participation in the habits of the spiritual life (disciplines)

---

1. John Siburt, "Crossing the Threshold: Catechesis as a Means for Discerning Relevant Christian Virtues at the Richardson East Church of Christ" (DMin thesis, ACU, 2005).

2. Ellen T. Charry, "Academic Theology in Pastoral Perspective," *Theology Today* 50, no. 1 (April 1993): 102.

3. Ibid., 91.

4. The heart of John Siburt's project thesis was published in *Good Shepherds: More Guidance for the Gentle Art of Shepherding*, ed. David Fleer and Charles Siburt (Abilene, TX: Leafwood, 2007) and is reproduced below with permission.

5. James W. Thompson, *Pastoral Ministry according to Paul* (Grand Rapids: Baker Academic, 2006), 22.

6. See John Mark Hicks, *Come to the Table: Revisioning the Lord's Supper* (Abilene, TX: Leafwood, 2002).

7. The following Statement of Virtues was distributed to the Richardson East Church of Christ by the elders and appeared as an appendix in John Siburt's thesis.

CHAPTER 2

Discerning the Call to Lead

AARON WALLING[1]

Imagine you are driving down the interstate on a Sunday afternoon when you receive a call from your congregation's elder-selection committee. Over the past few weeks, this group of individuals, empowered by the current leadership, has facilitated a process for the congregation to identify and appoint new elders. The first phase of that process concluded this morning as members put forward the names of potential elders. This call you receive pertains to that list; you have been nominated. A significant portion of the congregation thinks you would make a good elder, and the selection committee would like to know if you will consider serving in this capacity. Perhaps you have prepared for this moment; you have long felt God's calling on your life to serve as an elder in the church. Possibly, though, this call catches you by surprise. While you could easily recognize others in the congregation with this gift of leadership, you are surprised that you have been included, that others see the same gift in you.

Even as you maintain control of your car, you feel as if your mind is spinning. What should I say? What will my spouse think? What about my kids? How will this impact my family? Can I balance this with my work schedule? What will be expected of me? Can I really do this? Why would people pick me? In the span of a few moments, these questions and more swirl through your thoughts. However, before you are able to adequately reflect, the committee member indicates that an answer will be needed from you by the following weekend. The selection process necessitates that the committee announce potential candidates to the congregation by next Sunday. Therefore, you need to provide a response rather quickly regarding your willingness to serve. As you hang up the phone, you suddenly realize that you seem to have forgotten exactly where you were driving.

The Elder Selection Process at Cinco Ranch

One elder nominee at the Cinco Ranch Church of Christ gave such a description as his past personal experience of our process of selecting elders. Cinco Ranch was established in 1992 in a rapidly growing suburb of Houston, Texas. The accelerated growth of the community contributed to a significant increase in membership, necessitating a need for adding elders more often. In 2008 our four elders agreed that in order to effectively care for the church, they needed more help, and they commissioned a team to lead the congregation through a selection process.

At Cinco Ranch, the leadership invites the church to be part of this process, maintaining that God speaks through people to identify potential elders. Thus, over the years, Cinco Ranch has developed a formalized process of selection that consists of four distinct phases: nomination, introspection, resolution, and affirmation. Each of these phases is designed to allow the congregation adequate time for reflection and consideration. During the nomination phase, through a series of sermons and special announcements, the selection team encourages members to identify men within the congregation who exhibit the heart and qualities of a shepherd. By the end of this phase, members submit names, and the selection team then contacts those individuals receiving a certain percentage of nominations to determine their willingness to continue through the process as a candidate.

In the past, due to the amount of time needed for the next three phases of the process—phases in which the congregation would consider, approve, and affirm the candidates—the selection team asked nominees to decide within the week. Typically, members turned in their nominations on a Sunday. By the following Sunday, the leader of the selection team announced the confirmed candidates to the congregation. Unfortunately, this left nominees with little time for discernment.

Yet, the history of Cinco Ranch demonstrates that this particular week proves vital to the entire process. The congregation always responds favorably to those who accept their nominations. Over the years, all candidates along with returning elders have received the affirmation of the congregation; none have been denied. If a nominee accepts his candidacy, history indicates he will likely receive the congregation's affirmation. However, if because of his overwhelming questions or lingering hesitation he declines this opportunity, the congregation misses the chance to potentially affirm a leader otherwise identified as possessing the heart and qualities of a shepherd.

In 2008 members of Cinco Ranch put forward the names of fourteen men. Each of these were contacted and given a week to consider their nomination. By the following Sunday, only two accepted and agreed to continue through the subsequent steps. Guided by the official process, the selection team led Cinco Ranch through the next three phases, and the congregation installed the new men and reaffirmed the four already serving as elders.

While the four elders never placed numerical goals on the selection team, the post-selection assessment revealed a mutual sense of disappointment that so few men were willing to accept their nominations. The team admitted its desire to impact Cinco Ranch's leadership by facilitating the addition of more than two new shepherds. Through the course of their discussion, the team recognized a gap in the process. Why were those identified by the congregation as potential leaders so reticent to officially serve as elders? In what ways could the team enhance the process to encourage more men to accept their nominations? At the very least, how could the team ensure that nominees had the time to make an informed decision? It became clear to the team that while the process offered the congregation ample time to both nominate and affirm potential elders, it provided no formal structure for discernment among the nominees; it lacked any means by which to help them determine if they should indeed accept their candidacy. For this reason, Cinco Ranch needed to develop a fifth phase designed specifically to assist nominees through the process of discernment.

The Need for Discernment

Why would so many nominees hesitate to serve? Drawing on his extensive work in church consultation, Charles Siburt proposed three potential categories of influence that might produce negative responses among nominees.[2] Initially, various family considerations may affect a nominee's decision. He may assume that balancing family and career and serving as an elder will be too difficult, or he may wish to protect his wife and children from the pressures of church leadership. Or the nominee may in fact desire to serve as an elder but find his family less than supportive.

Misperception may also play a part in nominees' declining their candidacy. As outsiders to the leadership structure, they may misunderstand the role and functions of an elder. They may presume the congregation inundates elders with a wide range of problems and needs and thereby anticipate late nights spent counseling and caring for individual members. Even more, they may fear that serving as an elder means attending long, unpleasant leadership meetings.

Finally, nominees may simply find themselves plagued by personal misgivings. They may doubt their own abilities to rise to the task, uncertain of their own patience, wisdom, or leadership. Awareness of specific sins or struggles from their past, coupled with the misperception of elders as men with near-perfect records of life and faith, may lead them to believe their personal history precludes them from serving as an elder. Conversely, nominees may doubt the community of faith itself, questioning the congregation's ability to treat them with grace and understanding as they transition into their leadership role.

While only postulations, these categories highlight the variety of thoughts and concerns with which nominees might wrestle. Additionally, the previous selection process at Cinco Ranch added angst by requiring a hasty decision from nominees. Essentially, nominees had but a few days to learn of their nomination, wade through their apprehensions, and then accept or decline their candidacy. This lack of time and of a formal discernment phase forced nominees to draw their own conclusions about the demands of leadership. If the evidence of the 2008 selection process can be believed, the majority of individuals put into this position decline their nomination.

The commissioning of another elder-selection team in the fall of 2010 presented Cinco Ranch with an opportunity to adjust its process—specifically, to create a formal time of discernment during which nominees could openly discuss the theological basis and the practical aspects of serving as elders. Ideally, the elders already serving would provide valuable insight and candor regarding their own experiences. Additionally, this time of discernment would offer nominees adequate time to prayerfully consider the prospect of serving as an elder. Regardless of whether they would ultimately accept or decline the nomination, nominees would be afforded the opportunity to make an informed decision about their potential leadership within the community of faith.

The Practice of Discernment

Robert Kinast explains that regardless of the terminology, whether one calls it "spiritual discernment" or "theological reflection," the attempt to interpret the intersection between theology and experience ultimately seeks to disclose "the presence of God in people's experience, a presence that invites them to encounter God where they are and to participate in the divine life which is offered to them there."[3] As Kinast explores five contemporary expressions of spiritual discernment, with ideologies ranging across the theological spectrum, he identifies commonalities within their overall movement. Each expression begins with a lived experience, seeking to correlate that experience with the sources of Christian tradition, and to draw out practical implications for Christian living.[4]

Since this discernment phase assisted those encountering one such lived experience, namely receiving the congregation's nomination to serve as an elder, it needed to create a clear connection between their experience and the Christian tradition. Several sources of the Christian faith, including tradition, reason, communal perspective, and personal experience, could have introduced the prospective elders to this heritage. However, due to the time constraints of the selection process, this discernment phase needed to employ a manageable strategy for a six-week window of time. Therefore, while this phase utilized multiple angles of interaction with the Christian tradition, such as communal reflection and pastoral counsel, Luke Timothy Johnson ultimately provided the most helpful approach to discernment with his emphasis on the role of Scripture in the decision-making process.[5] In Johnson's assessment, unless believers understand what God performed in the past, they will fail to ascertain his current activity. Thus, believers must engage the Word of God in order to discover the necessary "interpretive tools for discerning the story of the present."[6]

Accordingly, we designed the discernment phase to help nominees frame their nominations within the parameters of Scripture as they determined their willingness to serve as elders at Cinco Ranch. If successful, such an approach would potentially provide nominees with a legitimate perspective from which to view their nomination—decreasing the chance that a nominee would respond in haste based on his own personal assessments or false assumptions or would miss the divine opportunity inherent in his selection by simply viewing his nomination as the result of a type of congregational democratic process. Rooting the conversations in Scripture would equip nominees with a biblical perspective as they maneuvered the discernment process.

Because some considerations would fall outside the scope of any particular scriptural response, biblical knowledge alone would prove inadequate for nominees. These men needed to sort through not only the theological foundations but also the practical implications of their service as elders, specifically as it would relate to their families and careers. They faced questions regarding the logistics of serving as an elder at Cinco Ranch as well as more personal inquiries into the impact of leading on their marriages, children, and jobs. Rather than ignoring this need for input from sources beyond Scripture, the phase provided opportunities for these conversations as well, namely through the use of specific group sessions and intentional mentoring relationships.

Nevertheless, a biblical perspective framed even these practical concerns. The men needed Scripture to inform their personal considerations. The selection process itself mandated that nominees base their discernment on more than individual concerns. The process is designed not as an election but as a contention that God often calls leaders into service through the voice of his people, as evidenced in passages such as Acts 6:1–7 and 13:1–3. To dismiss the congregation's nomination without intentional reflection on Scripture could potentially subvert this divine initiative. Again, as Johnson asserts, Scripture itself provides the necessary "interpretive tools for discerning the story of the present."[7] Thus for the sake of relevancy to the nominees, this discernment phase targeted those theological issues most applicable to the determining process.

I proposed three primary categories of consideration that nominees needed to explore. First, nominees needed to seek the source of their nomination, to decipher the voice inherent in their opportunity. Was the nomination simply from the congregation, or should they interpret any divine involvement? If they subsequently agreed to become candidates, nominees needed to identify the functions of serving as an elder. To what kinds of roles and activities were they committing? Finally, nominees needed to ascertain the goal of their service as elders. What is the ultimate purpose of serving in such a capacity?

Undoubtedly, the discernment phase could have employed a variety of passages to establish a theology for those considering serving as elders. For instance, the group sessions could have explored texts from 1 Timothy and Titus, which describe the character and quality of elders. However, while pertinent to the overall perspective, the specific questions addressed in those passages receive adequate attention in the introspection and resolution phases of Cinco Ranch's elder selection process. Instead of merely educating nominees on the biblical basis for church polity, this phase needed to establish firm theological foundations that would enable nominees to process their questions—namely, the source, the function, and the goal of their potential service as elders. Nominees needed a scriptural framework through which they could view their own nomination and explore issues relevant to their personal discernment. Ephesians 4:11–16 offered such a structure.

A Lens for Discernment

Set in the midst of a broader movement by the writer, Ephesians 4:1–16 serves as a connector between two main sections of thought. While the first three chapters pronounce for believers the privileges found in Christ, the author moves in chapter 4 to paraenesis, describing for his audience the way of life consistent with those privileges. Specifically, in this pericope, the author builds a case for both the unity and diversity existing within the church. Initially, in Ephesians 4:1–6, he establishes the call to unity among believers as they share many foundational claims of the faith. He then shifts in Ephesians 4:7–16 to describing the intentional diversity of giftedness within the body of Christ. Rather than creating potential conflict for the church, Christ intends this diversity to stimulate the complete growth and maturity of the body.

Christ serves as the writer's singular focus. Even in the midst of ecclesiological claims, Christology informs his rationale. At this point in the letter, the author has already asserted the place of Christ in the heavenly realms. Exalting him above all things, God appointed him as head over everything (Eph. 1:20–22). Now in this position of authority he shows care and concern for his people by giving gifts to his church.

This strong Christological emphasis and the segue in Ephesians 4:1–16 to the diversity of Christ's gifts triggers for the writer a recollection of a particular psalm, which he quotes in Ephesians 4:8. While the specifics of his usage fall outside the scope of this essay, the intended emphasis proves vital to the framing of what follows in Ephesians 4:11–16. Rather than receive gifts, Christ gives gifts to his church to confirm his superior place in the heavenly realms.[9] Therefore, while the writer may explore ecclesiological implications in this section, as well as in the duration of his letter, he establishes a firm Christological foundation.

With Christ's position firmly established, the writer continues by elaborating on the gifts Christ gives to his church. While other lists of gifts exist within Scripture, such as Romans 12:4–8 and 1 Corinthians 12:7–11, Ephesians 4:11 describes the gifts of specific people. Indeed, Christ blesses his body with individuals gifted to lead. Their leadership stems not from personal persuasion or even communal selection; they lead strictly by the appointment of Christ himself.[9]

While not an exhaustive enumeration of all forms of ministry, it behooves the modern reader to reflect on the identification of these specific gifts, especially given the explicit mention of *poimenas*. Often translated as either "pastors" or "shepherds," this term provides a potential connection point for elder nominees. What an incredibly significant realization for those entering the process of discernment—especially when the temptation arises to view their nomination as merely the result of the congregation's preference. Based on this passage, a nomination to local leadership could possibly convey a call from Christ himself;

he is the source. As Markus Barth states, "Christ gives the church the officers she needs, not vice versa."[10]

Understanding their role as such, these leaders refuse to use their giftedness as an excuse for ecclesial cloistering; rather, they recognize the need for intimate involvement in the life of the church. Christ gives them gifts not to establish positions of prestige but to provide his people with authentic leadership through service; that is their function. J. C. O'Neill compares the relationship between Christ and these ministers to the purely secular relationship between master and servants. Essentially, servants serve their master in two ways: they wait on the master, and they wait on the master's guests.[11] Their identity as servants of the master naturally orients them to a position of service to those within the master's care. Thus, these leaders given by Christ intentionally engage in ministry benefiting his church.

Few would disagree that these leaders should be oriented toward the service of the saints. But what is the exact nature of this function? Specifically, in Ephesians 4:12, does the author intend to describe three separate functions of leadership or to give a threefold description of one primary function? In other words, do leaders engage in the three distinct tasks of preparing God's people, performing works of service, and building up the body of Christ; or do they dedicate themselves to the singular task of preparing God's people to perform works of service that build up the body of Christ? According to the former interpretation, leaders engage in various forms of service that benefit the church, whereas the latter understanding suggests leaders primarily serve the church by helping the believers perform the actual works of ministry.

While the debate often involves grammatical, interpretive, and historical considerations, such discussion seems rooted in more recent ecclesiological concerns of the relationship between clergy and laity. While valuable for the contemporary church, this debate may, in fact, miss the writer's Christological intent. He aims not necessarily to establish a hierarchy within the church but to confirm Christ's ongoing provision for his people. Christ gives gifts to all believers (4:7). However, Christ also blesses his body with clear leadership as it grows up into him, the head. Functionally, these leaders ensure the growth and development of the church by proclaiming the word and performing acts of ministry. Christ specifically intends their service to prepare his people and to build his body.

Therefore, having ascended higher than the heavens, Christ gives leaders to his church for a particular reason. As Ronald Fung indicates, these leaders accomplish the "immediate purpose of equipping the saints and the ultimate goal of promoting the church's growth to maturity."[12] The leaders listed in Ephesians serve the church on behalf of Christ for a sole reason, namely to build up his body; maturing the church is their ultimate goal. For this reason, the author utilizes both body and building metaphors throughout his letter.[13] These images accomplish more than simply describing the church; they point to Christ. In each case, the writer uses the imagery to creatively portray the relationship between Christ and the church, whether as "head" or "cornerstone." Therefore, even in this ecclesiological imagery, the author makes Christological claims.

From his position of power and prominence, Christ gives leaders to his church for the purpose of maturing his body. These leaders recognize the goal of their giftedness, specifically to facilitate the growth of the body into the fullness of the head. Willingly, they dedicate themselves to teaching, training, proclaiming, preparing, serving, and building the community of faith; selflessly, they give of themselves so that the church might grow fully into the whole measure of Christ. Furthermore, even in the face of threatening pressures, rather than instilling dread or panic, these leaders mature the body by cultivating an environment of love. Such dedication, therefore, fulfills Christ's intent in giving the gift of leaders to his church.

Undoubtedly, those nominated in an elder-selection process deal with a variety of questions as they determine their willingness to serve. As they maneuver through the theological aspects of these questions, they are likely to find themselves seeking more information within three distinct categories: the source of their nomination, the function of their potential service, and the ultimate goal of their service as elders (should they agree to proceed). Personal practices of discernment, while necessary, are inadequate to the immensity of the task; the significance of a nomination to serve as an elder of Christ's church necessitates the implementation of a formalized discernment process.

Specifically, this process needs to provide perspective for potential elders by creating a connection between their experience of nomination and the Christian tradition, primarily that revealed in Scripture. In Ephesians 4:11–16 the author addresses all three categories of consideration by confirming that Christ gives the gift of leaders to his church to serve the body and build it up to maturity. This text, therefore, offers nominees a theologically informed lens through which they can consider their own nomination and discern their potential candidacy.

A Strategy for Discernment

The opportunity to serve as an elder presents nominees with a wide range of considerations. Not only must they determine a biblical basis for their decision, but they must also explore the potential impact of such service on their families, careers, and personal faith. Thus, in developing a formalized discernment phase, we wanted to address the theological foundations and the practical considerations of serving as an elder. Accordingly, our strategy involved two distinct components: group sessions and mentoring relationships.

Group Sessions

Upon completion of the initial phase of our process, the selection team contacted those identified by the congregation, notifying them of their nomination. In the conversation, the team expressed admiration to each of these individuals that the congregation deemed them worthy to serve in such a capacity. Furthermore, the team encouraged each nominee to refrain from making any immediate decision regarding his candidacy but instead to participate with other nominees in a formal time of discernment. Given the nature of such an opportunity, the team explained, this portion of the process aimed not to pressure a particular response but rather to afford each nominee the chance to make an informed decision.

Those who agreed to participate then met in group sessions for an hour and a half on Wednesday nights for six weeks. The six men already serving as elders also attended the meetings. Their tenure as elders of Cinco Ranch along with their own previous experiences of the nomination and selection process would prove invaluable for this group of men now facing similar considerations. As preaching minister, I served as facilitator of the group sessions.

While the discernment needs of nominees certainly varied among individuals, the sessions focused on four specific categories for reflection. Three categories related to the theological considerations of leadership, as identified above: the source of one's call into leadership, the function of those who accept such a call, and the goal of that call. The fourth, more pragmatic, category addressed the basic logistics of serving as an elder at Cinco Ranch. Although somewhat rudimentary compared to the divine implications of Ephesians 4:11–16, such practical considerations also substantially factor into a nominee's decision-making process.

The first session served as an introduction to our discernment process. Prior to that meeting, participants knew neither what to expect in regard to the class design nor who else might be in attendance. Thus, we provided time for brief introductions, and I gave an overview of our goals. From there, I shared Siburt's

list of possible hesitations to suggest in a non-threatening manner that a congregation's selection fills many nominees with a wide range of emotions. Furthermore,
I proposed that such questions necessitate a formalized time of discernment.

For the remainder of the session, I introduced our primary text in Ephesians,
along with our principle practice of *lectio divina*. Rather than structuring each
session around a lecture, I wanted to encourage participants to discover for themselves the significance of Ephesians 4:11–16 as it related to their task of discernment. Thus, for this first session, after familiarizing the participants with its
underlying premise, we engaged in *lectio divina* as a large group by reading the
text and sharing our initial responses.

Because I aimed in the next three sessions to explore the three categorical
implications of Ephesians 4:11–16, I utilized a similar format for each of the
meetings. After introductory comments, I divided the participants into smaller
discussion groups. Our numbers allowed for groups consisting of one elder and
two nominees. As much as possible, these groups remained consistent throughout the sessions. Within the groups, the participants interacted with the passage
through *lectio divina*.

For the purposes of the class, I imposed a sense of structure to this practice
by emphasizing particular questions raised by the text, questions that moved us
through the categories of the source, function, and goal of serving as an elder.
Thus, in our second session, which I entitled "Gifted by Whom?" participants
considered the question "What do we learn about Christ from this passage?" In
the next session, entitled "Gifted for What?" groups approached the text ponder-
ing "As Christ gifts his church with leaders, to what kinds of tasks do they devote
themselves?" Finally, in our fourth session, entitled "Gifted till When?" groups
interacted with the question "As Christ gifts his church with leaders, what is their
ultimate purpose?"

After the discussion groups engaged the text in their smaller settings, we
reconvened and shared our discoveries with the larger group. In facilitating the
conversation, I drew attention to those reflections highlighting our emphasis on
source, function, or goal. When pertinent to the discussion, I also added my own
exegetical observations gleaned from my preparations for the class. To conclude
each of these three sessions, I asked the group to consider specific ways in which
these conversations could influence a nominee's discernment.

In the final two sessions, I shifted our discussion to the practical aspects
of serving as an elder at Cinco Ranch. To keep our scriptural lens of discernment at the forefront of our conversations, we began each class with a reading of

Ephesians 4:11–16. Then during these sessions, we reviewed two specific leadership documents used by Cinco Ranch elders and staff: a covenant of leadership and an elder leadership model. The covenant of leadership enumerates the expectations for how elders and staff will interact with and support one another. The leadership model describes the protocol for meetings and the process for making decisions as an eldership. As we discussed these documents, we considered how they could facilitate the leadership's embodiment of the principles gleaned from Ephesians 4:11–16.

These last sessions also provided the opportunity to explore the implications of joining the leadership team. I facilitated a conversation regarding our current theological trajectory, conveying the need for those who serve as elders to generally embrace this direction, rather than attempt to drastically alter it. Because Cinco Ranch possessed a group of elders already in the process of leading the congregation, nominees needed to perceive their role as additions to the team rather than independent appointees with their own agendas.

During the remainder of our time, I opened the floor for nominees to ask the elders any questions they might still have. Whether they wished to inquire specifically about the eldership at Cinco Ranch or more generally about the personal implications of serving as an elder, we invited them to pose their questions. Again, the experience of our elders as both current leaders and past nominees offered a unique perspective and a depth of insight invaluable to the potential elders. Regardless of my skills to facilitate the sessions, our current elders alone possessed an ability to speak directly to the nominees' situation. For this reason, the elders' involvement throughout this process proved vital.

On a final note, spouses were not included in the group sessions. While the nominations presented considerations for the entire family, the nature of the group discussions aimed to provide a theological as well as practical basis for serving as an elder. This focus differs slightly from the potential concerns of the family unit, which it seemed likely would revolve more around issues of time commitment and the impact of church leadership on the elder's family. To ensure the discernment phase addressed these multiple factors influencing a nominee's decision, we included an aspect of intentional pastoral care for the nominee and his spouse through mentoring relationships.

Mentoring Relationships

Nominees inevitably needed more intimate interactions to complement their time of discernment. By design, group sessions focused primarily on foundational principles and practices related to serving as an elder. Yet nominees' considerations extended beyond the formalities of leadership. The men needed opportunities to discuss with seasoned elders the personal impact of such service on their families, their careers, and even their spiritual lives. Thus the establishment of mentoring relationships provided a forum for this aspect of discernment.

Accordingly, our current elders committed to personally mentor the nominees through this process. Upon completion of the nomination phase, the elders evenly distributed the nominees among themselves. As much as possible, they tried to base these matches on previous personal relationships. The numbers worked such that each elder mentored two nominees.

The mentoring relationships allowed too for the inclusion of spouses. The decision to serve as an elder involves more than the leader himself; it requires a family commitment. Therefore, recognizing the need for the nominee and his spouse to gain clarity through the course of the discernment phase, the elders asked their wives to join them in mentoring the nominee couple. Specifically, they committed to a particular plan of interactions over the course of the six weeks.

At our first group session, I explained to the nominees our desire to offer support not only to them but to their spouses as well. I described the mentoring relationships, and I identified for each nominee the elder serving as his mentor. Then, within the first two weeks, the elder couple met with their nominee couple to offer support, encouragement, and prayer during the time of discernment. The meeting also allowed for the elder couples to share their own personal experiences both as nominees originally and then as they transitioned to serving on the leadership team. Due to the nature of these conversations, the elder couples ensured the meetings happened in a rather intimate setting, such as an invitation to dinner, dessert, or coffee. Furthermore, since each elder couple had two mentoring relationships, they agreed to meet with each of their nominee couples separately. Because the discernment process would affect couples in different ways, the elder couples hoped to provide each couple with the most appropriate pastoral care.

After the initial meeting, the elder couple maintained regular contact with the nominee couple to address any questions and to express continued support. This contact could occur through phone calls, e-mails, and typical congregational interactions. Then during the last week of the phase, the elder couple offered the nominee couple the opportunity for another personal meeting to provide any final advice or encouragement, as well as prayer, as the nominee prepared to make his decision. Finally, in our last group session, we explained to nominees that their mentors would call them by the weekend to find out their decision regarding their willingness to continue through the selection process. Thus operating in conjunction with the group sessions, these mentoring relationships supplied a necessary breadth to the discernment phase.

The Value of Discernment

Because we modified the 2010 selection process with the addition of a formalized discernment phase, we wanted to evaluate its impact on the nominees' experience. Regardless of the number accepting and the number declining their nominations, the goal would be accomplished if nominees confirmed that the discernment phase aided them in their decision-making process. Therefore, throughout the six-week phase, I maintained extensive notes on the group sessions, recording any observations that might indicate nominees' perceptions of the process. Then upon completion of this phase, I conducted two group interviews, one with only the nominees and one with the existing elders. Utilizing both a written questionnaire and an open dialogue, I hoped to receive feedback on the process as well as suggestions for its improvement.

Through both their actions and their comments, nominees demonstrated from the start a sincere desire to participate in this process. Even though the discernment class started fifteen minutes earlier than our regular Wednesday gatherings, the men arrived faithfully on time to the group sessions for the entirety of the six weeks. Given that a typical Wednesday night at Cinco Ranch finds adult class members trickling into their classes ten to fifteen minutes late, the nominees' timely presence proved noteworthy and seemed to indicate their desire to engage in this process.

Beyond the attendance factor, overt comments also demonstrated the nominees' perceived need for discernment. In the first session when I led the group through Siburt's list of possible hesitations, participants indicated clear signs of identification with the various perspectives mentioned. In the conversation that followed, nominees seemed genuinely surprised that the congregation had selected them as potential elders. One individual jokingly said his initial thought upon receiving the call from the selection team was, "Am I being punk'd?"

Amazingly, each man could understand why everyone else in the room had been nominated. They could see the leadership qualities in others but were perplexed to find themselves in the same company. One nominee even used the word "uncomfortable" to describe his initial response to the nomination. Another man shared doubt about his biblical knowledge as well as his ability to lead. Thus, in our first session, participants confirmed the need for an intentional time of reflection to consider theological, practical, and personal aspects of serving as an elder. Fortunately, Siburt's list of hesitations seemed to release a considerable amount of tension for nominees as they discovered the normalcy of their fears.

Because these men all faced the same prospect of potentially serving as elders, they developed a sense of camaraderie over the course of the discernment phase. Within their written questionnaires, several emphasized their positive assessment of the group sessions, commenting on the value of meeting with "others like me" or the fact that they were "going to miss the sessions" once the discernment phase concluded. During the group interview, one nominee expressed how he was helped simply knowing others were dealing with the same concerns regarding their decision. Another appreciated the encouragement he received from the rest of the group. Thus, the discernment phase clearly provided the nominees with an opportunity to maneuver their considerations not in isolation but in community through a shared experience.

Besides connecting with other nominees, the discernment phase also allowed the development of relationships with the elders. Through both group sessions and mentoring relationships, the nominees gained a glimpse of future service as an elder by interacting with those already serving in that capacity. In the discussions on the practical aspects of serving as an elder, I noticed an impressive dynamic when one nominee expressed his concern about balancing time, and the elders gently reassured him as they spoke from their own experience. Later, one nominee shared his perception that serving as an elder "seems more manageable." In another evaluation, one of the elders spoke directly to this dynamic when he wrote, "The interaction between the prospective elders and those currently serving was invaluable." Therefore, the elders' involvement in the discernment phase provided nominees with essential insight.

While we designed mentoring relationships to enhance this dynamic between elders and nominees, we discovered the need for improvement. Even though one elder affirmed their value by calling the mentoring a "necessary part of the process," and another termed it the "most helpful part," some participants described a less than stellar experience. In one case, a nominee stated his mentoring relationship was "non-existent" because his mentoring elder had been out of town on business for much of the discernment phase. In other cases, two elders verbalized personal regret, stating they wished they had "met more often" or taken the chance for "more interaction." One of the nominees expressed a similar sentiment, saying that he "should have used [his] mentor more by calling and discussing [his] thoughts throughout."

For future purposes, I recognize the need for clearer expectations in regard to the mentoring. What are these relationships intended to accomplish? Such a conversation could help elders and nominees alike in knowing what to expect and how to take advantage of this intentional pastoral care. In fact, both nominees and elders independently expressed a desire for more structure to these mentoring meetings. They requested a "guide for discussion" or at least some "prompted questions," rather than an open-ended dialogue.

In spite of these shortcomings, though, nominees and elders alike agreed on the value of the mentoring relationships for the nominees' wives. Several nominees attested in their written evaluations to the impact of these meetings on their spouses. One indicated he could not have accepted his nomination without his wife's support and then wrote, "Her approval came after the time spent with our mentor two-on-two with his wife." The elders confirmed these assessments in their interview by stating that the "wives seemed to get more from the mentoring relationships." One elder shared his perception that wives had two concerns: the expectations placed on elders and the expectations placed on elders' wives.

As much as the mentoring relationships aided nominees' wives in the discernment process, the elders suggested the inclusion of more intentional opportunities for the spouses. One elder wrote frankly, "We need to involve the wives." Another proposed offering a group session devoted to wives, allowing them "to meet and discuss their fears and concerns." During the group interview with the nominees, one participant expressed his concern that he "felt like [his] wife was on the outside looking in." In response, someone proposed we "offer a similar class for spouses, at least something more official than mentoring." Such comments confirm that the decision to serve as an elder extends beyond the nominee's personal considerations. Discernment happens as a couple. Therefore, a formalized discernment phase should indeed include opportunities for both the husband and the wife to explore the implications of serving as an elder.

Other feedback revealed that the attempt to ground the discernment process in Ephesians 4:11–16 proved beneficial. Certainly the goal of the biblical discussions was not necessarily the imparting of new knowledge, as if one particular verse would magically lead to immediate discernment. However, these conversations served to remind participants that their nominations involved more than the human element, that the process was more than a congregational election. As the passage revealed, Christ gives leaders to serve his church. Therefore, in their discernment, the nominees needed to consider this divine component as well.

Furthermore, as both the nominees and elders grasped the Christological nature of their call, they discovered a natural orientation toward maturing the body. One of the shepherds described how this understanding helped him recover a view of elders as those who help "the flock grow in their walk." He further insisted, "shepherds should not focus too much on non-spiritual matters." The Christology revealed in Ephesians 4:11–16 hones a leadership's emphasis and creates a healthier eldership as it dedicates itself to matters of building and maturing the body.

When asked what effect this phase had on their process of discernment, nominees insisted it made a significant impact. Several men indicated that without this process, they would have immediately declined their nominations. One wrote, "I would have been an automatic 'no,'" while another stated, "Without this [process], I might have taken 'another pass' without sitting back and taking into account my invitation [by] the church to serve." Others described the process as "greatly beneficial" and "very helpful." They indicated the process gave them "specific areas to focus on" and "helped them understand God's perspective in a new and better way." Another nominee said, "This made me think more deeply about my nomination and my responsibilities as a church member."

Of the twelve men identified by the congregation in 2010 as potential elders, six accepted their nominations. At the end of the selection process, these six along with the six men already serving as elders were affirmed by the congregation and installed as the new eldership team. We created an intentional time of discernment not necessarily to increase our retention rate of potential elders, but to ensure nominees received adequate time to make an informed decision.

The nominees confirmed such an experience. One participant wrote that he had "ample time to reflect." Then in the group interview, a nominee stated, "My nomination is not a fluke. Something bigger is going on." Another nominee echoed this perception when he said, "I realized we are wanted. It is harder to take a pass on this process." Someone also asked, "How do you get to 'yes' in a shorter amount of time?" In his written evaluation, this same nominee indicated that the discernment phase gave him "time to learn, share, pray, and ask for help." In the end, he said with confidence, "I feel better about my decision." Two elders provided further confirmation when they stated that their mentees who declined their candidacy still benefited from the process and even expressed a desire to serve as elders in the future.

I concluded the evaluations by asking both nominees and elders whether this discernment phase should be repeated in future selection processes at Cinco Ranch, and every participant answered affirmatively. Nominees used such phrases as "absolute must," "enthusiastically recommend," "definitely keep," and "absolutely vital." Likewise, elders made comments stating it "should be a part of all shepherd selections going forward," and "I support one hundred percent continuing this type of class."

Regardless of a congregation's process of elder selection, the insertion of a discernment phase proves a viable strategy. It provides nominees and their spouses an opportunity to explore theological and practical considerations of serving as elders and thus make informed decisions about their nominations. Furthermore, a discernment phase offers nominees the chance to form deeper relationships with one another as well as with those already serving as elders. It also allows potential elders and current elders to establish a foundation for their eventual service together on the leadership team. Finally, the congregation itself benefits tremendously from such a phase by affirming and appointing elders who have discerned the call of Christ to serve his church and who will humbly dedicate themselves to building and maturing his body.

----

1. Aaron Walling, "Implementing a Discernment Phase for Those Nominated in the Shepherd Selection Process at the Cinco Ranch Church of Christ" (DMin thesis, ACU, 2011).

2. Charles Siburt, "Helping Those Nominated as Elders to Say Yes instead of No" (course handout, ACU, 2010).

3. Robert L Kinast, *What Are They Saying about Theological Reflection?* (New York: Paulist, 2000), 3.

4. Ibid., 1.

5. Luke Timothy Johnson, *Scripture and Discernment: Decision Making in the Church* (Nashville: Abingdon, 1983).

6. Ibid., 25, 31.

7. Ibid., 110.

8. Timothy Gombis compares the use of this psalm with the imagery of the Divine Warrior prevalent at the time. His assessment aids interpretation in that the leaders' being given as gifts to the church attests to Christ's position of power and prominence; see Timothy G. Gombis, "Cosmic Lordship and Divine Gift-giving," *Novum Testamentum* 47.4 (2005): 373.

9. Ernest Best, *Essays on Ephesians* (Edinburgh: T & T Clark, 1997), 172.

10. Markus Barth, *Ephesians 4–6* (Garden City, NY: Doubleday, 1974), 435.

11. J. C. O'Neill, "'The Work of Ministry' in Ephesians 4:12 and the New Testament," *Expository Times* 112, no. 10 (2001): 336.

12. Ronald Fung, "The Nature of Ministry according to Paul," *Evangelical Quarterly* 54 (1982), 143; also see Barth, Ephesians 4–6, 439.

13. The author of Ephesians uses body imagery in 1:23; 2:16; 3:6; 4:4, 25; and 5:23, 30. He also expands on this metaphor by referring to Christ as the head in 1:22 and 5:23.

CHAPTER 3

Listening to God
and to One Another

JOHN GRANT[1]

"You don't want to be an elder here."

That was the word on the street at College Hills Church of Christ in Lebanon, Tennessee. Church leadership is never easy, but some seasons are especially tough. The year 2007 was one of those anxious times. The elders needed fresh blood, but qualified candidates said no to eleven out of thirteen invitations to serve as shepherds.

An Emerging Problem

College Hills is an old church that began a new chapter. Established in 1836, it met at the same downtown location on College Street from 1874 to 2003. The congregation grew steadily during the twentieth century, with multiple additions to the facility. By the 1990s, the church had outgrown the site, with three Sunday morning services and with classes crammed into closets and nearby houses. The congregation purchased forty acres in 1997 and relocated to a spacious new facility at the beginning of 2003.

While the move to Leeville Pike alleviated space constraints, it created new problems because College Hills lost its identity as a mid-size rural church. Instead of offering three distinct services, the congregation transformed into a single "blended" assembly with a thousand worshipers. Members complained that they could not locate their seats or their friends in such a large crowd. While the new facility allowed freedom to move, members found it more difficult to meet newcomers. The narrow hallways and tight classrooms at the old site had promoted interaction. After a few weeks, thirty-five people left to start a new congregation because they missed the intimacy and informality of the worship service they had attended at the old facility.

The leadership was not immune to fallout from the transition. Within three years, five of the eleven elders resigned for various reasons and were replaced by six new men. An associate minister left in 2004. There were tense discussions regarding finances—builders made expensive errors, and the architect underestimated utility costs. Reacting to the sense of chaos, the shepherds banned the practice of members sharing testimonies during the sermon, only to restore the practice a year later. A long-term minister later reflected that "the first two years at the new facility were the most difficult time in my entire ministry career."

In spite of the difficulties, Sunday morning attendance increased by nearly one hundred during 2003. A staff member was added to develop a recreational ministry in the family life center. Wilson County's population was booming, and the building attracted newcomers who brought enthusiasm, energy, and fresh ideas.

The newcomers' impact became evident in 2005, the third year on Leeville Pike, when some of the new elders led a retreat that involved writing a mission statement. Leaders considered material about how the complexity of managing an organization increases with group size. After the retreat, the chairman appointed four shepherds to serve as an administrative subgroup to oversee day-to-day operations. The elders commissioned a committee of seven members to facilitate a strategic planning process, and this led to a ministry reorganization in which seventeen "ministry facilitators" were invited to serve. With four full-time ministers in a church of 1000, College Hills was short-staffed, but the changes of 2005 provided workers and momentum that increased the congregation's effectiveness.

As progress continued, the elders discussed how they could place greater emphasis on spiritual leadership and limit their focus on facilities and finance. They studied Lynn Anderson's material on shepherding and invited David Wray to coach them.[2] A new model for leading the congregation began to emerge, with elders devoting their main energy to caring for the spiritual needs of members and entrusting management questions to staff and other leaders.

Another significant transition occurred in early 2007, as Larry Locke, the pulpit minister since 1977, announced his retirement, moving into a part-time pastoral-care role. Leaders turned to Charles Siburt for coaching, and his "church transition packet" provided guidance for the search process.

By 2006, six of the elders were over age seventy and three were in their eighties. The multiple transitions of the previous decade left them spent, so they began to seek additional elders. They approached nine men and seven said no. The results were worse in 2007, as all four invitations were rejected. It was significant that in three attempts to add elders from 2004–2007, only one long-term member accepted. Long-term members led in multiple roles in the community and even in the church, but they refused to join the eldership.

Several anecdotes suggest that the problem was deeper than "too busy." One man stated in private that he was not interested in joining the eldership because of controversial decisions from the previous decade. Such negative perceptions were reinforced by the presence of three able-bodied former elders in the congregation who were openly relieved to be rid of their job. One of them claimed to be a more effective shepherd since he no longer had to attend so many meetings. Finally, a current elder told about two shepherds who quietly tried to discourage him from joining when he was a candidate. There was a widespread belief that serving as an overseer at College Hills was a thankless task to be avoided.

The elders were frustrated. One of the older men called the younger men irresponsible for shirking their turn to serve. He failed to realize that baby boomers do not volunteer out of loyalty to an institution; rather, they accept leadership opportunities that fit with their lives.[3] Many of the candidates were successful leaders, and it appeared to them that there was little chance of success as an elder at College Hills.

While there were no harsh words or visible battles between elders and potential elders, the situation had become stressful. Using John Paul Lederach's model, the conflict at College Hills had grown from level 1 ("we have a problem to solve") to level 2 ("you are the problem").[4] It was risky to address, but there was no way to move forward without an intentional response.

Developing a Response

When a conflict involves one mistreating another, a direct response often brings resolution in the form of an apology and an intention to improve. But this time there was no misbehavior; rather it was a difference of priorities and values. An appropriate intervention was needed to bring the two sides into conversation in order to develop common ground regarding biblical foundations and congregational goals. The conversation needed to be brief and safe, but it also needed to be substantive. Here is how it happened at College Hills.

The conversation included six elders with their spouses and six leadership couples who exhibited characteristics of shepherds.

Several factors converged in order for this project to get off the ground. First, most of the elders were eager to add to their number, so they were open to suggestions. Their readiness for change made it possible to hold the conversation. Second, potential elders could recognize the problem. While they did not want to get involved personally, they wanted the church to thrive and the elders' advanced age was an obvious concern. Third, a motivated facilitator was present. I had been with the church two years, which was long enough to gain credibility. As a small-group minister with an interest in effective leadership, I was well suited to guide the conversation. This unique combination of circumstances was important; church leaders often tolerate unhealthy situations because nobody is motivated to respond.

The Intervention

The conversation was scheduled for six Wednesday nights in September and October 2007, during the church's weekly Bible class time. Each session lasted one hour. Participants were encouraged to tell their friends what they were discussing. They were instructed not to share direct quotes from other participants, but rather to share questions and perceptions from the meetings. Since this was an academic project, a silent observer sat at the back of the room recording data during each session. This allowed the facilitator to focus on leading the group without worrying about taking notes.

One outcome of the group discussion was a document regarding the "Essential Functions of Christian Leadership." A nonelder group member recorded comments throughout the sessions, and during the fourth week he distributed a rough draft for the group to review. The fifth session included time for participants to discuss the document and propose edits. In their written evaluations, group members expressed satisfaction with how well the document captured key points of the discussion.

The conversation followed this general outline:

- Each meeting included time set aside to meditate on Ephesians 4:1–16, a text discussing how Christian leaders are part of God's cosmic plan for creation.
- Session one: Introduce the people. Easy questions in pairs to help participants ease into the discussion—who was a leader who invested in your spiritual growth? What makes a good Christian leader?
- Session two: Introduce the problem. An elder described the Anderson shepherding model and its implementation at College Hills. The group discussed benefits of the model and how it might create challenges. This was a non-threatening way for both sides to consider the problem.

- Session three: Listen to Ephesians 4:1–16. The heart of the intervention was a move away from the issue and into God's Word. This was not a diversion to avoid the problem but an attempt to focus attention on participants' common calling in Christ.
- Session four: Assess the problem in all its dimensions, then brainstorm responses.
- Session five: Develop recommendations. The group listed seven challenges facing the leadership at College Hills, along with recommendations. These were incorporated into the "Essential Functions" document.
- Session six: Review the group's recommendations and evaluate the process.

Participants reported that the conversation was a positive experience that helped them draw closer to one another and to understand the other side's perspective. The group's recommendations were presented to the eldership. The elders were appreciative of the material, but no specific response was planned.

College Hills Today

Five years later, College Hills is a stronger congregation, but it is difficult to say exactly what factors contributed to the progress. The major transitions of new building in 2003, new eldership philosophy in 2006, and new preacher in 2008 have calmed, and the church is back to a "normal" level of transition. There are clearer roles for elders, and they are working harmoniously with a team of six ministers to lead the congregation. A second worship assembly was added in 2012 without major turmoil, and early results indicate that both services are thriving.

The congregation still has twelve elders, but it is a younger group. Since 2007, five men whose average age was eighty have resigned, and they have been replaced with five men around fifty years old. The church is in the process of adding elders at the time of writing, and leaders hope to add two to four shepherds. Two of the new elders were project participants, and two other participants are on the list of current nominees. The elders are offering the congregation greater opportunities to provide input throughout the ordination process, a healthy sign of a willingness to listen.

Another reason the crisis has diminished is that the elders have developed better procedures for managing their work. After a consultation with Charles Siburt in 2009, the elders revamped the administrative team formed in 2005, splitting it into two separate functions. The Personnel Leadership Team (PLT) consists of two elders whose job is to oversee, encourage, and coach the staff. The Ministry Leadership Team (MLT) includes two elders, two ministers, three deacons, and a member of the finance team. They work with ministry leaders to coordinate the long list of details involved in leading a large and active congregation. Also, leaders redesigned the deacon program, shifting from a group of forty-six good guys with little direction to a group of twenty men assigned specific roles to support the elders. Many of them are working as assistant shepherds, who provide assistance for the elders and mentoring for the deacons.

There is room to improve in areas such as spiritual formation and leadership development. But overall, it appears that there is no longer a sense that being an elder is an undesirable job. The role will always be demanding, but now it appears achievable. The mood within the eldership has shifted from defensive and risk averse to an atmosphere where the group is learning and working together.

Assessing the Project Today

Reflecting on this project five years after its completion offers an opportunity to assess its effectiveness. My analysis in 2007 was that the project failed to address the central question: identifying core leadership functions. This was noted by the independent expert who evaluated the project, Carson Reed: "The first thing observed is the lack of any overt identification of essential functions of leadership!" He surmised that the group shared an implicit agreement about what leaders do, so they did not include that topic in the document they produced. Reed noted that the group bought Anderson's shepherding model and developed ideas for recruiting to that model, but their end product does not reflect the broader roles that Ephesians 4 recommends: apostles, pastors, evangelists, prophets, and teachers. Absent are the "functions that move beyond the pastoral care of people to the work of teaching, spiritual formation, resolving disputes, equipping, and discerning God's leadership in the congregation's life."

While conversation participants never shared my belief that College Hills was struggling to recruit elders because the role appeared to be impossible, leaders' actions over the subsequent five years clearly involved a reworking of the elders' role. Redefinition of leadership functions has been an ongoing project, while ironically the "practical" recommendations from the discussion group—ideas for training, recruiting, and retaining elders—remain unheeded. This might indicate that the conversation was more successful than it initially appeared. A small group under time pressure to produce recommendations moved into action points, but the deeper analysis of the problem has resonated within the congregation and shaped priorities for the last five years.

Leadership Principles

Several leadership principles that are helpful for College Hills and other congregations emerge from this project. First, it shows the *subtle nature of conflict*. If a researcher had asked anyone at College Hills to identify the top five points of conflict in the congregation, nobody would have listed tension between current and prospective elders regarding the shepherds' role. There were never any angry words exchanged. There was broad personal respect and good relations among the men involved. But one group's behavior (declining to serve) presented a roadblock to the other group reaching a goal (adding more elders), which meant conflicting priorities. The conflict came to light when the elders discussed whether or not they would approve the project: some were concerned that the conversation might spark disagreements or might put the elders in an uncomfortable spot of being scrutinized.

This situation demonstrates a second principle—the need for leaders to *listen when frustration is growing*. In spite of the concerns, this project gave elders and nonelders a safe place to discuss a touchy subject, and both groups expressed that it helped them understand the other perspective. The younger group got an inside look at the elders' hopes and plans, and the plans made sense once they were explained. For their part, the elders gained what one wrote in his evaluation: "It has helped me see the cause of my frustrations." Bringing together the two sides was powerful. Once they understood one another's position, they had a much greater chance of developing a satisfying solution.

Too often, church leaders brainstorm solutions before they have understood the problem. For example, every leadership group hears the criticism of "poor communication." But the charge is so generic that it could mean several things: "tell me more," "please listen to me," "I hear conflicting messages," or maybe even "I do not like what you are saying." Without a thorough understanding of the issue, efforts to improve communication might make the situation worse.

A third concept highlighted by this project is the potential value of *listening to Scripture as a mediator* of conflict. The Bible is often cited in conflict situations, with warring parties marshaling verses to prove a point. What if we brought Scripture into conflict situations as a point of reconciliation? Ephesians 4:1–16 filled this role beautifully in the conversation at College Hills. It helped the group bypass arguments and suspicion, moving more directly toward God's cosmic plan for the church. The right group listening to Scripture with humility can make significant progress.

The approach to Scripture was significant. It was not a detailed study of texts about elders' selection or function, which are sketchy and few, but rather it was a meditation on Ephesians 4. Participants engaged the ancient practice of *Lectio Divina*, literally "holy reading," where a text is read multiple times, with silent meditation or brief comments between readings. There was never an attempt to analyze precise meanings of phrases, such as a discussion of whether "pastors and teachers" in verse 11 refers to one function or two. The group read theologically, with an eye toward major themes demonstrating God's dreams for the church. This allowed participants to locate themselves in the grand scheme, in the ranks of the diverse leaders called to protect the unity God created and to work together to build up one another and the congregation.

Finally, this scenario illustrates the need for leaders to *be prayerful and discerning about timing*. The elders' goal of adding to their number was logical and appropriate, but they met resistance and that produced frustration. This project provided a helpful pause. It gave leaders time to assess the trouble, and it enabled them to look at deeper issues behind the reluctance of potential elders. Looking back years later, it is possible to see that the problem at College Hills might have dealt more with transition overload than with a leadership shortage. Taking six weeks to talk about what leaders can and should do was a helpful way to process the transition.

Toward a Theology of Christian Leadership

Going a level deeper, there is much that this project can say to help congregations today. Lynn Anderson's shepherding analogy has been a good remedy to call *church* leaders out of the boardroom and to a more biblical role of caring for the flock. But any model has gaps, and texts like Ephesians 4 can correct blind spots within the shepherding image.

Anderson's material taps into a rich biblical metaphor and offers a practical contemporary application. His works have made a positive impact in hundreds of congregations. An elder in one of those churches said that "shepherds' meeting is the spiritual highlight of my week." The Smell Like Sheep series provide redirection for leadership groups who have over-functioned as a controlling board and under-served as spiritual caregivers. Leaders can be confused about priorities, thinking that making decisions about money and programs is the most important thing they do. Anderson gently counters that true power—the place where the Holy Spirit operates—is in the lives of people, and then he casts a vision for how leaders might join that dynamic work.

The biggest questions from the Smell Like Sheep series regard how a church would apply the model. Anderson admits that shifting a congregation's leadership framework from board to shepherds takes at least a decade, but his ecclesiological reflection is thin. He offers little insight on what the final product might look like or how to make mid-course adjustments. Specifically, two structural questions go unanswered, and such issues could "block implementation of the vision" if they are ignored.[5]

First, this material lacks a discussion about the working relationship between elders and staff, a common source of friction. Should professional ministers be considered pastors alongside the elders, or do they serve a different function? Could it be seen as a power grab if a minister encouraged elders to move away from administration and toward shepherding? In what ways would the shepherding philosophy be compromised when a church changes preachers every two or three years? In Anderson's experience, a twenty-year partnership between a preacher (Anderson) and a gifted administrator (Wray) was vital for earning enough trust to implement the shepherding paradigm. Sheep get hurt when leaders operate out of competing ministry models, so the limited attention to team dynamics is surprising.

The other question left unanswered by Anderson's works deals with administrative issues. If elders devote themselves to shepherding, mentoring, and equipping, who provides for the physical needs of the flock? Who builds the pen, shears the sheep, secures supplies, and scours the countryside for greener pastures? Anderson's video curriculum suggests that elders should delegate administrative questions to a committee, and it offers a strategy for cultivating and supporting such a team. As a whole, though, Anderson's material understates the importance and difficulty of management tasks associated with a large group of people.[6] "Governance is a crucial part of our life together . . . Just as our bodies do poorly without food, bodies politic do poorly without governance. Communities, in order to be communities, must be ordered, cared for, led."[7]

In his effective effort to discourage a domineering style, Anderson has swung to the other extreme. *They Smell Like Sheep* is a better manual for member care than for missional congregational leadership. Many churches will not be able or willing to wait for a shepherding model to take root, and others lack the key players.[8] If their gifts are more administrative than pastoral or if they struggle to delegate, elders could view the call to shepherd as a burden. A consultant from another denomination highlighted this concern: "It is highly unusual to expect your governing board to provide pastoral care."[9] At College Hills, such issues posed a threat to congregational health as potential elders judged the role unmanageable. The shepherding model made leadership appear harder since there was not a strategy for moving personnel or administrative questions off the elders' table. Faithful shepherds need to pay attention to other voices.

Ephesians 4 offers one voice worth hearing. Ephesians 4:11 is the only instance of the word "shepherd" in the entire Pauline corpus.[10] With a variety of tasks clamoring for congregational leaders' attention, this text clarifies the primary job: to "prepare God's people for works of service, so that the body of Christ may be built up" (Eph. 4:12).

Putting chapter 4 in context, Ephesians is "notoriously silent"[11] about its occasion. There are no decisive clues to identify the first readers or the author's identity or reason for writing. Perhaps this lack of particularity accounts for the letter's positive message and simple structure. The mood is optimistic because God is at work in the world and in the church. God is calling creation to honor the reign of Christ, and the church stands at the forefront. The first three chapters of Ephesians describe the resurrected community called to mature into the fullness of Christ, and the last three offer instructions for developing this community. The two halves could be labeled theology and ethics, although this oversimplifies the rich theological nature of chapters 4–6: godly living is rooted in the character and actions of God.[12]

Ephesians 4:1–16 functions like a hinge between the two main sections of the epistle. It bridges theological and ethical sections with two crucial ideas: Christian behavior arises from God's actions, and God gives Christians to one another as gifts to promote maturity. The text plays a significant role in the epistle's logical development, offering a theology of ministry that reminds leaders of their calling and the resources at their disposal.

Ephesians 4:1–16 provides four insights into the nature of Christian leadership. First, Ephesians 4:4–6 specifies that Christian leaders preserve and demonstrate the unity that originates with the Father, Son, and Holy Spirit, and how believers share a common heritage through the seven "ones." This heritage leads to a shared mission: the church joins the Trinity in inviting all creation to grow into the fullness of Christ (1:9–10, 22–23; 3:10-11; 4:13).

Given this unity created by God, Christian leaders are called to preserve it. "Make every effort to keep the unity of the Spirit through the bond of peace" (4:3 NIV). "The calling you have received" expresses itself not in orthodox doctrinal propositions but in relationships in which believers are humble, gentle, and patient, bearing with one another in love (4:1–2). Leaders set the tone for such an environment. When they bicker and backstab, they destroy the unity created by God. But when they practice self-emptying, Christlike love, the church displays the "manifold wisdom of God" (3:10 NIV).

Just as unity originates with God so does diversity. It was the ascended Lord who gave apostles, prophets, evangelists, pastors, and teachers.[13] Christian leaders are neither self-made nor coerced by their peers; they are a gift from God. "The gifts are not gifts made to people but gifts of people."[14] This foundation gives them confidence for serving and motivation to work together. This idea was vital for believers facing the passing of pioneer leaders at the close of the first century.[15] All Christian leaders gain authority from Christ, not just the ones who experienced his physical presence.

Commissioned by Christ, leaders follow him down the path of selfless service. In pointing to the descent and ascension of Christ, Ephesians 4:9–10 reminds "readers of what was required on Christ's part to achieve this position of 'fullness' above the heavens."[16] A similar path of self-emptying lies before Christian leaders. The variety of gifts creates occasional frustration, but any sense of competition melts away when leaders humbly use their gifts to serve and edify one another, just like the Trinity. A spirit of submissive mutual service makes divergent voices a blessing worth hearing rather than a burden.

Diverse gifts serve the single goal of preparing God's people for ministry, which is the third insight on leadership found in Ephesians 4:1–16. Verse 12 says that leaders equip God's people, who all participate in ministry and building the body. Leaders do not carry out ministry on behalf of the saints. Rather, they equip God's people to be involved in ministry, and then they serve together. Christ gave leaders to the church so that all of God's people could be prepared for works of service, an important insight for overworked church leaders.

The fourth ministry insight is that God's gift of leaders serves an even larger purpose than equipping individuals because Ephesians 4 includes a corporate element. God uses leaders to equip the visible body of Christ (the church) to grow into the fullness of the cosmic Christ.[17] Leaders help congregations "grow up . . . into him who is the head" (4:15 NRSV). This fits with James Thompson's study of ministry in Paul's writings: "the center of Paul's thought is a theology of transformation," specifically, "transforming the community of faith until it is 'blameless' at the coming of Christ."[18] A theology of Christian leadership that addresses only the personal growth of individuals ignores a key biblical component and it feeds some of the worst impulses of Western society. Christ gives leaders so that the body can be a fitting partner in Christ's cosmic kingdom.

As a whole, Ephesians 4:1–16 states that God places diverse gifts, leaders, within the church in order to preserve unity and to promote the spiritual growth of individuals and the community.

An important thought follows: spiritual growth is integral to Christian living and salvation. The Christian life is not an ordeal to endure until departing for a blissful afterlife; rather, it is a rich, developing relationship with the Father, Son, and Holy Spirit, and with other believers. Discipleship is not merely an elective for the superspiritual but is for all believers, both as individuals and as congregations. Walking with and growing in Christ is salvation. This explains why prayer and Scripture meditation were an integral part of the project at College Hills, and not just a formality.

Placing Ephesians 4 beside the shepherding concept paints a fuller picture. Anderson summarizes one core task when he calls for an expanding community of disciples: "Bottom line: our mission is to make disciples who will make still more disciples who make still more . . . what could possibly be more important than spiritual formation and equipping?"[19] Ephesians responds that Anderson is correct, as long as the mission includes cultivating a community that is growing "up into him who is the Head." Strategies need to be developed to build healthy congregations, as well as healthy individuals.

Applying This Model in Other Settings

The project described above could be one of those community-building strategies. Church leaders might find it useful to apply this process of listening to Scripture and to one another in any situation where a group feels stuck or is struggling to reach a decision. When frustration is on the rise, the appropriate response is to listen faithfully, rather than to make something happen. It takes time and many voices to discern God's will for the community. A "recipe" for a healthy conversation might read:

Ingredients
- A group of 15–25 leaders who are struggling to resolve a situation
- A facilitator who is trusted by all parties—perhaps someone outside the congregation
- Six hours of discussion time—all leaders need to be present for every session

- A significant but accessible Scripture with broad meaning
- A comfortable, quiet environment

Directions

1. Begin each session with a reading of the key text and silent prayer or other centering exercises. Allow time for God's word to sink in.
2. Take breaks between sessions. These allow time for important "off-the-record" conversations in the hallways.
3. Session one: Introduce the people. Easy questions in pairs to help participants ease into the discussion—ask about positive past experiences and about success stories. Wrap up the session with participants sharing with the group.
4. Session two: Introduce the problem. Invite a nonanxious person to tell the background of the problem in a nonblaming way. How did we get to this point? Ask the group to assess where the problem stands at the moment—what is working and what could be improved.
5. Session three: Listen to God's word. Stop talking about the problem and listen to God. Read the Scripture at least three times, with silence between readings. What does this text say that God has done? What is God doing in the world? What does God have planned?
6. Session four: Assess the problem in all its dimensions. What are all the factors that have led us to this place? Brainstorm responses. List every possible response to this question, even outlandish or unlikely responses.
7. Session five: Develop recommendations. Look at all of the possible solutions and identify workable options.
8. Session six: Commit to an action plan. Each person articulates how he/she or their group intends to support the recommendation. During the last few minutes, evaluate the process.

The simplicity of this exercise makes it appropriate for a variety of situations, and not just a leadership shortage. This model would work well as a weekend retreat, although the multi-week approach allows more time for reflection. Stronger facilitation will be required in situations where conflict has grown to level 3 or 4,[20] because participants are keeping score about the other side's mistakes, and it would be of limited value at level 5 or above when participants are actively trying to harm one another. But for the lower level conflict that is common in most congregational situations, the guided conversation model is a useful tool.

Looking at College Hills five years after this project, it is clear that this conversation had a positive impact. It provided a mechanism for leaders to assess a point of contention that was holding back the congregation, and this helped leaders develop better responses.

Social Transformation of Conflict

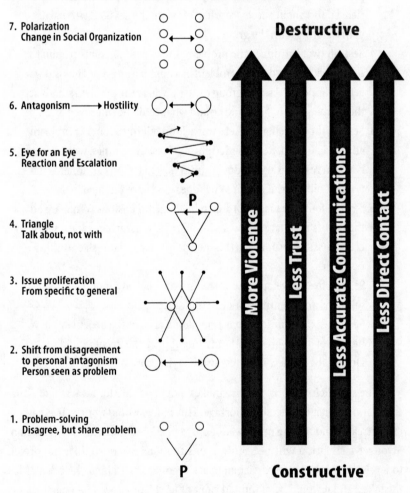

---

1. John Grant, "Facilitating a Conversation about Christian Leadership at College Hills Church of Christ" (DMin thesis, ACU, 2008).

2. Lynn Anderson, *They Smell Like Sheep: Spiritual Leadership for the 21st Century* (West Monroe, LA: Howard, 1997).

3. William Strauss and Neil Howe, *Generations: The History of America's Future*, 1584 to 2069 (New York: William Morrow, 1991), 306, 313.

4. John Paul Lederach, "Social Transformation of Conflict" (course handout from Charles Siburt, BIBM 706, ACU, June 2003). Included at the end of this chapter.

5. Jim Herrington, Mike Bonem, and James H. Furr, *Leading Congregational Change: A Practical Guide for the Transformational Journey* (San Francisco: Josey-Bass, 2000), 75.

6. Anderson, in *They Smell Like Sheep*, strips away the administrative aspects of the Greek word *episkopoi* by translating it as "'guides,' 'caretakers,' 'leaders,' or 'those who watch on behalf of,'" rather than the more literal "overseer," 128–29.

7. Larry Rasmussen, "Shaping Communities," in *Practicing Our Faith: A Way of Life for a Searching People*, ed. Dorothy C. Bass (San Francisco: Jossey-Bass, 1997), 120. Quoted in Peter L. Steinke, *Congregational Leadership in Anxious Times: Being Calm and Courageous No Matter What* (Herndon, VA: Alban, 2006), 93.

8. One preacher said his church gave up on the shepherding model after two years. "The administrative elders were doing fine, but the shepherding elders never could get organized."

9. Douglas Himes, president of Douglas Himes Associates, conversation with the author, May 2007.

10. Timothy S. Laniak, *Shepherds after My Own Heart* (Downers Grove, IL: Apollos/InterVarsity, 2006), 232n37.

11. Peter W. Gosnell, "Networks and Exchanges: Ephesians 4:7–16 and Community Function of Teachers," *Biblical Theology Bulletin* 30 (Winter 2000): 136.

12. For example, in Ephesians 6:1–3 children obey their parents "in the Lord," and slaves and masters treat each other well because of their new identity in Christ in 6:5–9.

13. We cannot know the exact function of these roles in the ancient church. Apostles and prophets were identified in Eph 2:20 and 3:5 as the foundation of the church, but evangelists, pastors, and teachers join their ranks in this text. The earlier references to apostles and prophets set them apart chronologically, and perhaps functionally. The force of Eph 4:11 is their common origin in Christ, not their distinctiveness.

14. Ernest Best, *A Critical and Exegetical Commentary on Ephesians* (Edinburgh: T&T Clark, 2004), 388.

15. Margaret Y. MacDonald, *Colossians and Ephesians*, Sacra Pagina 17 (Collegeville, MN: Liturgical Press, 2000), 298–99.

16. Thorsten Moritz, *A Profound Mystery: The Use of the Old Testament in Ephesians* (Leiden, The Netherlands: Brill, 1996), 84.

17. This universal aspect of Christ's reign is a repeated image in Ephesians (1:10, 20–23; 2:6–7; 3:10–11, 18–21; and 4:13, 15).

18. James W. Thompson, *Pastoral Ministry according to Paul: A Biblical Vision* (Grand Rapids: Baker Academic, 2006), 19–28.

19. Lynn Anderson, *They Smell Like Sheep, Volume 2: Leading with the Heart of a Shepherd* (West Monroe, LA: Howard Publishing, 2011), 141, 147.

20. See handout above from Charles Siburt, BIBM 706, Christian Leadership Development, June 2003.

CHAPTER 4

Scripture and Practice

CARSON E. REED[1]

My interest in the authority of Scripture first surfaced in a congregation I served during the early 1980s. A colleague and I were asked to teach a Wednesday night class on how to study the Bible. We selected for a text Gordon Fee and Douglas Stuart's book *How to Read the Bible for All It's Worth*. We should have known that we were in for a rough time when one class member grumbled about the title of this little volume and said, "It sounds like the authors don't think the Bible is worth much!"

But we stumbled through a quarter, teaching some things that helped many in the class and learning a lot ourselves. I moved on to another congregation soon after and my colleague continued to offer the course to others. Within a few weeks after my departure, several people had complained to the elders about this radical book. A couple of them reviewed the book and deemed it unfit. My colleague was then ordered to collect them all and destroy them. What is it about studying the Bible that can be so threatening?

Churches are facing an unsettling time of transition and change. Methodologies and ministries, worship and gender, the nature of marriage, outreach to the marginalized in our communities and to the world—these things and much more confront churches and church leaders. When the confrontation and trouble comes—and it will come!—then how will leaders decide?

Yet, more significantly, underneath these changes and challenges to the status quo lies a foundational set of assumptions rarely explored. Whenever matters of music, gender, or mission emerge, most everyone appeals to Scripture for their point of view. All choose to claim that Scripture is the authority. However, the fundamental question of *how* Scripture serves as the authority for congregational life and practice usually lies dormant. For those within the Stone-Campbell tradition, this dilemma is heightened by varied expressions of Scripture's authority that have developed. So between cultural shifts and changing congregational understandings, the interpretation of Scripture is left to the whims of whoever holds the floor.

Indeed, the need for a clear articulation of historical and biblical themes on Scripture's authority is highlighted by a fundamental reality: the assumptions one holds about Scripture affect interpretation. The project described here introduced how Scripture has been understood to function authoritatively by examining biblical material and the legacy of church tradition. This introduction was made into the particular congregational context of the Westlake Church of Christ in Indianapolis where I served as the senior minister from 1992 to 2004. I will also present the methodology used to introduce this material within the congregation. Perhaps others might find some usefulness in raising the question of *how* Scripture functions in order to help congregations and communities faithfully negotiate changing contexts and transitions.

Problem Defined

The issue of the authority of Scripture has occupied a prominent place on America's theological table since the late nineteenth century. Linked to the growing use of modern critical thought, this debate continues to generate both smoke and fire in American churches. At the heart of that debate is in the way and manner Christians proceed with the process of interpreting the Bible.

Underneath that debate are three principles that emerged in the nineteenth century—often attributed to the work of Ernst Troeltsch. Troeltsch, a German theologian, published a significant essay entitled "On Historical and Dogmatic Method in Theology" where he identified three principles that continue to serve as guideposts for contemporary conversations.[2] These principles are: (1) the principle of criticism or methodological doubt, which makes it necessary to observe history in degrees of probability; (2) the principle of analogy, which allows insight into present experience to be the method of knowing about the past; and (3) the principle of correlation, which implies an interconnectedness of all events, i.e., the role of cause and effect.

Basing historical research on these principles produced significant challenges in understanding the Bible's authority. Christians had traditionally affirmed their faith to be rooted in events that occurred in human history. But with the acceptance of critical thought, supernatural events and the possibility of the unique in history became suspect, calling into question the veracity of Scripture. Thus the polarization between verification and faith emerged, creating the need to establish, by the use of reason, a way of upholding the authority of Scripture.

By the late nineteenth century, two distinct postures emerged. For some persons the use of reason led them to embrace historical-critical methodology. This point of view anchored the authority of Scripture to whatever could be historically verified. Other people took reason and developed a framework to protect Scripture from the devastating effects of historical-critical thought, creating a framework of inerrancy that quickly became the hallmark of fundamentalists.[3]

The reality, however, is not simply divided into two clear categories. Within the Christian world, a great diversity exists concerning the authority of Scripture. However, one thing is clear: Scripture is primary. Yet, the clear skies turn to fog in contemporary settings when asking how Scripture functions. A person can no longer say, "the Bible says so," much less, "this is the clear historical-critical understanding of the text." With the rise of canon criticism and, more recently, the introduction of structuralism, the idea of a single meaning for a text has come under serious attack. Thus reason has fallen from grace; and objectivism, which was integral to both classical liberalism and inerrancy, is suspect.

In an attempt to mark signposts in the fog, Darrell Jodock delineates the plethora of positions being taken in understanding the authority of the Bible.[4] Of particular note are two primary assumptions that he makes. First, is that "each position was influenced by the context in which it was developed."[5] Second, "each position employs assumptions or makes theological assertions that influence the way the Bible is understood but that are not mandated by the Bible itself."[6] In other words, everyone comes to the table from some specific context, and everyone brings some philosophical or theological framework to begin the task of hearing Scripture.

The question is, how does the church hear Scripture in a way that it functions authoritatively for the church's proclamation and life? Indeed, the tension and debate about the nature of Scripture create a dilemma for contemporary churches and Christians. With a vast spectrum of approaches to Scripture, the temptation is simply to pick and choose from the menu offerings, or worse yet, to let go of a clear authoritative role of Scripture altogether. Jodock states the confusion well: "Persons wrestling with contemporary issues often work with unexamined, inappropriate, and sometimes even contradictory assumptions about the authority of the Bible. They are convinced that the Bible is important but, lacking a coherent explanation of its relevance, have patched together mismatched procedures and biblical interpretations."[7]

This crisis in the authority of Scripture has surfaced among Churches of Christ and has contributed significantly to an ongoing struggle to establish a clear identity in the opening years of the twenty-first century. Certainly, in recent years, reviews of hermeneutical assumptions within Churches of Christ have revealed the need for scrutiny, constructive critique, and new formulations. And yet, the nagging question remains, how does the Word of God function as the Word of God for congregational life and practice?

A Look at Ministerial Context

In the late 1960s no mainline Church of Christ existed on the west side of Indianapolis. Albert Galyan, an elder of the Franklin Road Church of Christ on the east side of the city, was a west-side resident and had a vision for a church to serve the community where he lived. In 1968, property was acquired on North High School Road. A group began meeting in the home of Albert and Naomi Galyan in April 1970. The Westlake Church of Christ congregation moved into a brick colonial-style building in October 1970. Highly visible to the community because of its location adjacent to the beltway that circles Indianapolis, Westlake quickly attracted a number of persons who lived on the west side of the city from other Churches of Christ.

For the first fifteen years of its life, Westlake struggled with a diversity originating from the Stone-Campbell Movement, which has flourished in Indiana since the 1820s. With that long history a broad spectrum of attitudes and beliefs has emerged, affecting fellowship, mission, direction, and leadership. In 1987, the minister and elders of Westlake began a clear call for a Jesus-centered life and ministry. This theme countered a tradition-bound, church-centered focus. About sixty people left over a six-month period. A new church formed, and another church received about twenty persons. Westlake then began to enjoy a sense of harmony and unity about its work and worship.

In 1994, Westlake was a relatively young church; seventy percent of the congregation was under the age of forty. Only four percent were over the age of sixty. The development of long-range planning and a recent restructuring of the leadership system brought focus and direction to the future of the church.

Perhaps due to the youthfulness of the congregation and its history, Westlake possessed a progressive, open spirit. Though Westlake has had some professional people, many members have been entrepreneurs. Westlake is a church of action, quick to perceive a need and respond to it. Nike's slogan, "Just do it," is emblazoned on a poster that hangs in one of the adult classrooms. Reflectiveness, deliberation, and planning quickly give way to immediacy, felt needs, and utilitarianism. More substantively, Westlake faced a number of significant issues during this season. The nature of evangelism, worship styles, and the role women played in the congregation's life were already on the table. For example, in the summer of 1993, leadership embarked on a major study of the worship practices and patterns in earliest Christianity. This resulted in three presentations to the church on music in August of that year. In the ensuing years, more contemporary forms of music began to be employed and by 1995, worship was typically led by a group of singers rather than a single leader.

In October 1994, Westlake hosted the first annual Christ and Culture conference. One hundred seventy-five registrants from Indiana and several midwestern states gathered to hear resource speakers address the topic "Women in the Church." During this same time period, Westlake began a relationship with a multi-denominational ministry to provide shelter for homeless persons. Such a commitment to the homeless demanded members' time, building usage, and a fresh understanding of the gospel. These issues illustrate the ongoing dialogue and focus of the congregation's life. Needless to say, such conversations were not uniform or unanimous. As these issues were explored, Westlake was forced to ask, how does Scripture function as an authority for life, ministry, and worship?

Simply affirming the Bible as God's Word was an inadequate response. Such naiveté resulted in an interpretation of Scripture that functioned no longer as an interpretation, but became biblical itself. Westlake's task to bring salt and light to Indianapolis and be faithful to Scripture required a careful and thoughtful understanding of how Scripture functions. On nearly every hand—leadership, worship, mission, and fellowship—Westlake was rethinking what it means to be the church. Given the legacy of Churches of Christ—"We are the people of the Book"—how will Scripture function as an authority in the congregation's life?

The critical nature of the problem surfaced in two distinct ways. First, as a young church Westlake has many persons whose link to traditional positions and interpretive postures within Churches of Christ was weak or nonexistent. Though they demonstrated a relatively high degree of loyalty to Westlake, loyalty to historical hermeneutics is low. Additionally, Westlake possessed a growing number of people who simply had no background with the Stone-Campbell tradition. Through various ministries, people came to faith and assimilated into the Westlake family. They knew more about noted Christian authors such as Charles Swindoll or Tony Campolo than they knew about Alexander Campbell or Walter

Scott. To this growing number a sensible, ordered understanding about Scripture was valuable for Christian nurture and maturity.

Second, Westlake had a small, but dedicated group of persons who were cautious about anything necessitating change to established patterns of thought and practice. Resistance to new ideas and beliefs was rooted in an appeal to tradition, often revealing a personal fear of stretched comfort zones rather than an informed understanding of the past. Among the older population, Stone-Campbell history and traditional understandings of hermeneutics were not well known—leading to a class in the summer of 1993 where I taught the history of the Stone-Campbell movement to a group that averaged forty persons and included many of the older members.

Thus, among those who were younger and had not been exposed to a clear understanding of Scripture's authority and to those whose understanding of Scripture's authority was deeply rooted in a traditionalism that was increasingly strained, the need for an informed doctrine of the authority of Scripture revealed itself. Ignoring this set of circumstances at Westlake would set the stage of unhealthy levels of conflict and the danger of losing Scripture's voice in the ongoing dialogue that supported the church's mission and life.

Theological Reflection on the Nature and Authority of Scripture

Scripture as Witness

What is Scripture? Scripture bears witness to the past revelation of God. That is its role. Karl Barth was fond of referring to a painting by Matthias Grünewald of the Crucifixion. John the Baptist stands to the side with his long index finger pointing toward the Crucified One.[8] That is the role of Scripture; the prophets and the apostles all attest to the work of God.

> Standing in this service, the biblical witnesses point beyond themselves. If we understand them as witnesses, and only as such do we authentically understand them, i.e., as they understand themselves . . . . They do not speak and write for their own sakes, nor for the sake of their deepest inner possession or need; they speak and write, as ordered, about that other . . . . Why and in what respect does the biblical witness have authority? Because and in the fact that he claims no authority for himself, that his witness amounts to letting that other

itself be its own authority. We thus do the Bible poor and unwelcome honour if we equate it directly with this other, with revelation itself.[9]

This posture points away from the chronic temptation of bibliolatry. By unequivocally affirming that authority is rooted in God's revelatory work and not in the Bible, Christians resist the propensity to practice a form of idolatry. By confessing that Scripture is witness to God's work, we confront the temptation to read the Bible as a compendium of propositional truth and open the possibility to hear the Word of God as did the primary, biblical witnesses.

Such a confession allows one to affirm that the Bible is indeed the Word of God—when we cease to procure for it some external authority and begin to listen. Perhaps much of the modern fundamentalist attempts to establish the authority of Scripture fall short simply because they have failed to take the historic Scripture principle seriously enough. In order to validate Scripture, external proofs and propositions are manufactured. Remembering Calvin and affirming the work of the Holy Spirit, the more biblical claim is that the Bible is the Word of God simply because it attests to God's saving work in Christ.

Thomas Long's book *The Witness of Preaching* presents a cogent argument for the metaphor of witness to be applied to the preaching task.[10] Long argues that it is the courtroom scene that makes the metaphor of witness viable. The preacher is not the judge, the jury, or the police officer, but the witness—one of the people who are called on to speak. "Now this witness is in every way one of the people, but he or she is placed on the stand because of two credentials: The witness has seen something, and the witness is willing to tell the truth about it—the whole truth and nothing but the truth."[11] This witness, the preacher, is the truth-bearer, speaking about what he or she has seen and heard. It is no mere mental or intellectual exercise; the witness, believing in the truth, stakes life itself upon the validity of his or her claims.

Long then notes how the image of witness shapes the preaching task. First, it locates the authority of the preacher in what the preacher has heard, not in the preacher's own personality or power. Second, the image speaks about the event and the encounter between God and humanity. It is not facts but a Person that the preacher proclaims. Third, the concept of witness relates to the rhetorical work of making known what has been seen and heard. What words, what forms, and what styles should be used? Fourth, the witness is not a neutral observer. Personal faith and the contours of the preacher's own past shape the testimony. It engages the preacher's whole life.

The witness metaphor is consistent with Scripture's own relationship to God. Preaching, like Scripture, can be the avenue by which the Word of God is heard today. But it is important to remember that the best that the preacher can do is to be a faithful and reliable truth-teller of what is found in Scripture. For even at his or her best, the preacher is removed from the primary witness of Scripture.

Scripture as Divine Words

Intricately connected to the affirmation that Scripture is the witness to the revelation of God is the affirmation that only through Scripture that we can come to know this Word of God.[12] To declare freedom from rationalism for a theological method does not mean that one casts off from shore without a compass. Rather, Christians adhere to an allegiance to hear Scripture speak. Though recognizing the historic confluence of authoritative sources—Scripture, tradition, reason, and experience—I am convinced of the priority of Scripture. It possesses that authority because it is the primary witness to God's work—most clearly in the revelatory work of God in Jesus Christ.[13]

Scripture has been and will continue to be the source of encounter with God. To understand that Scripture is inspired, that it is God-breathed, is appropriate. But to shape an understanding of inspiration in a mechanical way will reduce the Word of God to a mere codebook of propositional statements—as it did in post-Reformation scholastic Protestantism.[14]

Scripture as Human Words

Scripture is not only divine; it is also human. Luther made the comparison between the nature of Scripture and the incarnational nature of Christ. To ignore the historical realities of the texts that comprise the Bible is to practice a form of Docetism—of detaching the Word of God from the contexts of human experience.

When confronted by the critics with the human side of Scripture, many conservatives run quickly under the shelter of inerrancy. Then, to protect their shelter, they shore it up with attempts to harmonize and minimize the ambiguities of Scripture. I propose another approach. Between the giants of historical-critical results and the doctrine of inerrancy stands a David. Both modern critical study of the Bible and inerrantists rely on the Goliath-like strength of reason and logical thought, albeit expressed in radically different ways. But the David in the middle acts in faith. He admits that Scripture is human words (much to the chagrin of the conservatives), but he refuses to capitulate to liberal scholarship to thrash about in the modern muck and mire of subjective expression.

Certainly, historical inquiry, exegesis, and biblical theology are proper endeavors. Historical-critical methodology, textual criticism, historical and systematic theology are valuable and useful tools. But these endeavors are limited by and are subservient to the living Word of God. Bernard Ramm's maxim for Karl Barth is instructive: "Revelation generates history; history does not generate revelation."[15] Likewise, the priority of faith in the Word of God is necessary to negotiate the ongoing tension between biblical texts and our own personal, contextualized reading of those texts.

Discerning Scripture's Authority

Where do these observations lead? How does the present appropriate the past? In what way do we read the Bible? How do we determine what is authoritative and what is not? These and other questions beg for answers as one considers the contributions of Christian people throughout the ages. But perhaps most persistent is the question that is often just beneath the surface of many conversations about faith and Christianity—why should anyone turn to the Bible for an authoritative source?

Perhaps an answer begins to emerge when one asks yet another question: Where, or more properly, who is the ultimate source of authority for persons and communities marked by the term Christian? Such a question pushes beyond a text, or even an anthology of texts compiled by Christian people. It isn't the Bible that has authority; in reality, it is God.

Before an Old Testament or a New Testament existed, before canons of Scripture were debated or decided, God was. Scripture's authority is derivative—directly linked to the reality that discloses from God and about God. Historically, the church has always recognized that the power lies in the saving work of God through Christ. The Bible's role is witness; it attests to what God has done.

Significantly, Scripture as witness is rooted in the primacy of faith. Scripture does not need the authentication of reason, logic, or science to perform its divinely ordained task. Assured by the legacy left by earlier Christian spokespeople, the church begins with faith and seeks to understand God's work as disclosed through Scripture. Such an approach is particularly relevant in a day where the foundations of modernity show distinct signs of decay. Despite protestations from many Christian quarters, a return to the primacy of faith as a starting point to do theology is not only an appropriate approach biblically and historically, but it is a valid sociological method in our present world.[16]

With faith as the primary assumption regarding the authority of Scripture, the modern attempts to establish the authority of Scripture by positing its inerrancy seem particularly useless. To do so is asking an ancient document to stand under the criteria of a modern theory. As Paul Achtemeier noted: "One difficulty with inerrancy of the Bible in scientific matters it that scientific 'truth,' i.e., statements about 'the way things are objectively,' tends to change from time to time. Can the Bible be 'inerrant' for its contemporary readers in the time of *both* pre-Galilean *and* post-Galilean astronomy? Or was the Bible written to be inerrant only for late twentieth-century Western civilization?"[17] Surely another way exists.

Christ at the Center

What claims does Scripture make that are relevant to the issue of authority? Certainly 2 Timothy 3:16 is a clear reminder that Scripture is inspired—God-breathed—and is profitable for teaching, instruction, and doctrine. What is Scripture's "profitable" nature? If Scripture ultimately derives its authority from God, then perhaps those events that reveal God most clearly are pivotal. Taking a cue from Paul one learns that some expressions about God's work exist that prompt Paul's ire—namely a distorted expression of the gospel.[18]

In the earliest expressions of the nature of Christian faith, Paul wrestles with the Old Testament and the startling revelation in Jesus. As he does so, in articulates this notable statement:

> Now I would remind you, brothers and sisters, of the good news that I proclaimed to you, which you in turn received, in which also you stand, through which also you are being saved, if you hold firmly to the message that I proclaimed to you—unless you have come to believe in vain. For I handed on to you as of first importance what I in turn had received: that Christ died for our sins in accordance with the scriptures, and that he was buried, and that he was raised on the third day in accordance with the scriptures, and that he appeared to Cephas, then to the twelve.[19]

For Paul, the gospel—the message of Christ's death, burial, and resurrection—was paramount to his ministry, to his understanding of the Old Testament, to ethics, to preaching, and to faith.

But Paul was not alone on this matter. Peter and Jesus demonstrate an awareness of the difference between Scripture and the core of Scripture. The early church fathers, as they articulated the faith, merely continued this interpretive approach to Scripture. Any attempt to understand Scripture begins with some assumption. For the early church, that assumption was the message of the gospel. Therefore, any attempt to formulate a systematic statement about the authority of Scripture must recognize that its authority rests on the proclaimed message of Jesus Christ. Scripture itself attests to this all-important centering event. Karl Barth makes this point quite poignantly:

> If the crucified Jesus Christ is alive, if His community is the company of those among whom this is seen and taken seriously, . . . then the community cannot take account of any other word that God might have spoken before or after or side by side with or outside this word, and that He willed to have proclaimed by it. It accepts and proclaims this one Jesus Christ as the one Word, the first and final Word, of the true God . . . . It interprets creation and the course of the world and the nature of man, his greatness and his plight, wholly in the light of this Word and not vice versa.[20]

Such a Christocentric assertion steers a discussion away from utilizing categories of modern philosophy or historical method as fundamental assumptions. I would be quick to add that, of course, assumptions—both known and unknown—are at work in the interpretation of Scripture. However, as informed as we may be about our assumptions, the central theme that both constrains and unleashes those assumptions is a healthy Christology.

The Contextual Nature of Authority and the Church

As stated earlier, Scripture's authority is derivative; that is to say, Scripture's authority rests in and on the One who is disclosed in Scripture. Following this claim is a related one: Scripture functions as an authority only within a community of people who accept its authority, namely, the church. Jodock reflects on the connectedness of the church and authority in this way:

> A community also provides the context for the Bible's authority: the community of faith. In the community of faith the Bible makes its claim on persons—to be taken seriously in their decision making and to inform their sense of direction and purpose. Those outside the community of faith can respect the Bible as a document of religious significance for others, they can study it, and they may even appeal to it if they want to persuade Christians to act in a certain way (this frequently happens in political discourse), but for them it does not, properly speaking, exercise authority. It makes no claims on their own decision making or sense of direction.[21]

Jodock helpfully points out that even in the reading of Scripture faith is mediated through a member of the community of faith. Reading the biblical documents is an "overhearing" of a conversation between Paul or Luke or John and some church community. Thus, in observing the validity of truth claims in the life of the community and in the act of reading Scripture itself, authority comes as a result of these experiences, not as a presupposition to seeing and hearing.

Herein lies the poverty of prominent theories of scriptural authority that rely on external frameworks such as inerrancy. In an attempt to convince others of the Bible's accuracy and usefulness, a void develops at the heart of the issue of authority: Is it trustworthy? Will Scripture bring transformation, meaning, and hope? Instead, argument and debate often rule the agenda, making statements and offering conclusions about the Bible that many contemporary persons find intellectually dishonest and devoid of real meaning.

Stanley Hauerwas takes the disparity between the reality of Scripture's authority within the church and presuppositions made about the Bible's authority quite seriously. According to Hauerwas, the fundamental challenge facing American Christianity is the casual way in which all people are encouraged to read the Bible for themselves—independent of any church community.[22] By making the Bible its own standard, "then the authority of the Bible is not privileged. Instead the authority of our private judgment will prevail."[23] And, as explored earlier, at the center of the community is the presence of Jesus Christ, living among his people, the church.

The Relational Nature of Authority and the Church

Authority implies relationship. Authority defines the relationship between a person or persons and another person, persons, or, as in the case of this conversation, a collection of texts. It requires time and experience to develop. To the community of God's people, it is not merely texts, but it is the presence of God's Spirit, "who works through the message of grace proclaimed by human beings belonging to the community."[24] Thus, Scripture does not possess authority; Scripture is the conduit for the authoritative work of God within the church. As Darrell Jodock relates:

> No contemporary theory of the authority of the Bible can assume that a person will be convinced of the Bible's authority apart from participation in the community of faith. As Jaroslav Pelikan observed after hearing his eight-year-old daughter sing, "Jesus loves me, this I know, for the

Bible tells me so," the lyrics of the children's song were incorrect for her. She had not read the Bible. She knew that Jesus loved her because her mother, her father, her Sunday-school teacher, her pastor, and others in the Christian community had told her so. Only later would she come into contact with the Bible.[25]

The Tradition of Authority and the Church

At first glance, the following observation is simple enough: the Bible functioned authoritatively in the church because the church allowed it to do so. But underneath that simple observation lies a significant reality. Before a Bible existed, the work, ministry, and life of the church were upheld by the gospel message and the rule of faith. Indeed, the church developed a canon out of a response to a series of factors in the second and third centuries. Through consensus and usefulness, Scripture's authoritative role evolved in the life of the church.

Jodock utilizes a term from Michael Polanyi to describe this reality. Jodock asserts that authority is tacit. By "tacit," he means that authority is "established not consciously and deliberately but implicitly as attention is focused on the tasks of the community."[26] In the life of the early church, the documents that comprise the New Testament canon came to be seen as God-breathed—useful and profitable. Why does the contemporary church turn to the Bible? With the passing of each generation, the church would be hard-pressed to reject the claim of tradition to the authority of Scripture in offering guidance to present day issues.

Ministry Intervention: Method, Summary, and Implications

After the ministerial task of addressing the issue, the concrete situation of people still remains. To address the dilemma of Scripture's role as the church's book and to engage in a proactive intervention, the following approach emerged.

Since the question of the authority of Scripture develops in the context of ministry, I first engaged significant historical sources to gather some insight to the church's voice on the nature and authority of Scripture. Then, I developed a theological reflection on the nature of Scripture, the authority of Scripture, and some interpretive trajectories for an approach to Scripture that is consistent with its nature. This activity set the framework for the project and engaged significant literature in the areas of inspiration, authority, and revelation that have been presented here in a summary form.

Using the historical review and the theological reflection as a foundation, I compiled another document. Entitled *The Work of Witness: An Introduction to the Nature and Authority of Scripture*, this document served as an introduction to Scripture's role in the church. Its design and content were to assist lay persons in assimilating an informed understanding of the nature and authority of Scripture.[27] To accomplish this task, *The Work of Witness* was rooted in historical and theological issues. Comprised of eight units, *The Work of Witness* included a collection of readings from various primary sources; they were introduced and intertwined with my own reflection and analysis. Generally, each unit possessed three components: (1) an introduction and summary statement, (2) a reading or readings from primary sources, and (3) a set of thought questions suitable for group discussion.

A group of eleven persons at Westlake formed a discussion group to read *The Work of Witness* and engage in discussion. Eight weekly, one-hour meetings were held during the months of October and November 1994. One unit of *The Work of Witness* was assigned each week; every participant read the materials and considered the thought questions before the next meeting. The group, identified as the Focus Group, was composed of both opinion leaders at Westlake who were specifically selected and others who responded to announcements in the church bulletin. The group began and concluded with the same eleven participants.

Evaluation occurred in three ways. First, through the informal feedback and interaction of the weekly meetings, I received an immediate response to the materials presented. Second, the Focus Group completed a questionnaire designed to measure the clarity and utility of *The Work of Witness*. The questionnaire also assessed what the Focus Group learned and the strengths and weaknesses of the facilitator. Third, one week after the completion of the study, the group reassembled for a one-hour session to assess and evaluate *The Work of Witness* and the process.

Based on the feedback of the Focus Group and the results of the questionnaire, I made minor revisions to *The Work of Witness*.

Results

The Work of Witness guided eleven people to explore some of the historical and theological issues that surround the nature and authority of Scripture. What now? Did the document, or this subject, have any ongoing role to play at Westlake and for Churches of Christ? What value can the study of the nature and authority of Scripture possess for the church as it moves into a new century?

Initial Data

One way to begin to answer the questions raised above is to review the response of the Focus Group to their experience. At the conclusion of the eight-week study, each participant was asked to fill out a questionnaire. On a scale from one to ten (one meaning "disagree strongly" and ten meaning "agree strongly"), they responded to several statements about the written materials. The average scores ranged from 8 to 9.3, indicating a high degree of agreement and satisfaction with the experience.

In addition to responding to each statement, participants were provided space to make comments. Through those written comments and through informal conversation, several themes emerged. First, reading from primary sources such as Augustine or Luther was a profound and powerful experience for most of the group. Second, historical awareness and some sensitivity to theological issues created an entirely new way of looking at doctrinal and ecclesiastical issues. Rethinking Scripture's authority opened new vistas for hearing the Word of God afresh. Third, the study established a new respect for Scripture. Scripture is a living voice, not dead words.

In addition to the statements that each participants was asked to score, six open-ended questions were asked. These questions elicited several significant observations. Through the reading of *The Work of Witness* and through class discussion times, participants found learning about the formation of the canon to be a new experience and helpful in understanding Scripture's role for the church. Being able to connect history with faith was affirming for several participants. The concept of accommodation and the function of the rule of faith were often noted as important discoveries. As one person stated, "I love the idea of God accommodating himself to us. It amazes and thrills me."

Inerrancy was often mentioned in participants' responses. Understanding the historical development of the doctrine presented opportunity for people to consider its validity and truthfulness. For two of the participants who had never had a name for this approach to Scripture, raising questions about inerrancy was disturbing: "The inerrancy materials infuriated me—probably because I have heard these arguments all my life and have seen what is does to churches"; and, "Inerrancy bothered me the most because in the past I have seen how the church has used this to support doctrine."

Perhaps the way to understand what *The Work of Witness* and the class discussions provided is capsulated by this response: "This study forced me to stop and consider what I really believe rather than just take things for granted. Then

I had to find out why I believed it and what I was basing my faith on. It gave my faith a much firmer foundation and bolstered my belief in the changes I've been going through as being good changes."

Reflection on Focus Group Response

What sort of summary and reflection can be made from the participation and response of the Focus Group? One clear thought to emerge from both the written response and the oral discussion that followed the class was the value of this kind of study for a larger circle of people at Westlake. One person suggested that the course should be required for all teachers in the education system. The high regard for this subject matter reflects an awareness from participants of the value of one's paradigms and the interpreting task.

Being able to read and discuss concepts about the nature and authority of Scripture offered the opportunity for faith development. As one participant said, "The class made me think through why I place trust in the Bible. But I found a growing confidence in expressing what I believe about the Bible." Another stated, "Though I have often taken Scripture for granted, I now have valuable reasons for turning to Scripture and listening to what God is saying." Yet another said, "It is okay to ask questions. Our faith makes it okay to live without all the answers." Rather than simply accepting what has always been said, participants in the Focus Group entered into an environment where it was safe to explore. The result was stronger faith in God and confidence in Scripture.

As the Focus Group repeatedly observed, encounters with history and persons from history created a structure wherein reflection could safely and positively occur. One participant put it this way: "I can't explain the impact of the primary readings; they affirmed my own thoughts and instilled confidence in our attempts to understand the Bible today." Because of the interest in historical material, I taught a class on early Christian writings within the year.

In practical terms, *The Work of Witness* and the discussion it engendered developed a healthy respect for thoughtful and prayerful exegetical work. Though beyond the scope of this present work, learning about literary and historical methods was a clearly expressed interest. Understanding the nature of Scripture and its vital role as witness heightens its value and promise to the church.

Implications of *The Work of Witness*

Several trajectories developed from this work in 1994. What follows is a brief synopsis of those possibilities.

Education

The Work of Witness found its way into the adult education curriculum at Westlake within the year. Expanded into a thirteen-week study, in part with some additional hermeneutic material, the course was presented to the congregation. Additionally, Morris Cromer, who served as the monitor for this project and is one of Westlake's elders, has continued through the years to emphasize the selective use of primary historical material in Westlake's educational program. In recent correspondence, Morris noted:

> The principles of this project found their way into teaching methods in both classroom and pulpit, the results of which were evidenced by a greater number of folk opening their mind to potentials never before considered . . . . [T]he end results of this approach served to strengthen and enlighten a congregation which, like Paul perhaps, had become used to "scales covering their eyes" where biblical interpretation was concerned.[28]

Nurturing Faith among the Youth

Nurturing the faith and spiritual development of our young people is a vital task for the church. In addition to the usual educational programs that offer instruction to children, Westlake encourages all children to participate in a program called REACH (Racing for Excellence at Church and Home). REACH provides yet another setting for spiritual formation. In particular, REACH offers an opportunity for Scripture to be heard. REACH was initially a way for students to memorize Scripture. However, in light of this work, REACH was broadened to incorporate some other features. In particular, REACH included structured times for parent and child interaction, for the oral reading of Scripture in group settings, more opportunities for artwork to express Bible stories, and some teaching about the role and life of the community.

Community

Significant to the thesis of this work is the role that the community plays in hearing Scripture. Scripture, as the church's book, must be given voice within the church's worship and life. Likewise, within the faithful community, the work of the Spirit nurtures and supports the Word. For Westlake, the role of the community in hearing the Word with authority found at least three distinct opportunities.

First, Westlake's worship developed an expanded role in the use of Scripture in worship. Scripture is an active, vital part of what is heard each week. Through responsive readings, congregational readings, and dramatic readings, Scripture received a significant hearing each week in worship.

Second, preaching takes on new life when rooted in understanding that God, mediated through the Son, is the sole source of authority for the church. Thus, working through the themes of this project, a clearer vision about preaching emerged. Notably, as a result of this project, I am becoming aware of the vital role that the proclamation of the gospel has for creating and nurturing the community. During the years I preached for the Northlake Church of Christ and in Tucker (Atlanta), Georgia (2004–2012), this developed into a coordinated program of sermons, Bible classes, and Wednesday evening offerings that focused on a particular book of the Bible through literary and historical studies, *lectio divina*, and proclamation.

Third, Westlake utilized small groups that are centered in Bible study. Each week approximately eighteen groups meet for study and fellowship. The purpose of these groups is to nurture one another through study and "care-giving." As a result of this project, a renewed emphasis on community development will be advanced. These small groups are ideally suited for Scripture to be heard within the context of real living. Additionally, small groups provided the context for accountability to the word that is heard each week.

Conclusion

One implication of this work is the awareness that theological controls supporting the interpretive process need expansion and development. Though the message of Jesus or the rule of faith stands as the starting point for all reflection, some other validation must take place for interpretive work. I suggest community as the place of validation because the community is the place of God's Spirit. From earliest times the church has affirmed the work of the Spirit affirming the proclamation of God's message. Should not the practice and life of the church today be seen as the place to see whether the voice of Scripture is affirmed? The life of the community becomes the place where the word of Scripture converges with the work of the Spirit.

The role of community as the place where an authoritative word is heard heightens the significance of discipleship. Obedience and distinctive Christian lifestyles will be the evidence of Scripture's authority. Saying that the Bible is authoritative possesses little power; only when a community of people live out the truth does the truth find validation.

Much lies ahead for Stone-Campbell churches that seek a lively future. For underneath all the talk about worship, women, small groups, mission, and all the other issues that are creating points of tension is the fundamental concern about authority. Though Churches of Christ have long claimed the Bible as the sole source of authority, *how* the Bible functions and *why* it functions as an authority, receives poor and inadequate response. And if understanding the authority of Scripture is foundational to the church's concerns, then what is to become of a fellowship whose awareness and articulation about Scripture suffers historical and theological anemia? Only by a robust turn to hearing the voice of God through the witness of Scripture in community will the church's mission find hope and vitality.

----

1. Carson E. Reed, "The Nature and Authority of Scripture: Historical Sources and Theological Engagement for Congregational Awareness and Reflection" (DMin thesis, ACU, 1995).

2. Ernst Troeltsch,"Über historische und dogmatische Method in der Theologie," in *Zur religiönsen Lage, Religions-philosophie und Ethik*. 2 Aufl., Gesammelte Schriften (Tübingen: J. C. B. Mohr, 1922), 729–53.

3. George M. Marsden, *Fundamentalism and American Culture* (New York: Oxford, 1980).

4. Darrell Jodock, *The Church's Bible: Its Contemporary Authority* (Minneapolis: Fortress, 1989), 31.

5. Ibid., 32.

6. Ibid.

7. Ibid., 2.

8. See the Frontispiece of Eberhard Busch, *Karl Barth: His Life from Letters and Autobiograhical Texts* (Philadelphia: Fortress, 1976); Barth's comments in Church Dogmatics, ed. Geoffrey W. Bromiley and Thomas F. Torrance, vol. 1, pt. 1 (Edinburgh: T. & T. Clark, 1936–77), 112, hereafter cited as CD.

9. *CD*, 1.1:111–12.

10. Thomas Long, *The Witness of Preaching* (Louisville: Westminster/John Knox, 1989).

11. Ibid., 43.

12. Barth, *CD*, 1.2:462.

13. One of the quandaries of presenting material in 2013 that was originally framed in 1994 is that learning continues to evolve and so does my own thinking. Rather than try to reflect that by doing a major rewrite of what is said here, I would simply point astute readers to a few sources that indicate where my own thinking is headed. See: Ellen F. Davis and Richard B. Hays, eds., *The Art of Reading Scripture* (Grand Rapids: Eerdmans, 2003); William J. Abraham, et. al., eds., *Canonical Theism: A Proposal for Theology and the Church* (Grand

Rapids: Eerdmans, 2008); N. T. Wright, *Scripture and the Authority of God: How to Read the Bible Today* (New York: HarperOne, 2011).

14. Jack B. Rogers and Donald K. McKim, *The Authority and Interpretation of the Bible: An Historical Approach* (San Francisco: Harpercollins, 1980), 147–99.

15. Bernard Ramm, *After Fundamentalism: The Future of Evangelical Theology* (San Francisco: Harper & Row, 1983), 75.

16. Thomas Oden made this point well in AFTER MODERNITY . . .WHAT? AGENDA FOR THEOLOGY (Grand Rapids: Academie Books, 1990).

17. Paul J. Achtemeier, *The Inspiration of Scripture* (Philadelphia: Westminster, 1980).

18. Gal. 1:6–9.

19. 1 Cor. 15:1–8 (NRSV).

20. *CD*, 4.1:346.

21. Jodock, *Church's Bible*, 106-7; see also David H. Kelsey, *The Uses of Scripture in Recent Theology* (Philadelphia: Fortress Press, 1975), 91, 208ff.

22. Stanley Hauerwas, *Unleashing Scripture: Freeing the Bible from Captivity to America* (Nashville: Abingdon, 1993), 15.

23. Ibid., 29.

24. Jodock, *Church's Bible*, 110.

25. Ibid., 74.

26. Ibid., 111.

27. Carson E. Reed, *The Work of Witness: An Introduction to the Nature and Authority of Scripture* (Kindle Direct, 2012).

28. Morris Cromer, e-mail message to author, September 21, 2012.

CHAPTER 5

Deep Calls to Deep

BERT REYNOLDS[1]

Many Christians are thirsting for God, panting for authentic connection to the living God. They resonate with the image of the psalmist in 42:7—"deep calls to deep." The deep hopes of their hearts cry out for the depths of God's life. The deep struggles they have with sin cry out for the fullness of God's salvation. The deep voids in their souls cry out for the depths of God's meaning. Like the psalmist, many wonder when they can go and meet with God, and not just when but how, and who might accompany them on this journey.

For two millennia, Christians seeking greater participation in the life of God have committed themselves to the practice of spiritual disciplines as a means to open the door to God's transformative work. Most Christians know some disciplines like prayer, worship, and the study of Scripture, but too often the full depths of these paths go largely underused. Due to limited teaching or a lack of training, people's experience with these practices remain narrow or shallow. Unfortunately, other practices such as solitude, silence, the prayer of *examen*, and fasting (to name a few), remain as hidden or all but forgotten paths, undiscovered and unexplored by many.

Rediscovering and reengaging these practices is not a guarantee of growth. Only God can grant that (1 Cor. 3:6). However, as Marjorie Thompson suggests, like garden tools, spiritual disciplines "make it more likely that growth will be unobstructed" as they remove the "stones and roots, aerate the soil, weed and water the garden" of our hearts.[2] As Thompson goes on to suggest, this deliberate work of developing healthy habits of the heart is necessary if we want to experience true depths of life in God.

It would be nice if we could simply "practice the presence of God" in all of life, without expending energy on particular exercises. But the capacity to remember and abide in God's presence comes only through steady training. If we wish to see, name, and love Christ "in the flesh" of daily existence, we will eventually need some kind of intentional practice of spiritual discipline.[3]

The Chenal Valley Church of Christ was planted in a growing section of west Little Rock, Arkansas, in 1989. It began with the vision of being a church in which Christ would be preached in an atmosphere of love, kindness, and acceptance. Deep within the church's DNA is a desire to be a grace-filled body that maintains an open door for all people. That open-door approach stems both from the steadfast love of God as well as a wish to move beyond what founding members perceived to be closed-minded, judgmental legalism of their past.

Unfortunately, the gracious attitudes that helped create a warm, welcoming church also contributed to a few problems as well. As many well-intentioned, grace-focused churches can discover, spiritual maturity and growth can unintentionally become separated from salvation. Emphasizing working with God in the process of transformation can be treated as suspect, as some fear that spiritual labor could lead to legalism or works-based salvation. The result can be a church better equipped to welcome people in their brokenness than help them on the road to God's transformation. Moving away from a perceived identity of closed-mindedness does not guarantee moving toward being a people of renewed minds (Rom. 12:1–2).

The church was in need of deeper levels of spiritual formation, but many of our members seemed underequipped to seek those levels. Further, in the face of some serious, public sins on the part of a few prominent members, the church started to realize that emphasizing an incomplete understanding of the love and grace of God can foster spiritual immaturity and sin. The atmosphere seemed ripe for engaging the spiritual disciplines as a means of deeper participation in the life of God and consequently greater transformation into the image of Christ.

My project set out to equip church leaders and teachers of adults to facilitate classes on spiritual disciplines at the Chenal Valley Church of Christ. More than offering teaching methods and training materials, I aimed to deepen the teachers' understanding and practice of spiritual disciplines so as to broaden their participation in the life of God. While I hoped to enhance their abilities as teachers, I was more interested in empowering spiritual formation in their lives.

Thus, I taught an introduction to spiritual disciplines workshop, but also I provided opportunities and training to practice the spiritual disciplines. The introductory nature of the series meant that only some of the spiritual disciplines could be taught to and practiced by the teachers and consequently the members of adult classes. The spiritual disciplines explored by Marjorie J. Thompson in *Soul Feast: An Invitation to the Christian Spiritual Life* comprise the disciplines covered in this series.

My intent was that through this process teachers would grow in their knowledge and practice of spiritual disciplines. Through teaching about and modeling spiritual disciplines, teachers, class participants, and ultimately the church will seek to participate more fully in the life of God by developing a lifestyle of devotion to the practice of at least some of the disciplines. When the church seeks to collaborate more fully with the transforming grace of God, we will continually and increasingly be spiritually formed into the image and likeness of the triune God.

Theology

Salvation as Participation in the Life of God

Both the theology and the practice of the church are severely stunted when salvation is primarily understood as an individual's escape from condemnation postmortem. In this scenario, spiritual formation—while desired—is optional and ultimately unnecessary. After all, God is primarily concerned with judgment at the eschaton, and like a good life insurance policy, grace offers comprehensive coverage. This project, however, sought to reframe a theology of salvation to reveal how it is better understood as participation in the triune life of God that leads to transformation into the image of Christ beginning now.[4]

God created us as image bearers to be in communion with God. Sin is living in denial of our designed purpose of participating in eternal fellowship with God. By seeking and allowing the Spirit of God to transform us into the image of Christ, we collaborate with God's work of bringing all creation, starting with ourselves, back into loving relationship with the Divine. When we are baptized in the name of the Father, the Son, and the Spirit, we open ourselves to a lifetime of God's transforming work that pulls us deeper into God's life.[5]

Transformation into the Image of Christ

Thanks to God, humanity is not left to its own devices to decide what communal connection to God looks like. Jesus is the image of the invisible God (Col. 1:15), and he is the incarnational exemplar of human participation in the life of God.[6] Our goal and means for living full life is through transformation into the image of Christ.[7] We know that we will not fully realize that goal until Christ comes again (1 John 3:2), yet we strain in cooperation with the Spirit so that Christ may be formed in us (Gal. 4:19). This is the plan of God, that all humanity whom God created in the *imago dei* would reembody that image through being conformed to the *imago Christus* (Rom. 8:29).

Jesus insists that becoming like him means daily walking with him down the self-emptying path of the cross (Luke 9:23), in the path of love (1 John 3:16), and in the path of his mission.[8] To live as he lived means to train as he trained, because his ability to think and act rightly was the product of the overall life he adopted.[9] Transformation into the image of Christ then requires imitation of Christ's nature and ways (Eph. 5:1). The more we act and think like him, the more we look like him.

The Necessity of Communal Connection

Spiritual transformation that enables and flows from participation in God's life certainly involves each Christian, but full participation in God's life requires communal connection because the triune God by nature is communal. To be created in the image of God and transformed into the image of God in Christ through the Spirit is to reflect and embody the divine *koinonia* (fellowship).[10]

To grow into the image and likeness of Christ is to grow in fellowship, communion, and loving connection to God and all God made. Certainly God is interested in individual spiritual formation. Yet even individual spiritual formation is not experienced in isolation, nor is it experienced for the sole purpose of edifying the individual. God is forming a people, not just a person (1 Pet. 2:4–12).

Collectively, we seek to empower and encourage one another to participate in God's life. This is important because we are neither born nor "born again" knowing how to live the Christian life. Alone we lack the skills, knowledge, and power. Thus "we need mentors, teachers, and partners who will provide the advice, challenge, and support to enable us to extend and deepen our participation."[11] While personal spiritual practices are formative, it is often deep connection to a community of faith that is "the most powerful and determinative factor in Christian spiritual formation."[12]

Christians occasionally walk the path of spiritual formation in solitude, yet we never walk it alone. Even private experiences are shared experiences. In Christian community, we have room to search for authentic communion with God, but we do so in connection to one another, encouraging and edifying one another (Heb. 3:13; 1 Cor. 14:12). We share common as well as diverse experiences; however, in our diverse practices and explorations, the church can achieve a common goal through combining those individual efforts.[13]

Grace as a Means of Participating in the Triune Life of God

God's salvation is a gift (Eph. 2:8–9). In Gods' gracious love, God created us in God's image (Gen. 1:26–27). Through gracious love, God reached out to us as we were in a state of ultimate spiritual powerlessness (Rom. 5:6–8; Eph. 2:4–5). Even our movement toward God stems from a natural desire instilled in us in the gracious gift of creation.[14] By the sacrificial nature and actions of Jesus, God offers all humanity the possibility of reconciled, abundant, eternal life (John 10:10). God's gift of life is salvation.

Unfortunately, some of the meanings we ascribe to God's gracious gift of salvation actually rob salvation of its full meaning. Too often one component of salvation (gracious forgiveness of sins) replaces salvation (new life in Christ). Instead of aligning all that we are with the life and ways of God, salvation becomes a mere mental assent, a private belief between the individual and God.[15] Rather than pursuing and embracing full, eternal life in God that begins now and is brought to completion in the eschaton, we equate eternal life solely with heaven and make it our only target.[16] We need God's grace to help us overcome the obstacles of sin and draw us deeper into fellowship, but God does not withhold grace until the end of life. God gives it now that we might be presently, persistently transformed to enter God's life.

The Necessity of Collaboration with God to Participate in God's Life

Participation in the life of God, while a gift, is also a choice. Because of love, God created humanity with freedom to accept or reject that love. God's presence is "empowering" rather than "overpowering."[17] God does not force God's desires on us; instead God woos, entices, and invites. This is true prior to and even after baptism. Conversion does not equal transformation, and transformation does not occur automatically. We still retain our proclivity to sin, and we still retain our choice. Spiritual formation requires an intentional, disciplined approach.[18] Transformation is something that will be done neither to us without our openness nor for us without our collaboration. We must choose to make ourselves vulnerable and available to God. Yet our kenotic act of self-emptying is not a "negation of self, but the place of the self's transformation and expansion into God."[19]

When we choose to join God in a life of transformation, God joins us. Our need for God is not a sign of being weak; it is a sign of being created. The very nature of the triune God revealed as maker, redeemer, and sanctifier reminds us that God knew and created us to need God.[20] Nonetheless, God chooses to work with us, not just for us. Christians are certainly God's workmanship, God's creative works of art and beauty (Eph. 2:10), but we are also God's fellow workers (1 Cor. 3:9) who join in God's work in the world and the task of actualizing our own salvation (Phil. 2:12–13).[21] Collaborating with God in the work of transformation does not always come easily. At times it seems so formidable that some refuse to seek it out of discouragement. Yet as we respond to the grace of God by joining in the work of transformation, we find that holy living becomes more and more natural and delightful to practice.[22] This is how it should be, for God created us so that participating in God's life should be our natural state.

Spiritual Disciplines as a Means of Collaborating and Communing with God

Spiritual disciplines can function as a transformative way to collaborate with God in spiritual formation. Though all humanity is created with a spiritual fire inside and that fire finds fulfillment only in fellowship with God, people choose to deal with it in different ways. Yet as Rolheiser contends, "How we channel it, the disciplines and habits we choose to live by, will either lead to greater integration or disintegration in the way we are related to God, others, and the cosmic world."[23] Spiritual formation is more than verbal or mental declarations of surrendering our lives to God. While formation may include such declarations, it is choosing to cultivate "practices, habits, and ways of seeing and knowing" that make us attentive to the gracious work of God's Spirit.[24] Contrary to notions of grace that equate practicing the disciplines with works-based salvation, rightly practiced spiritual disciplines serve as conduits of grace. Some misunderstood approaches to spiritual disciplines can become a form of slavery[25] or simply devolve into mere technique.[26] Nonetheless, authentic disciplines in the Spirit are entered into and received as God's gracious vessels for drawing us deeper into fellowship.

Training to become Christlike is also an apt description for the practice of spiritual disciplines. The process of cooperating with the Spirit for transformation into the image of Christ requires intentional effort. Beyond trying, those who truly desire Christlikeness need to train (1 Tim. 4:7–8).[27] Jesus practiced most of the spiritual disciplines advocated in this project. Thus since Jesus was sinless (Heb. 4:15), practicing spiritual disciplines is clearly more than moving away from sin. These exercises are a means of embracing godliness and communing with God. Though Jesus is the Son of God, preparation to fulfill his calling was an integral part of his life.[28]

The transformation that can come as a result of the practice of spiritual disciplines leads to deeper union with God. Still, the communal nature of God necessitates that the disciplines draw us deeper into fellowship with the rest of humanity and all of creation. Within the church, we find commonality in our mutual efforts to enter the life of God. At times our training involves corporate commitments; at other times our efforts are individual. Sometimes we succeed, riding the waves of the encouragement and prayer of fellow pilgrims. At other times we struggle and lean on the forgiveness and healing of a loving community. Through this, the Spirit reminds us that God is forming more than individuals; God is forming a body.

Further, life in deeper communion with God and fellow Christians is by no means limited to specific moments of the gathered church or particular times of practicing spiritual disciplines. Indeed, engaging in disciplines that truly deepen communion with God enables active and full enjoyment of the love of God and humankind in all of daily existence. Communing with God through the disciplines is not then an act of escape; it is a way to explore and experience the presence of God.[29] Rather than pulling us into ourselves, disciplines ultimately push us out into God's life and God's creation.[30] All of these elements of practicing spiritual disciplines—a means of collaboration, transformation, and corporate and individual communion with God and creation—are the desired outcomes of the disciplines practiced in this project.

Methodology

The participants in this project were teachers of adult classes and their spouses, and many served in multiple leadership roles within the church. Spouses were invited to be full participants in the project because I desired the couples to enter into a shared spiritual journey. Participants were asked to commit to a retreat and five, two-hour sessions that took place every other week.

Retreat

The retreat was three hours on a Friday night and three hours on Saturday morning. Both the weekend retreat and Monday night sessions were in a member's home, creating familiarity and comfort with the setting.

We began with a brief time of prayer and worship to focus our thoughts. I then introduced David Wray, an outside expert whom I brought in to help facilitate the retreat. He made a few instructional comments concerning the spiritual exercise of *lectio divina* in which we were about to participate and then led the group through a meditative reading of Matthew 4:1–11. Wray then led the group in an introductory lesson concerning spiritual disciplines, using personal stories and a handout entitled "Disciplines for the Journey: Growing in Christlikeness." In our last segment of the evening, we divided into small groups of four to five people to take communion.

The next morning, we began with worship. Wray then led the group in African Bible study.[31] Lesson One was entitled "Participation and Transformation: The Purpose of the Christian Life." Wray led the group through the essence of the study, modeling an effective way in which one can take prewritten material and meaningfully engage the content and questions without working verbatim through the handout. Wray ended the session by offering insights as to how to improve our teaching ministry.

The final session began with contemplation and commitment. Participants wrote a three-faceted prayer seeking transformation in our lives, guidance as we teach or participate in the classes, and transformation of the church. As we wrote these prayers, I played the song "O Lord, Hear My Prayer," to help center our hearts.[32] Next, I encouraged people to put together a spiritual formation group of two to four people. I encouraged participants to fill out a covenant card, committing as teachers and leaders in the church to journey together in the practice of the spiritual disciplines during the series.[33] Wray concluded our morning praying for our church and our group.

Session One

In order to quiet and focus our minds as we began, I invited the group to practice a centering prayer in which they were encouraged to focus on a sacred word such as a name of God or Christ. Next I led them through the prayer exercise "Palms Down, Palms Up."[34]

Then, I took them through a shortened version of Lesson Two: "Everybody Needs Somebody Sometime: The Necessity of Community for Christian Spirituality." I utilized the first planned experience, inviting them to express formative experiences that church had provided through their life. Next, I asked them to cite biblical examples that reveal God's interest in forming not just individuals, but a people. Conversely, I inquired about ways in which our society in general and Christians in particular both approach faith and church in ways that suggest that Christian communal connection is optional. Drawing on the previous week's discussion, I asked in what ways growing to greater reflect Christ draws us closer to other Christians (the church) and non-Christians alike.

Moving toward personal application, we explored ways in which Christian friends can serve in the spiritual formation process. Following up on the encouragement for group members to find a spiritual formation partner or two, I invited some to share in what ways that relationship will serve in the spiritual formation process. We closed the lesson reading aloud in unison the Lord's Prayer as an act of communal expression and as an example of a prayer that uses plural language as opposed to individual language.

To begin the next part of the session, I invited them to close their eyes and listen as one of our participants read a paraphrase of St. Patrick's shield. After a moment of silence, we started working through Lesson Three: "Training vs. Trying: Avenues for Entering the Life of God." We paired up with a partner and brainstormed for two minutes to come up with as many positive and negative images as possible that they associate with words such as *discipline*, *training*, or *exercising*. As was expected, it was a lively discussion, uncovering both the perceived benefits and the many negative impressions of the words, including concerns when the concept was connected to legalism, judgmentalism, and guilt-inducing, joyless Christianity.

I distributed a handout that contained a list of spiritual disciplines that the teachers and class members could practice. I read some descriptions of spiritual disciplines intended to reframe our view. I then I read from Philippians 2:12–13; 3:12–13; and 1 Timothy 4:7–8 and encouraged them to discuss ways that our life with God is described in terms of collaboration and cooperation.

Next, we discussed training for godliness, considering ways in which we could train to grow in Christian knowledge and practice. I reminded them that as in physical training, when we look to train spiritually, we will often find that this too is an arena in which communal connection can aid in success and growth. I concluded the session by asking the participants to close their eyes and listen as I read Ephesians 1:15–23 over us as a prayer seeking God's blessing in the transformation process.

Session Two

We started session two with the "Jesus Prayer." I guided them through the prayer several times, and inviting them to alter the words of the prayer while following the same pattern.[35] We proceeded to work through Lesson Four: "Communicating and Communing with God: Expanding Our Lives of Prayer." I had arranged for two volunteers to help with the first planned experience, a role-play designed to reveal how we approach prayer more as a monologue than a dialogue.

Next, we identified the various types and approaches to prayer found in Scripture. We also explored the types of prayers we thought were employed most frequently by Christians. While the responses varied, overall we recognized that a significant portion of our prayers are relegated to requests, especially for physical wants or needs either for ourselves or others. We discussed both the validity and the deficiencies that exist in our prayer lives if request constitutes our primary content.

I then introduced the concept of prayer as communicating and communing and asked in what ways our prayers might be enhanced if we entered prayer seeking communication and communion with God. The group concluded that request would still have a place, but relationship might become a more dominant theme. To aid in expanding our lives of prayer, I passed out a sheet that had a few self-reflection questions and an opportunity for the participants to make specific commitments in regard to where, when, and how they might put some of the concepts we discussed into practice. The backside of the sheet provided a brief list of prayer exercises intended to facilitate participants' expansion of their prayer experiences. To close, I led the group through the prayer experience "Palms Down, Palms Up."

Following a brief break, we began our equipping session for Lesson Five: "Beyond Bible Study: Meditative Scripture Reading." Engaging the first planned experience, participants discussed an experience they had had in which they had gone too quickly or distractedly and it had caused problems. After sharing humorous examples ranging from driving to cooking to following directions, we discussed in what ways similar problems hamper Scripture reading.

Next, I invited participants to close their eyes and listen to a brief series of passages that allude to deep thought, meditation, devotion, and love for the word of God.[36] After a moment of silence, we discussed our thoughts when we hear the word *meditation*. The word evokes images of slowing down, spending time, stilling the heart, mind, and body, and deep thought and reflection.

To illustrate one method of meditative reading, I guided the group through the practice of *lectio divina*. First, we closed our eyes and spent a moment in silence, preparing to hear the word. I read slowly (*lectio*) from Psalm 1, allowing another brief moment of silence. Second, I guided the group through a time of reflection (*meditatio*), encouraging them to meditate on the words, God's message to them, and their place in the passage. To help them find how God might be using the passage to speak to them, I invited them to draw on their memory, experiences, thoughts, feelings, hopes, desires, intuitions, and intentions. Third, after a few seconds of silent meditation, we prayed as a response (*oratio*) to the Spirit's leading during their time of reading and meditation. Fourth, we entered a time of quiet rest (*contemplatio*) in the presence of God. During this time I instructed them that the only expectation was for them to enjoy the presence of God, receptive of whatever God desires to do with them. To conclude, I encouraged them to allow the message of the text and the moments of reflection and communion to continue to serve as an anchor, grounding them in the life and love of God throughout the evening.

Next, I read a brief quotation from Eugene Peterson and expressed why this type of approach was especially important for a room filled with teachers and leaders of the church.[37] We concluded our time together by listening to a prayerful song entitled "Breathe" that celebrates God's presence and word.[38]

Session Three

I began by passing out note cards and soliciting feedback as to how the practice of the disciplines was going so far. These cards represented a chance to offer reflection on the experiences, as well as identify hopes, fears, and obstacles to continued growth. We entered into a brief time of prayer, presenting our hopes for the evening to God. To assist our time of prayer, I encouraged them to respond audibly in unison "Lord, hear our prayer" at the conclusion of reading each note card. When the prayer ended, I explained that one way to stay more engaged in prayer is to join more intentionally in the prayer, silently or audibly, by saying "amen," "let it be, Lord," "that's right," "Lord, hear our prayer," or something similar.

We moved next into our equipping session for Lesson Six: "Search Me, Oh God: *Examen* and Confession." For the first planned experience, I passed out a sheet with pictures of optical illusions and questions associated with each. I asked the participants to answer the questions silently, and individually, with only about forty-five seconds to look. I then asked them to pair up and answer them together, this time giving them several minutes. We compared the two experiences, and as expected, they responded that additional time coupled with the varied perspective of another person helped them see things they would have otherwise missed.

Next, we meditated on Psalm 139:1–12, 23–24. In particular, we considered how and why God, and trusted Christian friends, can help us examine our hearts more accurately. I proceeded to introduce the spiritual exercise of *examen*, explaining that it is often practiced in two forms: 1) *examen* of conscience (a time of self-exploration through the grace and guidance of God to recognize our personal sins and strengths), and 2) *examen* of consciousness (a time of self-exploration through the grace and guidance of God to grow in awareness of the daily presence of God and our response to his presence).

Next, I encouraged the participants to close their eyes as I walked them through a succinct experience of *examen*. I invited them to ask God for the light of insight to reveal sins and God's presence during the day. Additionally, I suggested that they ask God for forgiveness of their sins. Finally, I challenged them to resolve through the grace of God to do better. After a break, we begin our equipping session concerning Lesson Seven: "Hungering for God: Fasting." I instructed them to form groups of two or three. After a lighthearted introductory discussion of times of hunger, I asked for images, feelings, or reactions they associate with fasting. A few descriptions were positive, but most were negative, such as pain, fanaticism, unnecessary restriction, eating disorders, and hunger strikes.

Attempting to identify the biblical underpinnings for fasting, I asked the group to share passages that came to mind that referred to fasting and the purposes associated with fasting. Examples such as Jesus in the desert, David's response to the impending death of his son, and Jesus' discussion of fasting with religious leaders in Mark 2 were mentioned as positive examples. Jesus' chiding those who fast for show in the Sermon on the Mount was identified as a negative example. Following this line of thought, we discussed other ways that fasting could be inappropriately practiced.

While recognizing the potential distortions of fasting, I pointed out that it was and has been employed as a common discipline throughout the Bible, early church years, and up until recent times. I proceeded to ask why they thought the practice might have fallen out of favor for modern Christians. Further, I inquired what beliefs, values, or practices in our society might make fasting especially unpopular or difficult. We identified that our consumeristic surroundings; the desire to have what we want, when we want it; and the challenge of seeing how restriction and voluntary limitation of certain comforts could create possibilities for deeper spiritual lives were all contributing factors. I also pointed out that in a time when some popular notions of God are that God wants to make us happy, keep us from hurting, and give us what we want, the concept of voluntary abstinence works against this distorted understanding of the good news of the gospel.

We concluded by considering ways that entering occasional, if not regular, times of voluntary restriction could provide opportunities for deeper spiritual formation. We also discussed the way in which fasting is often coupled with prayer. Understanding that some people cannot fast from food, we identified some other types of fasts (media, purchasing, etc.) that one could practice to allow similar spiritual benefits. I ended our evening together by passing out a teacher's aid: a list of types of fasting found in Scripture. We concluded in prayer, asking God to help us learn how to let go, scale back, or give up some things even temporarily so that we could create greater space for God's work.

Session Four

Session four began with a time of breath prayer. Next we began our equipping session for Lesson Eight: "Gathered in the Spirit: Worship." Utilizing the first planned experience, I asked them to divide into groups of two or three and discuss an event, activity, or competition in which the judging at times seemed fair and at other times seemed subjective. Participants shared many humorous examples, including experiences of judging beauty competitions and watching Olympic gymnastics. As a follow-up question, I inquired about ways in which people judge the quality or effectiveness of corporate worship, exploring both times when that might seem appropriate and times when those judgments can devolve into discussions of little more than personal preferences and individual experiences.

In preparation to hear the Scripture, I invited the group to close their eyes and listen to the song "The Heart of Worship."[39] Next, I asked the group to listen to a few passages while considering the following question: "Why do we worship?"[40] Amending the question I asked, "Why are we called to *come together* to worship?" Complementing the previous discussion, participants recounted our need for encouragement and accountability to live lives of worship. They also recalled that life in God is communal by design since God is forming and calling a people, not just individuals. Finally, they recognized that loving, serving, welcoming, and similar activities that accompany gathering together are acts of worship to God.

I then encouraged them to discuss in what ways our attitudes or actions enhance or hinder the spiritually formative nature worship has on our lives. During the discussion, participants suggested that we as individuals could have a significant impact on the ways in which corporate worship does and does not form us. God is the transformer of our hearts, and the facilitators of worship and the elements included in worship also play an important role. However, participants admitted that their attitudes and actions impact the way in which they are formed by worship. We proceeded then to discuss specific ways in which each person could approach the time before, during, and after corporate worship as a discipline to enhance its formative potential in their life.

After a short break, we began exploration of Lesson Nine: "Where Do We Go from Here: Developing a Rule of Life." I reminded the group that one of the goals was that some of the disciplines introduced and practiced in this series would become regularly practiced exercises. I informed them that developing a rule of life was a practice from Christian tradition that has aided many in pursuing a deep life in God.

Next I encouraged them to work on a quadrant exercise. Participants spent a few minutes filling in each quadrant, identifying those activities that they already do on a daily, weekly, monthly, and yearly basis that nurture their spirit. I then read aloud sample rules of life and pointed out the varied lengths, content, and form of the samples provided. We examined several tips for developing and keeping a rule, and I made comments about the suggestions when needed. I encouraged the participants to look back over their quadrant sheets with the samples and suggestions in mind, paying attention to what they should affirm, what they should adjust, and what they should add.

I asked them to work prayerfully and thoughtfully to complete their personal rule of life before our next session together so we could share them with one another. I went on to suggest that all of those who would be teaching on the Sunday in which we introduced the rule of life should attempt to finish their rule of life to offer at least a portion of it as another sample for their class. I also suggested that they consider asking if the members of their class would be willing to bring completed copies of their rules of life the following Sunday. We concluded with a prayer in which I asked for God's wisdom and guidance as we seek to develop a personal rule of life.

Session Five

The last session was set aside for reflection and wrap-up. I asked each participant to fill out a brief questionnaire answering the following questions:

1. What effect, if any, did practicing spiritual disciplines have on me as a teacher during the course of this series?
2. What effect, if any, do I anticipate the practice of spiritual disciplines will have on me as I teach in the future?

After allowing time to complete the questionnaire, I asked them to form groups of two to three. I then encouraged them to share at least some, if not all, of their rule of life with those in their group. After allowing enough time for all to share within their groups, I called everyone back together and invited participants to share with the entire group. After each person shared, I thanked them for sharing, affirmed what they had shared, and asked that God would bless them in living out that rule.

We ended the evening and our equipping sessions by taking communion together. Partaking together of the communal meal was a reminder of our series-long desire to share more fully in God's life and in one another's life. At the end of communion, we stood in a circle and one of our elders closed our time with prayer.

Suggestions and Conclusions

Numerous aspects of this project could be beneficial for those who are interested in embarking on a similar journey filled with excitement and trepidation, especially if the disciplines are new. The very word *discipline* can evoke negative connotations. While the word need not be discarded, it may have to be rehabilitated. Further, the exercises themselves can prove inviting and intimidating. It takes time for people to grow in their comfort and stamina with new spiritual exercises.

Additionally, facilitators should equip teachers of classes on spiritual disciplines through modeling, studying, and experiencing the disciplines together, not just through disseminating curriculum. While many teachers will require greater knowledge of the disciplines, much of what they need to learn comes through experience and observation. The teachers will have a difficult time leading class members through disciplines they themselves have yet to practice.

Further, one should encourage and when possible equip the formation of small groups that can aid in the practice of the disciplines. Teacher-equipping sessions can help on one level, but creating spiritual formation groups among both the teachers and the rest of the church offers the potential for a deeper, longer-lasting impact.

While the rule of life initially evoked the strongest reaction of fear and inadequacy, I recommend that anyone looking to introduce a similar study offer gentle but strong encouragement for participants to complete a rule of life. Developing a rule of life takes time, thought, prayer, and recognition that one is entering a commitment by the grace of God. These realities surface anxiety in the hearts of those who fear failure, setting the bar too low or too high, or the increased sense of commitment. These concerns are understandable, but all the more reason to guide participants toward formulating a rule of life. While not a necessity to the practice of spiritual disciplines, developing a rule of life compels increased intentionality. If possible, one should look for a way to allow group members to share at least a portion of their rule of life with others. Sharing provides an opportunity for encouragement and loving accountability.

One should also make a concerted effort to connect the practice of spiritual disciplines with individual and communal living for the sake of the world. Due to the limits of time, some disciplines such as service, hospitality, giving, and evangelism were not included in the course of this intervention but were covered congregationally afterward. Even without the introduction of some of these disciplines, participants will be helped by hearing and witnessing how transformation into the image of Christ should always draw us deeper into the mission and nature of Christ—living, serving, and sacrificing for the sake of others.

Finally, churches should plan ways to practice and teach the disciplines after the series concludes. Find ways to incorporate some of the exercises, such as different approaches to prayer and meditative reading of Scripture, into corporate worship settings. Utilize regular seasons of the year (Lent, for example) to invite the church to practice the disciplines as well as inform them of ways to do so. Finally, look for ways to practice and model the use of spiritual disciplines in the context of teacher training, small-group leader training, and leadership gatherings within the church.

This project proved rewarding for our church. Most of the participants concluded that the experience of practicing the disciplines impacted their approach to teaching the disciplines. One reported that developing a deeper appreciation for the subject matter made for deeper wells to draw from. Another shared that his passion for teaching increased, and with it a greater sense of the presence of God in the midst of teaching. A teacher who teaches older members wrote that he was pleasantly surprised by how much more they participated than he had anticipated. He closed by writing: "I think leading by example helped." All of them mentioned how they could imagine continuing to use some of the disciplines in their ongoing task of teaching, in particular new approaches to prayer and slower-paced, meditative reading of Scripture.

However, participants expressed that the biggest impact of our sessions and study was on their personal spiritual formation. More than half admitted having little exposure to spiritual disciplines prior to this experience. This study gave them a greater awareness and appreciation for the varied avenues of spiritual growth that are available. All the participants anticipated continuing to practice some of the exercises explored in this study.

I also benefited from the experience on a personal level. One of the project's basic assumptions—effective teaching ministry requires practicing the disciplines—holds true for my ministry as well. I am grateful that in addressing the needs of my church, God graciously continued transformation in my life.

---

1. Bert Reynolds, "Deep Calls to Deep: Equipping Teachers for Facilitating Classes on Spiritual Disciplines in the Chenal Valley Church of Christ" (DMin thesis, ACU, 2006).

2. Marjorie J. Thompson, *Soul Feast: An Invitation to the Christian Spiritual Life* (Louisville: Westminster John Knox, 1995), 10.

3. Ibid., 11.

4. C. Leonard Allen and Danny Gray Swick, *Participating in God's Life: Two Crossroads for Churches of Christ* (Orange, CA: New Leaf, 2001), 70.

5. Ellen T. Charry, "Spiritual Formation by the Doctrine of the Trinity," *Theology Today* 54 (1997): 372.

6. Nonna Verna Harrison, "Human Community as an Image of the Holy Trinity," *St. Vladimir's Quarterly* 46.4 (2002): 349.

7. Robert P. Meye, "The Imitation of Christ: Means and End of Spiritual Formation," in *The Christian Educators Handbook on Spiritual Formation*, eds. Kenneth O. Gangel and James C. Wilhoit (Wheaton, IL: Victor, 1994), 199.

8. Sandra M. Schneider, "Biblical Spirituality," *Interpretation* 56.2 (April 2002): 134.

9. Dallas Willard, *The Divine Conspiracy: Rediscovering Our Hidden Life in God* (New York: HarperCollins, 1998), 4.

10. John Zizoulas, "The Church as Communion," *St. Vladimir's Theological Quarterly* 38.1 (1994): 6.

11. Darrell L. Guder, *Missional Church: A Vision for the Sending of the Church in North America* (Grand Rapids: Eerdmans, 1998), 155.

12. John Mark Hicks and Greg Taylor, *Down to the River to Pray: Revisioning Baptism as God's Transforming Work* (Siloam Springs, AR: Leafwood, 2004), 328.

13. Ibid., 9–10.

14. L. Gregory Jones, "A Thirst for God or Consumer Spirituality? Cultivating Disciplined Practices of Being Engaged by God," *Modern Theology* 13 (Jan. 1997): 5.

15. Dallas Willard, *The Spirit of the Disciplines: Understanding How God Changes Lives* (San Francisco: Harper San Francisco, 1991), 23.

16. Willard, *Divine Conspiracy*, 47.

17. Charles J. Sabitino and Daemen College, "Spirituality: Experiencing the Everyday World as Grace," *Horizons* 25 (1998): 85.

18. Glen G. Scorgie, "Yearning for God: The Potential and Poverty of the Catholic Spirituality of Francis de Sales," *Journal of the Evangelical Theological Society* 41 (Sept. 1998): 439.

19. Sarah Coakley, *Powers and Submissions: Spirituality, Philosophy, and Gender* (Malden, MA: Blackwell, 2002), 35–36.

20. Charry asserts that the "second and third *hypostases* of the Trinity are not afterthoughts, but their co-eternal and co-existent state speaks to God's anticipation of our full need." Charry, "Spiritual Formation," 377.

21. Bernard of Clairvaux. *On Loving God* (Grand Rapids: Christian Classics Ethereal Library), accessed March 16, 2005, http://www.ccel.org/ccel/bernard/loving_god.html.

22. Jones, "Thirst for God," 8.

23. Ronald Rolheiser, *The Holy Longing: The Search for a Christian Spirituality* (New York: Doubleday, 1999), 11.

24. Stanley P. Saunders, "'Learning Christ': Eschatology and Spiritual Formation in New Testament Christianity," *Interpretation* 56.2 (2002): 156.

25. John Ackerman, *Spiritual Awakening: A Guide to Spiritual Life in Congregations* (New York: Alban, 1995), 32.

26. D. A. Carson, "When Is Spirituality Spiritual? Reflections on Some Problems of Definition," *Journal of the Evangelical Theological Society* 37 (Sept. 1994): 388.

27. Willard, *Spirit of the Disciplines*, 98.

28. Ibid., 5.

29. Saunders, "'Learning Christ,'" 156.

30. Susanne Johnson, *Christian Spiritual Formation in the Church and Classroom* (Nashville: Abingdon Press), 55.

31. We read Luke 10:38–42 from three different versions: NRSV, NIV, and The Message. In line with the tradition of African Bible study, he invited the participants to listen to the text with their eyes closed, and before each reading, he instructed us to listen for slightly different words, phrases, or concepts. Between the readings, we were asked to turn to a person next to us and discuss for about a minute various aspects of the text.

32. "O Lord, Hear My Prayer," *Taize: Wait for the Lord* (GIA, 1987), compact disc.

33. The covenant card, while encouraged, was presented as a voluntary commitment to be entered into on the part of the participants. Language of invitation was used throughout the process to model that spiritual formation cannot be forced.

34. This is a slow-paced prayer in which participants engage body with mind and spirit. I first invited them to place their palms flat on their knees. I led a prayer encouraging them to release to God such things as the anxiety, anger, sin, and distractions of the day. The participants then turned their palms up. I guided them in a time of asking for peace, comfort, quiet, and the leading of God so that we could be formed and filled through our time together.

35. The "Jesus Prayer," borrowed from the prayer of the tax collector in Luke 18:13, has a long history in the Christian tradition for those seeking to center their hearts on God. It is a simple prayer that synchronizes one's rhythms of inhaling and exhaling as one prays (exhale—"Lord Jesus Christ, Son of God"; inhale—"have mercy on me a sinner").

36. Josh. 1:8; Ps. 119:15, 23, 24, 48, 97, 148.

37. Eugene Peterson, *Working the Angles* (Grand Rapids: Eerdmans, 1987), 87.

38. Michael W. Smith, "Breathe," Worship, Reunion Records, 2001, compact disc.

39. Zoe Group, "The Heart of Worship," *The Heart of Worship*, Christian Music Resources, B007IUF0GY, 2000, compact disc.

40. Ps. 100; John 4:21–24; Col. 3:12–13; Rom. 12:1–2.

CHAPTER 6

Equipping Parents

CHRIS SMITH[1]

The phone call comes on Monday. The mother wants me to talk with her pre-ten-year-old about baptism. Invariably she means, "We want our child to be baptized this Sunday and you need to talk to the child for one hour." Sometimes, the child shows an appropriate level of understanding of the significance of baptism. Often, the child is woefully unprepared for immersion. Yet, I have never refused to baptize a child, even when I considered the youngster unready. For this lack of pastoral guidance, I have no excuse except my reluctance to thwart the enthusiasm of youth. But I have never felt good about it. I have always thought there had to be a better way.

As a preaching minister for the last two decades, I have not been especially involved in ministry to children or adolescents. However, at least two factors led to my interest in more adequately equipping parents of younger children for baptism. In 2006, I preached a sermon on baptism to my congregation, the Harpeth Hills Church of Christ. In this sermon, I expressed concerns about the decreasing baptismal ages of our children; this segment was five minutes of a twenty-five-minute sermon. For the first time, I publicly expressed dissatisfaction over our casual and almost flippant attitude toward baptizing clearly unprepared children. I intentionally planted the seed that parents should consider waiting rather than rushing their pre-ten-year-olds to the baptistry. The sermon served as a genesis for conversations among members concerning the appropriate age for baptism. In the fall of that year, one of our children's ministers, Melissa Roe, and I taught a four-week class on preparing children for baptism.

The second influence was the memory of a multi-week Bible study with a young couple several years before. The parents knew they were not prepared to teach their son, a ten-year-old already talking about baptism; in fact the husband had questions about his own baptism years before. I worked with the parents, teaching them to teach their son. As a result of this mutually satisfying experience, the father did not feel a need to be rebaptized, and the young man's immersion occurred two years later. Working with these parents to teach their son just seemed right.

Over the last decade, I have noticed an increasing lack of confidence among parents for the task of training their own children in discipleship. When studying something as simple as the conversion stories in Acts, parents often displayed a lack of familiarity with the biblical record, giving the impression that they were learning as much as their youngsters were.

In addition to a lack of parental confidence, I have also noticed a lowering of the baptismal age. When I moved to Nashville in 1997, I noted an immediate difference from my ministry context in Duncanville, Texas, a suburb of Dallas. At Duncanville, children were baptized at an average age of thirteen or fourteen. At HH, the average age was nine to eleven.[2] Southern Baptists have noted a similar decrease in age as well, with the number of six-to-eight-year-old children baptized increasing in the 1980s and 1990s while the number of nine-to-twelve-year-olds has declined.[3]

Today's parents have greater difficulty in telling their children no or wait than older parents. "Generation X" (1961–1981) and "Bridger" (1981–2000) parents seem to be more likely to acquiesce to childhood pleas for baptism than previous generations. The following stereotype, perhaps harsh, contains elements of truth: parents do not want to hurt their children's self-esteem, so if little Johnny wants to be baptized, let him. The reasoning? "We do not want to discourage youthful devotion." I can certainly understand such a sentiment. However, a more damaging unspoken assumption says, "Well, it won't hurt anything." The second assumption betrays a low view of baptism.

This parental indulgence perhaps displays a shift in spirituality styles among Churches of Christ. Many have moved from a crisis model of conversion, requiring a deep sense of guilt prior to baptism, toward a more personal, pietistic approach that seeks to affirm the faith of sincere children. The current spirituality style no longer emphasizes the child's comprehension of spiritual truth or his capability to commit. Now parents and others look to the heart; since children are capable of great love and devotion, many assume that baptism must follow, even at a young age. "Yet if we have not helped them understand the place of baptism in their ongoing journey of faith," notes Childers, "they may come to believe that baptism is the only and most natural way to express those first self-conscious urgings of love toward Christ."[4]

Parents display contradictory attitudes toward baptism. They strongly desire their children to be baptized, even insisting on immersion at the first sign of youthful faith, yet they inadequately prepare their children to take this step. Parents say to their children, "Baptism is the most important step you will ever take" but seldom back these words by actions. If baptism epitomizes the most important thing a child can do, one would think parents would spend significantly more time and effort in leading their children to baptism.

Since parents remain the primary influencers of their children in the decision to be baptized, scoring higher in surveys than youth ministers or peers,[5] the purpose of this project was to equip parents. A failure to train the greatest influencers of children—their own parents—simply misses the mark.

Theological Framework

The Status of Children

This project was based upon the theological assumption that children are neither lost nor saved but innocent until they reach an age of responsibility, or accountability. While one cannot explicitly support this view from the New Testament, it does mirror the view of children in the Old Testament. Under the old covenant, children were a part of the community but accepted a more responsible position upon reaching adolescence. Likewise G. R. Beasley-Murray writes of children in the first century: "The children of Christian parents, nurtured within the fold of the Church, are certainly not outsiders nor 'little pagans,' though they may be little terrors. But neither are they, in the fullest sense of the term, 'in the church' in the sense of members of the Body, that is, in Christ."[6]

A declaration of innocence does not answer every question about the proper treatment of children in the church. Thomas Halbrooks analyzes Southern Baptists and details four views of children held in that denomination: nonmembers, prospects, potential disciples, and maturing participants.[7] The maturing participant approach treats children as catechumens—"included as participants in the community, learning, being nurtured, and maturing in the faith, but becoming full members of the church only upon a personal profession of faith."[8] Children participate in the community of faith but are not treated as adults. They are allowed to be children.

These children of the church are safe, not because they are immersed at age eleven, but because we serve a God who loves our children. If we as parents remain patient with difficult teenagers under the onslaught of hormones, can we not imagine God as having patience as well? Did not God display great patience with the children of Israel? Do we believe in a God who condemns children or adolescents before the age at which they can possess a driver's license, go on a date, balance a checkbook, or make a host of other decisions for themselves? We need not immerse them at an early age to relieve our fears. Instead, parents and the church community bear the responsibility for making sure our children understand the deep significance of baptism prior to baptism.

The Significance of Baptism

The conversion stories in the book of Acts portray baptism as an initiation into the Lord. In the stories of the Ethiopian eunuch, Saul, and the Philippian jailor this initiation is dramatic and sudden. Yet viewing baptism only through the lens of initiation or crisis conversion provides an incomplete picture. Baptism can also be seen through the lens of continuation. For many people who grew up in a church, a continuation theme gives a more accurate assessment than a decisive-turning-point explanation. These people do not experience baptism as a U-turn from a life of sin and debauchery but as another step in the journey with God. Baptism can legitimately be seen not just as a destination but as a point of departure.[9] While the crisis conversion model predominates in the book of Acts, an element of dynamism also pervades the stories.

The Ethiopian eunuch lives a life devoted to God; his story is no three-hour conversion experience from start to finish. "He had come to Jerusalem to worship" (Acts 8:27 NRSV)—most likely not for the first time. Owning a portion of Scripture in New Testament times indicated not just personal wealth and prestige but passion and interest as well. Weatherly observes that both the Ethiopian eunuch and Cornelius already recognized the God of Israel as the one true God. "Their devotion to him was nothing new, though their understanding of their access to him and membership in his people was radically altered by the gospel."[10]

Saul of Tarsus is steeped in the Jewish Scriptures, trained since childhood to know God. With the gift of hindsight, he acknowledges that the Lord has set him apart even before his birth (Gal. 1:15). Saul travels the Damascus Road that day, not as a pagan or neophyte before the Lord, but as one who knows of the Messiah, believes in a Messiah and only needs to be convinced that Jesus is indeed that one. Much work has been done on Paul prior to the blinding light on the road. Ben Witherington says we are "dealing with a process of enlightenment and change, not an instant conversion and commissioning at Damascus with Spirit Baptism and/or water baptism added three days later."[11] So while Saul and the eunuch had dramatic and sudden conversions, these conversions were a long time in the making.

Scripture does not speak exclusively in a punctiliar tense when it comes to salvation. Witherington points out salvation "is something about which one must say, 'I have been saved, I am being saved, and I shall be saved' if we are to be true to all the New Testament says about soteriology."[12] Numerous texts like 1 Corinthians 1:18, 2 Corinthians 3:17–18; 5:17; Ephesians 4:13, 15; and Philippians 3:10–14 reveal the nature of salvation as dynamic and organic.

To speak of salvation as both present and aorist tense is not to confuse justification and sanctification—although the line between the two is blurry at best. Using both tenses does, however, emphasize the work of God as opposed to the activity of humankind. Salvation is something that God does for people. Some people God saves in a dramatic fashion, such as the thief on the cross or the jailer at Philippi. A host of others come to the Lord gradually and unperceptively.

As we lead our children to the water, we invite them to continue on a journey. Most will not have a dramatic experience but will simply take another crucial step toward God. They will walk in the same direction in which they have been headed since their parents brought them to church at one month of age. Since the conversion may not be an intense crisis filled with emotion, we must train our parents to recognize growing faith and adequately prepare their children for baptism.

The Role of Catechesis

Baptism is an event; events require preparation. Unlike the Philippian jailer, who came to the Lord in one evening, or the hardened sinner marching down the sawdust trail after being convicted by the persuasive Walter Scott or Charles Finney, our children gradually grow in faith and one day make a decision to cross over. Glen Stassen writes, "We do not believe that baptism is a magic ritual but that it is a deep expression of faith in Christ who was dead, buried, and raised for us; therefore, we need not rush baptism but should be concerned about the growth in faith that goes with baptism."[13]

The early church took seriously the responsibility to prepare believers for baptism. In fact something quite remarkable happened from the first to third centuries of Christendom. The church moved from the model of rapid crisis conversion in the book of Acts—seemingly one sermon and proceed to the water—to lengthy preparations for baptisms. In *Apostolic Traditions*, Hippolytus detailed the mid-third-century practices of the church, including a three-year catechetical period of instructions.[14] The early church wanted to ensure that new converts, many coming from pagan backgrounds, were prepared to take up the cross of Jesus. The early church showed less apparent concern for precisely when catechumens were saved and more concern for their commitment to a life of discipleship. The church of the third century gauged immediate baptism upon confession of faith less important than the problem of converts falling away from the faith.[15] We too should take seriously the readiness of our own catechumens.

We should consider the maturity level of the child. All children, like Jesus, "[increase] in wisdom and in years, and in divine and human favor" (Luke 2:52 NRSV). Some, however, mature more quickly than others, as any parent with more than one child can bear witness. However, even parents of precocious and spiritually minded preadolescents should take note that Jesus himself was twelve before the first mention of his involvement in religious activity.

Our sincere efforts not to discourage a child must not strip baptism of its meaning and significance. Of course, children of the church love Jesus; we want them to and teach them to. But baptism means more than devotion. We do not delay baptism in anticipation of future sophistication or eloquence, but we do have the responsibility to expect some level of mature faith. Indiscriminately offering immersion at the least sign of faith strips baptism of its deep meaning.

Common sense tells us there is nothing inherently wrong in delaying baptism until greater maturity occurs. Parents tell children no all the time. Even the most permissive parents do not allow children to date or drive just because they beg persistently. So why would parents allow children to be baptized just because they ask twice and seem sincere? As Claudia Dickson states, "In the early centuries of Christianity no one would have assumed that a person was ready for baptism simply because he or she expressed an interest in being baptized."[16]

If the "essence of Christian baptism is deeper than the cleansing forgiveness of sins, the act of joining the church or the experience of personal renewal,"[17] then we should take care not to blithely allow young children into the water before they can fathom such depths of meaning. Martin Jeschke notes that in a society that does not allow adolescents to drive until the age of sixteen or vote until eighteen, "we are deluding ourselves if we ask them [children] to make authentic decisions with respect to personal faith at a much earlier age."[18] If the decision to follow Jesus in baptism is, as most parents tell their children, "the most important decision they will ever make," parents must think seriously about the appropriate age for such a momentous decision.

Parents can become uniquely qualified to fulfill the role of spiritual mentors—teaching, modeling, and leading their children to a responsible decision concerning baptism. Moreover, these same parents can continue to lead their children in a maturing walk with the Lord, recognizing baptism as not only a destination but also a point of departure. As we live into, and out of, our baptism, we pray for ourselves and we pray for our children the words of Paul: "And all of us, with unveiled faces, seeing the glory of the Lord as though reflected in a mirror, are being transformed into the same image from one degree of glory to another; for this comes from the Lord, the Spirit" (2 Cor. 3:18 NRSV).

The Project

This Bible class coincided with the beginning of a new Sunday school class at HH, begun in the fall of 2007 for parents of elementary-age children. Melissa Roe, one of our children's ministers, and I taught the class. Roe's role as co-teacher for the new class was important since she is highly respected among our parents. Her ongoing relationship with our parents and her understanding of children and their needs far exceed mine. The new class coordinators began each session with announcements and prayer so that the three coordinator couples could build a sense of community within the group.

Week one served as an introduction to the class. After opening comments, I encouraged parents to tell the stories of their baptisms. Since faith formation involves personal testimony, it was important for the class to recount the movement of God in their own lives. They answered three questions in small groups: Were you adequately prepared for your baptism? Why were you baptized? Who influenced you the most? Toward the end of class, I solicited additional feedback. We asked the groups to discuss briefly two questions: Are you prepared to teach your children, and what are you looking for in this class? I concluded the class with a reminder of the power of parental influence, citing both Scripture (Deut. 6) and survey results.[19]

Week two focused on the theme "children are a part of the community of faith." To develop a working theology of children, we looked at both the Old and New Testaments to find out how children were viewed. Then, I briefly described how the church has viewed children through the centuries, particularly as it relates to original sin and innocence. I concluded class by introducing Thomas Halbrooks's study of Southern Baptists and how that denomination has viewed children through the years. Halbrooks's fourfold description (non-members, prospects, potential disciples, maturing participants) closely tracks Churches of Christ as well. I encouraged the parents to consider the maturing participant model and more appropriate terminology for our children, such as journey, story, growth, disciple, or follower of Jesus—instead of in/out, lost/saved, and/or member/non-member.

Since I had lectured the entire time the previous week, we devoted week three to questions and answers. Questions from the class included:

1. What about the role of the Spirit?

2. Are we denying our children the Spirit's help if we delay baptism?

3. How do we establish a balance between the emotional and the rational concerning baptism?

4. What are we teaching our children at church about baptism?

5. What about the child who is afraid of going to hell?

6. How do we find the balance of working with our children?

7. If we give our children a checklist, are we somehow interfering with what God is doing?

The healthy feedback reflected a group still working through the issues. I intended to begin teaching on baptism as initiation, but since the questions and answers took so long, we revised the schedule. Receiving feedback and answering questions seemed more important than remaining on task. I concluded class by encouraging the students to study the stories of Saul of Tarsus, the Ethiopian eunuch, and the Philippian jailer before the next class.

Week four introduced baptism as initiation. Looking at the stories of Saul of Tarsus, the Ethiopian eunuch, and the Philippian jailer allowed the students to glimpse the breadth of the conversion experience as detailed in Acts. We discussed the difference between the crisis conversions in Acts and the gradual conversion experiences of most of our children. Since the New Testament is a missionary document dealing primarily with first-generation Christians, we face the challenge of determining how to adapt a crisis model of conversion to our second-generation children.

On week five, I introduced the idea of baptism and salvation as continuation. Several texts (1 Cor. 1:18; Eph. 4:13–15; Phil. 3:10–14; 1 John 3:2; 2 Cor. 3:18; 5:17) remind us that salvation is dynamic and ongoing, not static. One objective of this class involves helping parents see baptism as one step on the journey rather than the destination. The goal is not to get our children baptized by the age of thirteen; the goal is for our children to become lifelong disciples. I also recounted a brief history of catechesis in the early church to provide parents with another way of looking at children and baptism. I pointed out that the early church would have forced the jailer to wait two to three years before baptism. The key point of week five was that baptism should not be rushed but thoroughly prepared for and anticipated.

On week six, Roe discussed how parents can discern their children's readiness for baptism and the four ways people relate to God—affective, cognitive, engagement, and observation. She briefly lectured on childhood development as it relates to faith development, pointing out in particular that some studies indicate that, until around the age of twelve, for most children right and wrong are what the mother says they are. Roe detailed what to look for in spiritual maturity and readiness by listing three key concepts: understanding right and wrong, understanding obedience, and understanding what it means to choose God and make a statement of faith.

On week seven, I solicited input from parents through small group discussion. The four groups discussed two questions: What do children need to understand before they are baptized? and what instructions or activities have we done in our homes that have been beneficial? We discussed the responses at the end of class, and reporters from each group emailed me the groups' more exhaustive lists later in the week. The groups shared eighteen different answers for the first question and sixteen for the second. Significant responses to the first question included:

1. A good understanding of why we need God's grace and forgiveness
2. Cognitive recognition of right and wrong
3. Desire to be a child of God, not necessarily fear of hell
4. Spiritual longing/compulsion/desire to be right with God
5. The reality of baptism as opposed to make-believe
6. Understanding of remorse and repentance

A sampling of the responses to the question about what their family has done that has been successful in teaching their children included:

1. Praying real prayers
2. Engaging in family devotionals where children ask about baptism
3. Encouraging service to others
4. Making it a daily walk—when they lie down and rise up
5. Assigning passages to look up and tell what they mean

The interaction among the students was lively and instructive.

Roe led week eight's discussion of how to make the baptism day memorable. She stressed a planned, celebratory (vs. haphazard or nonchalant) approach to baptism. Such planning begins well before the day itself as parents share their dreams with their child, planting seeds early. Baptisms should be planned events, taking into consideration the personality of the child and the communal aspect of baptism. Consideration of the child's love language—gifts, words of affirmation, quality time, acts of service, physical touch—helps determine how parents might express their love and the love of the community on this day.

Roe offered several suggestions for making the day special: providing a favorite meal, scrapbook or video, a cloud of witnesses, and a program. Many of these suggestions honor the communal aspect of our faith. Parents help each other lead their children in the footsteps of Jesus. Since our walk is a walk, a journey, Roe discussed ways to celebrate other steps along the journey, such as early professions of faith by pre-teens and more mature expressions of faith by young adults. The guiding principal was that baptism is a significant step, but it is not the only step. At the conclusion of class, we provided four devotionals suitable for pre-teens.

On week nine, we began class by asking, "If baptism is just one step along the way, why are we advocating making such a big deal out the baptism itself?" Some of the class responses included:

1. Baptism symbolizes the birth and death of Jesus.
2. Baptism is a declaration of faith.
3. We should do a better job celebrating all the steps of faith.
4. Baptism is the beginning of a journey that is worthy of being noted, though it is not the end.
5. Baptism refers to all the other steps of faith.
6. Baptism is ceremonial, much like a groundbreaking.
7. Baptism is stepping through the doorway.

Roe then followed up on the conversations from the week before and talked more about celebrating the baptismal event. She and I stressed the communal aspect of baptism and the importance of including family and friends on that day. In that context, I observed that for centuries people never considered baptism to be a private event. We also discussed the pros and cons of allowing children to participate in the Lord's Supper prior to their immersion.

The tenth week provided the opportunity to distribute questionnaires to the class. While they completed the questionnaires, I asked a father to tell of a recent meeting involving his twelve-year-old son, his wife, and me. His son had expressed an interest in baptism and a concern about where he would spend eternity if he died. According to the father, hearing me say, "It is not a matter of if you will be baptized but when" seemed to relieve the pressure the young man felt at the time. I shared with the class my willingness to meet with any child who was expressing interest in baptism.

Roe then discussed four general topics of conversation parents need to have with children—sin, obedience, repentance, and counting the cost. We made this addition to the curriculum when we learned some parents have trouble conducting any kind of spiritual conversation with their children. The problem was not just a failure to lead their children to baptism, but difficulty in talking about spiritual matters in the ordinary course of life events. Those parents lacked either the ability or the inclination to put into practice the admonitions of Moses in Deuteronomy 6.

On the eleventh week of class, we invited Jennifer Pagel, one of our two youth ministers, to talk about her experiences with our teenagers over the last decade of ministry. Specifically, she addressed baptism and rebaptism. She noted that the ministers and coaches exert little pressure on youth to be immersed because most of the children are baptized by the time they enter the youth group. The teens themselves exert most of the pressure, such as assembling prayer groups at camp to intercede for an unimmersed tenth grader and going so far as to tell the teen that the group is praying for them. Pagel also discussed the issue of rebaptism. According to Pagel, most children do not question the legitimacy of their first baptism. Yet when they have sinned in a particularly public fashion, they feel a need to make some kind of public statement. For many of these teenagers rebaptism provides the only viable option. The Pagels work with these teenagers individually and generally counsel them to trust in their initial baptism. They also provide different faith-proclaiming opportunities throughout the year so that a public face can be given to sin, repentance, and recommitment.

Conclusion

This project taught me three important lessons. First, the levels of spiritual maturity and parental skills vary widely among parents. Most parents may be motivated, but some parents are motivated far more than others. For example, the difference between the core group who attended 75 percent of the classes and those who were present occasionally involves more than travel schedules and the number of sick children on Sunday. The commitment levels of individual families vary significantly. Some parents lead their children spiritually from the cradle while others are not as comfortable in directing their children at any age. (Roe assures me, based on her interaction with children, that the level of parental involvement in spiritual matters at home is not directly correlated to church attendance.) The less proactive parents are not necessarily bad parents, just less spiritually mature. Not all parents are created equal.

Second, the importance of peer teaching cannot be underestimated. We should have taken advantage of the opportunity and allowed more time for small-group discussion and interaction. The list the parents came up with on week seven proved they had something valuable to contribute. The participants needed to hear from each other, not just from the designated experts. Possibly some students felt overwhelmed or guilty because of all they had done or not done. More input from other parents might have encouraged them. In addition to traditional question-and-answer sessions, I recommend more small-group discussion in future classes.

Third, I became convinced the key in talking to children about baptism lies in the verb, not the noun. The importance of parents' talking to their children outweighs the subject matter. While the class members need teaching on baptism, they need even more the encouragement to start talking to their children. Those who develop the habit of addressing spiritual matters with their children from infancy will, I am convinced, figure it out somehow when the time comes to talk about baptism. I assumed when I started the class that parents need a few more theological tools to give them the confidence to lead their children to the water. I now think many parents do not need more tools but the tool belt itself—the ability or desire to talk about spiritual matters. For this reason, when we gained additional weeks of instruction time, we added to the curriculum sessions on having spiritual conversations with children.

The proposed material cannot be adequately covered in eleven weeks. We dealt insufficiently with the biblical evidence and needed more time for small-group discussion. An additional two weeks of class time would facilitate the repetition of some material, made necessary by sporadic attendance. A weekend retreat presents another option. A three-day period would provide time to cover much information in a more intensive way. This retreat could be a stand-alone event but would be even more helpful if held toward the end of the class, thus providing opportunity for more instruction, prayer, discussion, and debriefing. The last two times we have taught the class (2009 and 2012) we first used a Friday night/Saturday morning format and then six weeks on Wednesday night. Neither of these formats is adequate but is all that we can do. I now preach three times on Sunday morning and am unavailable to teach a class.

In addition, I recommend a separate class on the meaning and significance of baptism. In this project, we devoted only two sessions to what the Bible says about baptism, and the material came almost entirely from the book of Acts. We passed over many key issues due to time constraints. A ten- to thirteen-week supplementary class on baptism would afford time to deal with more of the biblical material concerning baptism and conversion and to deal with the questions my class raised about other religious groups. Developing a well-rounded and healthy view of baptism requires more than two or three teaching sessions. The format we used required an assumption that the students brought to the discussion a more than adequate grasp of the meaning of baptism, that they only needed assistance in adapting the accounts of crisis conversions in Scripture to their own children. I consider this assumption questionable.

For this class to be successful, the teachers must be older. I frequently referred to experiences with my own children, as did Roe. Some comments made references to positive experiences; other expressed "I would have done this differently." In addition to the wisdom that can only come through experience, the teacher should possess, in the words of Edwin Friedman, a "non-anxious presence." Although an important trait for all congregational leaders, such calmness would be especially helpful in teaching this class. Parenting produces anxiety. Parents worry whether their efforts are adequate to the many challenges. An anxious presenter could sabotage the class through promoting guilt and shame. Certainly parents could do a better job in training their children. The very premise of the class implies this. But the approach in the class should radiate encouragement and support; anxious people find such gifts difficult to offer. Parents need to hear "You can do this."

Through the centuries many have accepted God's gift and come to the waters of baptism through dramatic conversion experiences. Yet this is not the only way people come to the Lord. Children who grow up in the bosom of the church are led to the Father in a more gradual way. While they may not undergo a dramatic encounter—and even because they may never undergo such an experience—baptism signifies a crucial step for them. This step should not be taken lightly. Parents possess the marvelous opportunity to train their children, teaching them the meaning of the water and the power of the God who waits for us there.

---

1. Chris Smith, "Equipping Parents at the Harpeth Hills Church of Christ to Prepare Their Children for Baptism" (DMin thesis, ACU, 2008).

2. Baptism of children under the age of ten at HH has decreased over the last ten years.

3. John Warren Withers, "Social Forces Affecting the Age at Which Children Are Baptized in Southern Baptist Churches" (PhD diss., Southern Baptist Theological Seminary, 1997), 192.

4. Jeff Childers, "Moving to the Rhythms of Christian Life: Baptism for Children Raised in the Church," in *Like A Shepherd Lead Us*, ed. David Fleer and Charles Siburt (Abilene, TX: Leafwood, 2006), 105.

5. In a 1990s survey of children in Churches of Christ, the top two greatest influencers on baptism were mother (76 percent) and father (68 percent). Youth minister (65 percent) was third, followed by close friends (58 percent). David Lewis, Carley Dodd, and Darryl Tippens, *The Gospel According to Generation X* (Abilene, TX: ACU Press, 1995), 143.

6. G. R. Beasley-Murray, *Baptism in the New Testament* (Macon, GA: Paternoster, 1972), 372.

7. Thomas Halbrooks, "Children and the Church: A Baptist Historical Perspective," *Review and Expositor* 80:2 (1983): 179–88.

8. Ibid., 185.

9. Jeff W. Childers and Frederick D. Aquino, *Unveiling Glory: Visions of Christ's Transforming Presence* (Abilene, TX: ACU Press, 2003), 69.

10. Jon A. Weatherly, "The Role of Baptism in Conversion," in Evangelicalism and the Stone-Campbell Movement, ed. William R. Baker (Downers Grove, IL: IVP, 2002), 161.

11. Ben Witherington, *Troubled Waters* (Waco, TX: Baylor University Press, 2007), 73.

12. Ibid., 133.

13. Glen H. Stassen, "Preparing Candidates for Baptism," *Review and Expositor* 80 (1983): 251.

14. Hippolytus is often referred to in discussions of infant baptism because of this one statement: "And they shall baptize the little children first. And if they can answer for themselves, let them answer. But if they cannot, let their parents answer or someone from their family." Hippolytus, *The Treatise on the Apostolic Tradition of St. Hippolytus of Rome*, ed. Gregory Dix (London: SPCK, 1968), 28–37.

15. Hippolytus considered church discipline paramount, as seen in several charges such as this one to the church: "If a catechumen or a baptized Christian wishes to become a soldier, let him be cast out. For he has despised God." Hippolytus, 26–27.

16. Claudia A. Dickson, *Entering the Household of God* (New York: Church Publishing, 2002), 90.

17. Childers, "Moving to the Rhythms," 98.

18. Marlin Jeschke, *Believers Baptism for Children of the Church*, rev. ed. (Eugene, OR: Wipf and Stock, 2000), 113.

19. Lewis, Dodd, and Tippens, *Gospel According to Generation X*, 143.

CHAPTER 7

Faith Decisions

TOMMY KING[1]

Churches of Christ have traditionally taught and practiced adult baptism by immersion. One of the identifying marks of the tradition is that the path of conversion, at some point, goes through the water. This model works well in the case of an adult who has recently come to faith and repentance. However, the baptismal records of the typical Church of Christ will reveal that most of its baptisms are not administered to adults from outside the faith, rather more often to the children of the church. We instinctively realize that the baptism of our children differs from the baptism of an adult convert—especially one who has led a life ignoring the will of God, but how to define that difference remains problematic. We know that our children began the process of discipleship the day they were born. The journey has continued through the practice of faith in the family and the interaction with the church. Yet, we also believe that their baptism remains a vital milestone in their spiritual formation and their relationship with both God and the church. Where does it fit? What does it mean? How can we insure that baptism addresses the reality of their experience of God, Jesus, the Holy Spirit, and the church rather than attempting to impose an alternative reality?

The challenges encountered in bringing children of believers into the full fellowship of Churches of Christ in a meaningful way are complicated by a poorly developed theology of children and the focus on only one or two of the biblical images to describe the meaning of baptism. The theology of children among Churches of Christ is delimited to an avowal of the innocence of infants and the rejection of infant baptism as an effective rite. The church instructs its children to postpone baptism until an age of accountability, the determination of which is left primarily to the discretion of the parents and children with occasional consultation with church leaders. Thus, the focus on baptizing our children falls on when rather than how. While giving no direct answer to the question, Scripture does provide many images illuminating the meaning of baptism. However, the preaching and teaching of churches has tended to emphasize only two of these images—baptism as death, burial, and resurrection (or regeneration), and baptism as the washing away of sin. While these pictures are biblical and meaningful, we might ask whether they best address the reality of our children as they enter the water.

This lack of a theology for the baptism of believers' children is rooted in one of the strengths of the Restoration Movement—the desire to return to primitive Christianity as described in Scripture. While the writing of the New Testament spans more than one generation of the emerging church, its attention to baptism and conversion remains primarily on first generation disciples. This is particularly true in the book of Acts, which serves as the most available resource on baptism. In Acts, the examples of conversion and the teachings accompanying baptism are found exclusively in the context of adults who are coming into the church from Judaism and paganism.[2] At best, there are only meager indications of how a child of Christian parents was assimilated into the fellowship. Thus, a theology of initiation based solely on New Testament pattern is only applicable to bringing adults from outside into the fellowship of the body. Such a pattern presents definite problems for believers' children who are not abandoning a pagan lifestyle, religion, or god.

This problem was also not an immediate concern of the leaders of the Restoration Movement in the early nineteenth century. Their mission had much in common with the mission of the early church, as they set out to restore the form and practices of primitive Christianity. They preached their message of believers' baptism by immersion to people on the American frontier who had either never been baptized or were sprinkled as infants, a rite rejected as valid baptism by the new movement. The pattern seemed relevant under such circumstances, and the leaders of the movement gave little consideration to its application to second-generation restorationists.[3] This resulted in a doctrine of baptism cast in the mold of radical conversion with a strong emphasis on repentance and regeneration. This model did not distinguish between those entering from outside the church and those who were children of the church. Such imagery is certainly biblical and the emphasis on forgiveness of sins, repentance, and regeneration is meaningful today for someone leaving behind a life of sin and death. However, a child of the church should find it difficult to experience a radical conversion of New Testament proportions. Initiation implies change, and the change must be from one reality to another. Indeed, the church must confess failure in its nurture of children when all children entrusted to its care must experience such a conversion to enter its fellowship. It is ironic that a tradition that so values baptism finds itself without a meaningful statement on baptism for those who comprise its most promising hope for the future.

In order for the church to present the rite of baptism in a manner that addresses reality in the life of a child of the church, the church must work to develop a clear and biblical theology of children. This theology must address the status of children within the church and define the change in that status that is initiated and represented by baptism. Also, the church is called to develop a method of effectively preparing its children for initiation into its full fellowship.

A Theology of Children

Before discussing how to prepare children for baptism, one must wrestle with the question, what place in its fellowship does a church grant unbaptized children? If a church judges infants to be innocents and denies them the rite of passage until a time deemed proper, where do such unbaptized children fit into the life of the church body? The answer, whether spoken or tacit, produces widespread effects. A precise and biblically informed answer to this question provides the opportunity for the church to celebrate its wholeness and to rejoice in the process of baptizing its children. An imprecise definition of the relationship between the church and its children results in a confusing process of initiation and inner turmoil during a time that should be filled with peace and joy. The church that has developed the language to name the relationship it shares with its children is the church that is able to develop a thoughtful and theologically sound approach to baptizing its children.

Historic Christianity has proposed two descriptions of the status of children: (1) all children are born bearing the guilt of sin and sharing in the separation between fallen humanity and God; and (2) all children are born innocent of sin and live in relationship with God until they are capable of choosing evil over good—a choice that all humans eventually make. Augustine is credited with bringing the first position to prominence, and its resulting doctrine of original or inherited sin has dominated Christian thinking since the fourth century. Some churches adhere to this teaching by baptizing their infants soon after birth. Proponents of the doctrine of innocence and free will cite Tertullian as evidence that the apostolic church reserved baptism for those who could make a conscious statement of faith and confession of sin. These churches defer baptism until the individual is capable of making that decision, when he or she has attained an age of accountability. The problem of describing the status of children in the church would seem to rest with those who refuse baptism to their children. However, even those who practice infant baptism (e.g., Anglican, Lutheran, Reformed) do not afford their baptized children full membership in the church. Full membership and admission to the Eucharist await confirmation, a practice developed as an attempt to address this issue. Thus, all traditions face the common problem of describing the status of children, baptized or unbaptized, in the church.

Of the two positions described, Churches of Christ affirm the second. Since the early days of the Restoration Movement, Churches of Christ have been united in their belief that children are born into a state of innocence. The churches have also been united in their relative silence concerning what position their children occupy within the church. Children are not considered church members, but most adult Christians share the general feeling that they are a part of the church family. D. M. Baille insists that such an ambiguous status is not acceptable: "Christians have to face the alternative whether their children are in the church or are outsiders, whether they are children of God or children of wrath, whether they are Christian children or 'little pagans.'"[4] While Baille's insistence that the church bring precision to the description of its children is well founded, the alternatives he proposes are not valid. The belief that children are born in innocence implies that no children in this world are children of wrath. There is no such thing as a "little pagan." All children, whether children of Christians or non-believers, are children of God and are, therefore, children of the kingdom.

This line of reasoning uses Matthew 19:14 as support, "Let the little children come to me, and do not stop them; for it is to such as these that the kingdom of heaven belongs" (NRSV). James Thompson observes, "Jesus' words, 'For to such belongs the kingdom,' refer not to childlike disciples, but to children. Whereas children were not officially counted in the synagogue until the *bar mitzvah*, Jesus gives them a place in his kingdom. In the same way the kingdom of heaven belongs to the poor and the helpless (Luke 6:20), it belongs to the children."[5]

To describe all children as citizens of the kingdom of heaven has biblical precedent but is rarely mentioned in Churches of Christ. The reluctance to assign kingdom status to children could lie in a tendency to identify the kingdom with the church. If the church is synonymous with the kingdom, then all members of the kingdom would be members of the church as well. Such a view limits the boundaries of the kingdom of God. Rather than the simple statement that the church is the kingdom, a more accurate description is that the church exists within the kingdom of God. Certainly the kingdom is larger than the earthly church. The boundaries of the kingdom encompass the heavenly beings known as angels, cherubim, and seraphim as well as the great cloud of witnesses who have gone before (Heb. 12). The boundaries of the kingdom also encompass the church, which is composed of those who are justified, cleansed from sins, participators in Christ and the Spirit. The boundaries of the kingdom encompass children.

Therefore, Christians and children have much in common to celebrate as well as some differences to note. Recognizing each other as kingdom residents is a celebration of beauty and freedom, and the purity of children enables them to model many behaviors of the kingdom that adult Christians tend to discard with age. However, the fallen but forgiven nature of adults provides them with the wisdom to know that the children will someday find righteousness no longer in their own innocence but only through the blood of Christ. A part of the calling of Christians is to prepare their children for that time.

This last realization returns us to our problem. If children are fellow members of God's kingdom yet destined to retain that status only through the redeeming work of Christ in the church, how is that transition made? How do children move from innocence to redemption? Must they first leave the kingdom and endure a period of "lostness" in order to reenter the kingdom as members of the body of Christ? The model of crisis conversion would suggest an affirmative answer. Such a model of conversion requires that the church determine a time when it no longer tells its children that their relationship with God is strong and secure and warns them that they are in danger of the fires of hell. Children who have felt a part of the community must now feel that they stand outside that community. The determination of this time in a young person's life (commonly referred to as the age of accountability) has been the subject of numerous studies. The age of accountability is crucial if the church bears the responsibility of creating an awareness of crisis at that age so its children may address the crisis in conversion.

In one form or another, the practice of initiation for children in Churches of Christ has followed this process: (1) an age of innocence; (2) upon reaching the age of accountability, an awareness of crisis; (3) the resolution of that crisis in baptism and full church membership. The first stage of this process has been discussed above and has not proven to be problematic other than in the church's failure to celebrate fully the kingdom status of its children. The second and third stages do produce problems. For some young people, a real point of crisis does indeed arise in their lives. No one can deny that some children of the church rebel against family and church and reject both faith and the lifestyle inspired by faith. For these young people, hope lies in recognizing their crisis and seeking to return to the people of God through repentance and baptism. But the mission of the Christian family and the church is to nurture faith in its children. What happens when the family and church succeed in their task? What happens when a child of the church never feels a loss of continuity with the people of God? Is the only alternative to convince them of their peril so that the model of crisis conversion will function properly, or do other models of initiation better align with the reality of their lives?

In his book *Believers Baptism for Children of the Church*, Marlin Jeschke suggests that there is a second model of conversion that is much more appropriate for the church's children.[6] This is the pattern of nurture in Christian principles from childhood, nurture in the "discipline and instruction of the Lord" (Eph. 6:4 NRSV). Jeschke compares the situation of children of the church to that of the children of the nation of Israel.[7] At one point, God found it necessary to deliver Israel from the bondage of Egypt. Freeing them from slavery, God created a covenant community and brought them safely to the Promised Land. The descendants of those who experienced this dramatic deliverance were expected to grow up in the understanding of all that God had done in blessing the people. In Deuteronomy, God admonishes Israel, "Keep these words that I am commanding you today in your heart. Recite them to your children and talk about them when you are at home and when you are away, when you lie down and when you rise" (Deut. 6:6–7 NRSV). Israel was commissioned to teach its children that their lives depended on the mercy of God. However, the children "did not need to return to bitter Egyptian bondage in each generation in order to make their own difficult crossing through the Red Sea and the Jordan. Later generations had the privilege of growing up under the blessings of covenant life in the land."[8] The purpose of God's deliverance was that the people could live and grow in a redeemed community—the kind of society God had intended in creation. Such a concept does not suggest that later generations had no responsibility to the covenant. They understood that there would come a time in the life of each Israelite when he or she would personally appropriate the meaning of the covenant and assume responsibilities within the community.

In one sense, the children of the Jewish community were born into the covenant; in another sense, the community initiated them into the covenant through the circumcision of the male children at the age of eight days.[9] No biblical evidence points to any other ceremony involved in bringing a young person into the full fellowship of the community. Personal acceptance of covenant responsibilities appears to have been a process of maturation and participation within the community. Roy Honeycutt recognizes three elements contributing to this process. Each generation renewed its commitment to the covenant (1) by participating in group ceremonies that told the stories of the creation, the exodus, and the giving of the law, (2) by displaying character consistent with the demands of a covenantal relationship with God, and (3) by sharing in the worship of the family.[10] Through these interactions, the child matured into an adult role in the community. No single rite signified the completion of this process. Instead, rejection of the covenant required action, and this procedure was considered a great dishonor to the community and to the family.

Later Judaism did develop a rite to mark the transition from a child of the covenant to an adult of the covenant. The ceremony of *bar mitzvah* (and, even later, a parallel ceremony for girls) granted this status in the community. Becoming a "son of the covenant" (*bar mitzvah*) was reserved for the age of puberty and followed gradual, intentional preparation that began as early as five years of age.[11] This was a communal process—the community opening itself, giving of itself, and establishing accountability as its young members matured to take their places beside their elders. Personal faith was not inherited, but the blessing of being reared within the covenant community was—and the end result of that blessing was faith.

The old covenant is not the new covenant. Differences do exist, some of which have been emphasized to the point of obscuring the similarities. The latter prophets Jeremiah and Ezekiel both spoke of a coming age when God would deal with humanity on a more individualistic basis. Jeremiah told his people that one day "every one shall die for his own sin" (Jer. 31:30 RSV). This stand in contrast with such communal punishment as is evident in the story of Achan (Josh. 7). God's new covenant would bear similarities to the old, but "its individualistic nature is such as to underscore that God will deal with a man on the basis of his own relationship with God and the covenant written 'upon their hearts'" (Jer. 31:33 RSV).[12] The preaching of the apostles bears out this appeal to individuals: "Everyone that believes is freed" (Acts 13:39 RSV). Yet, the new covenant also created a community. Under the new covenant, people of all races and nations are called as individuals to community (cf. Eph. 2:11–22). This community becomes a force in shaping the lives of those within it. This shaping is particularly true for those children privileged to be born physically into its realm.

If the model of the covenant community of Israel has any bearing on the new covenant community, then we must make an emendation to the discussion of children within the kingdom. As stated above, all children are citizens of the kingdom, but not all children are privileged to be associated with the redeemed community of the church. This is comparable to the situation under the old covenant where the children within the nation of Israel had special status—even before they came of age and assumed full responsibility in their covenant relationship. Though God was concerned with the welfare of all the children of the world the children of God's people enjoyed a special blessing. Paul acknowledged this privilege in Romans 3:1–2. Does this imply that the status of children of the church can be distinguished from innocents outside the church? Paul indicates so in his discussion of the Corinthian families in which one spouse was not a believer. In imagery that parallels the situation of the Old Covenant, Paul comments, "For the unbelieving husband is made holy through his wife, and the unbelieving wife is made holy through her husband. Otherwise, your children would be unclean, but as it is, they are holy" (1 Cor. 7:14 NRSV). Some scholars have argued that Paul's language indicates that the children of Christians are already full members of the community of faith, but others are quick to point out that there is a difference between holiness and sanctification. While holiness does indicate special status, it does not preclude the necessity of baptism.[13] Children are holy in the same way as the unbelieving spouse is holy. Both live in the sphere of the covenant community, but both remain candidates for baptism to receive the full blessing of the covenant. As Jeschke notes, the option of not baptizing children of the church has never been seriously entertained citing that the common denominator in the meaning of the baptism of an adult convert and of someone nurtured in the church is that baptism calls for the appropriation of faith.[14] Thus, the church is called to initiate through baptism children who initially carry the status of being in the kingdom and who have the distinction of being holy—yet who must affirm their own commitment to the covenant God has made with the community through the gift of his Son.

By casting children of the church as holy and children outside the church as unclean, Paul indicates that children of the church have the distinction of already being dedicated to God in some manner. Unfortunately, the language of the New Testament does not go further in describing the status of children of the church. In the search for a term to facilitate the church's understanding of its relationship with its children, a careful examination of the writings of the early church in the years following the close of the canonical writings is helpful. Such a term must acknowledge that the covenant community is nurturing the children in the faith and that they are not unbelievers but young believers,[15] and that they carry with them the status of being holy. The early church did have a term that described its children's relationship with the community. Within the church was a group who lived in the sphere of the community but just outside its full fellowship. They were the catechumens.[16] In describing the catechumens in the time of Cyril of Jerusalem, Edwin Gifford states, "Such persons were either converts from Paganism and Judaism, or children of Christian parents whose Baptism had been deferred."[17] The catechumens were a recognized group of learners within the church. They were admitted to all services of the church except the Eucharist and were the subjects of intense training leading to baptism. According to *Apostolic Tradition*, when someone was accepted into the class of learners, or catechumens, that person was considered a convert and regarded no longer as a pagan. He or she was an incipient Christian.[18] To recognize the children of the church as catechumens, learners, incipient Christians, or Christians in process would deliver both parent and child from the duplicity of crisis conversion. As catechumens, the children would be recognized as the believers they are. Faith can be affirmed, celebrated, and nurtured. The wholeness of the people of God can be realized. The day when the child's faith is appropriated and owned in baptism and is eagerly anticipated as a day of fulfillment rather than crisis, is a day recognizing the saving process of conversion that is the life of community.

Initiation of Catechumens: A Model for Community

The church that grants the status of catechumen to its children presents the rite of baptism to them not in the context of crisis but in the context of fulfillment and maturity. The conversation between church and catechumen includes discussions about growing up in faith and becoming an adult in the church. When children are young, the church speaks simply, but as children grow older, the church invites them into more adult conversation. They hear of the problem of sin in the lives of the faithful. They discover that even those who intensely love God fail him and that their lives are incomplete without the abiding presence of God's mercy. They are told that the gift of wholeness of life (salvation) is claimed in baptism.[19] Children learn about the covenant and hear the words of Jesus, "This is my blood of the covenant which is poured out for many" (Mark 14:24 NRSV). They know that covenant members must contact the blood that initiated the covenant. Children of the church hear adults talk about the working of the Holy Spirit in the lives of Christians, and they are told that the Holy Spirit is the gift of God in baptism. Children hear of the blessing of the Eucharist and how the presence of Christ is made visible in the partaking of the Supper. They know that only those who have been baptized are called to the table. In other words, catechumens enjoy the life of the community as children, but they are made aware of the greater blessings of life as adults in the church. Their desire for such blessings is the result of the information (or conversion). Just as an adolescent anticipates the privileges and responsibilities of an adult in the social and political culture, a child of the church learns the privileges and responsibilities of maturity in the covenant community. An adult Christian is what the child is in the process of becoming.

In this context, the decision to enter the full fellowship of the church through the act of baptism is not a decision that awaits an emotional crisis but is an event eagerly anticipated years in advance. Since the decision is a result of an ongoing conversation between church and catechumen within the realm of community, the process of deciding can be trusted to the church as well as the individual. To ask some within the community, do you think I am ready for baptism? becomes a valid inquiry for a catechumen whose faith is acknowledged and who has been nurtured in the atmosphere of belonging. For the church to have the conviction to answer no as well as yes to that question would show that the church has accepted its role of nurturing young disciples into mature disciples and embraces the act of baptism as the communal event it is.

If a church decides to address its children as catechumen, then the church must shape its catechesis to lead young believers to adult faith and action. More suggestions on catechesis will be offered below, but two issues immediately come to mind. First of all, though baptism will have been discussed and witnessed throughout the life of the catechumen, at what point in the catechumen's development will the church begin calling for baptism? Secondly, what meanings of baptism will the church make available to its catechumen?

As mentioned above, the discussion of the timing of baptism for those traditions that practice believers' baptism has revolved around the issue of accountability. If we view maturity as a process, it follows that we will also view accountability as a process. Parents instinctively understand this. They certainly hold a two-year-old child more accountable for behavior than they do a two-week-old. Their ten-year-olds are held to an even higher level of accountability. To paraphrase Jesus' words in Matthew 7:11, if we as parents know how to do this, how much more does our Father in heaven. We do not envision our children going to sleep one night as innocents and awaking the next morning fully accountable before God. Thus, the question about age of baptism can be better stated, "At what point in the process of maturing as disciples does baptism become meaningful?"

American culture recognizes several markers in the process of maturity, such as the beginning of formal schooling, transitioning from elementary school to secondary school, the onset of puberty, receiving a driver's license, graduating from high school, registering to vote, reaching the legal drinking age, and graduating from college or vocational training. Which of these correlates best with becoming fully accountable before God? It can also be noted that over the past century, American culture has prolonged the period of adolescence. In generations past, a person was considered an adult at the age of eighteen. Not many American parents today would agree. Laws have been passed raising the legal drinking age and the age of marriage and sexual consent. Though the age of full maturity remains vague and varies with individuals, it is obvious that for most the process continues into one's early to mid-twenties. If this is the judgment of parents and our legal establishment, can we imagine that perhaps God reserves the full weight of accountability that long as well? If so, at what point does the act of baptism make the most sense?

The Christian communities of different times and cultures must answer this question to the best of their ability. The most accessible guide in this decision is the one other covenant community created by God—Israel. As noted above, Israel did initiate their infant boys into the covenant community through circumcision, but they reserved the full right of adult members until the age of puberty. They must have found it difficult to believe that a child was in the process of becoming adult until this physical process began. Given our current culture that is extending the age of maturity, this marker would appear to be the earliest time a church could begin to call on its young disciples to profess their maturing faith in baptism. Actually, an argument could be presented that such an age might be too young rather than too late.

Another factor in baptizing children of the church as catechumen is deciding how we will explain the act of baptism itself. We have proceeded under the assumption that believers' baptism is the crucial step of initiation into the full fellowship of the church. We have also observed that the image of crisis conversion with baptism interpreted in terms of death, burial, and resurrection does not fully represent the situation of a child of the church. Dramatic conversion implies dramatic change, yet for a child nurtured in the faith, disciplined in its behaviors, and acculturated by its story, the change experienced following baptism falls short of the drama portrayed in our standard teaching. If we present only one or two of the biblical images of baptism to them, then we are preparing them for a clash between expectation and experience; and, in effect, we are devaluing their baptism. While the act of baptism is normally an emotional experience, such emotions begin to fade when the realization sets in that little has changed. At least, little has changed in the way we may have led the believer to think. Perhaps what the believer needs is a different way of looking at baptism and thus different expectations.

A quick survey of Scriptures discussing baptism reveals that there are many images that shed light on what is happening in the act. Below is a partial list:

1. Union with Christ in death, burial, resurrection – Rom. 6:3–4

2. A washing away of sin – Acts 22:16

3. A washing of regeneration – Titus 3:5

4. A new birth – John 3:5

5. An adoption process – Gal. 3:26–27

6. An act of consecration to God – 1 Cor. 6:11

7. A covenantal act (as circumcision in OT) – Col. 2:11–15

8. Incorporation into Christ's body on earth, the church – 1 Cor. 12:13

9. A change of clothes – Gal. 3:27; Col 3:1-17

10. A rescue experience, as in the flood – 1 Pet. 3:21

11. Receiving the Holy Spirit – Acts 2:38; 1 Cor. 6:11; 12:13

The meaning of baptism rests neither on any one image nor in the total of all of them. Baptism, like salvation in general, is essentially something God does. These scriptural pictures shed light on what God is doing in baptism. One picture may more appropriately address the situation of one believer while another picture better fits the reality of another believer. We make a mistake if we hold only one or two images as the most important. If maturing in faith is a process, then the act of baptism must address the situation of the believer at the time of the baptism. As the baptized believer continues on his or her faith journey and faces the experiences of life, one or more of the other images of baptism may become more meaningful. Certainly a seventy-year-old man can better appreciate baptism as renewal than can a twelve-year-old girl. This is one reason that Paul continually urged the recipients of his letters to remember their baptism and appropriate it for their current situations. As we grow in our faith we continue to grow in our baptism. As the church, we must provide room for that growth.

Suggestions for Catechesis

Churches today must make an effort to catechize young disciples in a manner that is relevant to their lives. However, insight can be gained in looking at how the church in generations past approached this task. Several passages in the New Testament have been identified as catechetical material. In his article "Catechesis, Catechumenate" in the *Encyclopedia of Early Christianity*, Everett Ferguson points to 1 Thessalonians 4:1–5:11, Colossians 3:5–15, and the epistle of 1 Peter as reflecting blocks of catechetical material.[20] In addition to these Scriptures, two of the earliest Christian writings outside the New Testament canon, *The Didache* and Irenaeus's *Proof of the Apostolic Preaching,* have been identified as catechesis. Beyond these, we have several third- and fourth-century documents that reveal a more organized program of catechesis for the church. The apostles and church fathers summoned the learners to encounter the story of salvation, the ethical demands of the story, and the liturgy of the church as it interacted with the story. If the church of today is to enter the task of catechesis seriously, it must make every effort to see that its catechesis adequately addresses these three areas.

Story

The story of salvation begins with the creation in all its goodness. Of particular interest is the fact that humanity was created in the image of God. The story includes the fall of humanity with its consequences and the beginning of God's plan for redemption in the choosing of Abraham. The deliverance of the people of Israel reveals the merciful and saving nature of God and sets the stage for the crowning act in the story—the revelation of Jesus Christ. In relating the mission of Jesus, the story speaks of what was done in his life, death, and resurrection; but it also continues by telling what Jesus is doing today and what the end of the story will be. Throughout the process of narrating the story, one concern is always evident. This is not a story about others; it is the story of the teacher and the listeners. The appropriation of this story in a real and personal sense is the initial step of living with the kingdom of God.

Ethics

Moral behavior and ethical principles grow out of the story. For those who identify with the story, questions of right and wrong do not find resolution in human logic or in societal trends. Ethics is not a study of rules or even the endeavor to be good. For Christians, ethics is the call to become part of a story that grants significance and calls to specific behaviors. The standard behavior for people of the story is the revelation of God's own nature and the working out of that nature in the lives of God's chosen people. God's concerns are their concerns. God's holiness is their goal. And it is a way of life made possible through the redemptive act of God in Jesus and the presence of God in the Spirit.

Liturgy

People of the story view their liturgy sacramentally. The act of worship is the point at which the invisible realities of God become most visible. The sacraments of baptism and the Lord's Supper make visible the saving death and life of Christ. It is worship that allows people of the story to maintain a grasp on reality so that they might continue to serve and love their God and their fellow humans. When Christians are struggling, they are called to reexamine their acts of worship because in those acts of worship reality is enacted and appropriated. It is suggested that while the story and ethics inform the believer, it is the liturgy that is most actively forming the believer. Any serious attempt at catechesis should involve the communication of these three elements: story, ethics, and liturgy, and seek to demonstrate how the three are interdependent.

An Example of Catechesis: Faith Decisions

The Glenwood Church of Christ in Tyler, Texas, put the principles discussed in this chapter into practice in the mid 1990s. While each faith community should shape catechesis within its own context, the following brief description of Glenwood's Faith Decisions program can demonstrate the form such an approach can take. The church decided that Faith Decisions would be offered as a thirteen-week study for young people completing their eighth-grade year in school (thirteen to fourteen years of age) and their parents. The decision to include parents (or mentors for those children whose parents were not available for the study) was an attempt to integrate the faith formation of the home and the church. A curriculum was developed based on the preceding discussion of the role of story, ethics, and liturgy in faith formation. Each lesson attempted to involve parents and children interacting to explore segments of the story, the ethics that flowed from such a story, and how the worship of the church reflected elements of the story. With these preparations made, the course was designed as follows.

Parents' Orientation

We discovered that students received the inclusion of parents in this vital discussion more enthusiastically than the parents. Many parents were apprehensive about their ability to share their faith with their children in such a setting. The purpose of the orientation was to equip the parents for the weeks ahead and to assure them that their own faith journey was relevant to their children. In the orientation, parents were instructed to prepare for their child a letter in which they shared the most important elements of their faith that they desired to pass on to the children. Each letter was to also include a blessing of the child.

Opening Banquet

The banquet was prepared as a way to emphasize that the church considers Faith Decisions an important moment in the lives of the children. At the dinner, an elder blessed the families, and the instructors of Faith Decisions made a statement of commitment to the families. One by one, each family stood and the parents read aloud their letters of faith to their children. The letters were then presented to the children with the request that they keep them; the children were told that the importance of what is expressed in the letters will become even more significant in the years to come.

Presentation to the Church

The students and their parents were presented to the church on the first Sunday morning of the Faith Decisions program. The church was instructed to pray for the families and to encourage them personally during the following weeks. An elder delivered a charge to the families and to the church.

Teaching the Curriculum

Families were exhorted to attend as many sessions of the Faith Decisions program as possible. In a culture where travel is frequent, this was a meaningful commitment for families to participate fully in this significant formational time of their children's lives.

Concluding Blessing

At the end of the thirteen-week Faith Decisions program, the families were once again presented to the church. The elders commended them for their dedication and love for the Lord and the church. The elders also indicated that they and the church now prayerfully encouraged each of the young people to consider taking the next step of their faith in baptism.

These were the basic elements of the Faith Decisions program as it began to be practiced by the Glenwood church. Over time, elements have been adapted and changed. Other congregations have developed their own approaches. What is of importance is that intentional efforts are being made to prepare our children for baptism.

Conclusion

The process of a church bringing richness, meaning, and reality to the baptism of its children begins with the church thinking through its theology of children and adopting a language that accurately describes its children's role and place in the community. The church must also be able to describe how the baptism of its children embraces the will of God for this act in their lives. The church that spends the time and energy to address these issues should be able to develop within its context a method of leading its young believers through the waters of baptism and onto the path of spiritual maturity.

———————————

1. Tommy King, "Faith Decisions: Christian Initiation for Children of the Glenwood Church of Christ" (DMin thesis, ACU, 1994).

2. An exception might be the references to households being baptized (Acts 16:33), but there is not clear indication that the household included the children. Some suggest children were viewed in the ancient world as non-entities until they approached adulthood; and, thus, an "entire household" would refer only to the adult members of the family, including slaves.

3. Both Thomas Campbell and J. W. McGarvey gave some attention to the faith of children. Thomas Campbell, "Family Education: The Nursery," *Millennial Harbinger*, n.s., 4 (1840): 340–345. J.W. McGarvey, "Religious Duties of Children," *Millennial Harbinger*, n.s., 7 (1843): 536–539.

4. D. M. Baille, *The Theology of the Sacraments*, quoted in G. R. Beasley-Murray, *Baptism in the New Testament* (Grand Rapids: Eerdmans, 1962), 371.

5. James Thompson, "The Education of Children in the Early Church," *Institute for Christian Studies: Faculty Bulletin* 4 (November 1983): 17.

6. Marlin Jeschke, *Believers Baptism for Children of the Church* (Scottsdale, PA: Herald, 1983).

7. Ibid., 67.

8. Ibid.

9. Under the old covenant only the male children were ritually identified with the covenant, through the male rite of circumcision. Females were members of the community through their relationship with a male, either as daughter or wife.

10. Roy L. Honeycutt, Jr., "The Child within the Old Testament Community," in *Children and Conversion*, ed. Clifford Ingle (Nashville: Broadman, 1966), 25.

11. Thompson, "Education of Children," 17.

12. Honeycutt, "Child within the Old Testament," 29.

13. Reginald E. O. White, *The Biblical Doctrine of Initiation* (Grand Rapids: Eerdmans, 1960), 362.

14. Jeschke, *Believers Baptism for Children*, 71.

15. The concept of children as believers is also a concern in the interpretation of Titus 1:6. While the exact meaning of the phrase "believing children" is open to interpretation, it presents the possibility of acknowledging the faith of young children.

16. Paul and Luke each use the word *katecheo* (to inform, instruct) four times. Primary among Luke's usage is Luke 1:4 ("that you may know the truth concerning the things about which you have been *instructed*" NRSV). Paul employs the word exclusively in the sense of instructing someone regarding the content of the faith (1 Cor. 14:19; Gal. 6:6; Rom. 2:18). Some scholars have suggested that Paul introduced the term to designate the teaching of the faith. By the time of the writing of 2 Clement in the middle of the second century, the word had already become the normal term for instruction given to those preparing for baptism. If early English translators had chosen to transliterate the Greek verb *katecheo* rather than translate it, the Restoration churches long ago might have discussed the need to catechize those who were growing in the faith and knowledge.

17. Phillip Schaff and Henry Wace, eds., *A Select Library of Nicene and Post-Nicene Fathers of the Christian Church*, vol. 7, *The Catechetical Lectures of S. Cyril*, by Edwin Hamilton Gifford (Grand Rapids: Eerdmans, 1978), xiii.

18. *Apostolic Tradition* 16, quoted in Aidan Kavanagh, *The Shape of Baptism: The Rite of Christian Initiation* (New York: Pueblo, 1978), 55.

19. The church must strive to communicate definitions of "sin" and "salvation" to its youth that are more comprehensive than the common understanding. Children must become aware that sin is more than misdeeds, small and large, and salvation is more than rescue from danger. Rather, sin is better described to adolescents as brokenness and inadequacy and salvation as fullness and completion of life.

20. *Encyclopedia of Early Christianity*, 2nd ed. Everett Ferguson, ed., (New York: Routledge, 1990), s.v. "Catechesis, Catechumenate," 223–225.

CHAPTER 8

Welcoming the Stranger

JERRY SHIELDS[1]

For most churches, the organizational and cooperative efforts of doing missions and ministry are a given. Most churches meet regularly and seek to engage in worship, grow disciples, minister to needs, foster fellowship, and share the gospel. However, many churches face the challenge of moving members beyond the organizational and cooperative efforts to more personally and intentionally engage in the practice of reflecting God's presence by participating in God's ongoing work in the world. If we are not careful, we can end up writing checks, giving assistance, and offering programs that fail to help us engage in relationships that God may use to transform lives. As a result, this intervention sought to engage individuals in the ongoing work of Christ through the practice of hospitality, with the goal of extending God's welcome to people encountered every day.

The intervention was enacted in the small, west-Texas, county-seat town of Colorado City, in a church that has been in existence for over 125 years. Colorado City is a declining town of fewer than 5,000 people in Mitchell County, which has a population of less than 9,500. While great economic, cultural, and ethnic diversity is evident throughout the community, that diversity fails to be reflected in the membership and participation of most of the local churches.

Historically, the church has made joint mission and ministry efforts a priority and has given generously to share the love of Christ in other parts of the state and throughout the world. In addition to worldwide and state-wide partnerships, the church has been active in the community, serving as a temporary hospital after a devastating tornado hit Mitchell County in 1923 and locally televising services since 1978. For over thirty years, the church has provided an at-cost childcare program that provides ministry to parents and children on Tuesdays and Thursdays. Since 2003, the church has worked with others to provide clean and comfortable weekend housing and meals, all free of charge, to family members of inmates who come from out of town for visits to the local prisons, providing a Christian setting and opportunities for Bible study and worship. In addition, the church seeks to provide ministry to local needs through the local food bank, clothes closet, ministerial alliance, and other action programs that assist with home repairs.

During the past twenty years, the community appears to be transitioning from a stable agrarian community to a community characterized by temporary residents and highly mobile workers. The construction of two prison units during the early 1990s as well as the recent revitalization of the oilfield and construction of wind turbines throughout the area has brought an influx of people, from prison workers to field personnel. Furthermore, the local lake has become a busy place for vacationers as well as a popular retirement spot for senior adults. As a result, despite the continuing decline in population, an opportunity exists in the community to reach new people and break down existing barriers.

Though the transition within the community and the opportunities present are increasingly evident, several assumptions common for small towns have to be overcome. If we have lived in a small town for a number of years, we have a tendency to assume we know everyone. We tend to assume we can identify local people of faith who go to church, where they go, and that those who are open to church are already involved. We tend to assume that everyone in the community knows where the church is and what the church is about. We assume that others know they are welcome, and we tend to sit back and wait for them to come.

The problem addressed by this intervention is a lack of personal practices that help us to welcome strangers. The church is a friendly church, and a number of ministries seek to connect with those around us, but we face the challenge of practicing hospitality in a way that crosses boundaries, reaches out to others, and personally welcomes them. The church members who sense the challenge of reaching outside our walls are often pulled in one of two directions. Some are pulled toward the consumer model that seeks to create excitement by engaging in special events or by seeking to produce a particular religious experience. The motive is pure, but the method employed is plagued with the potential pitfall of forming pious-appearing consumers rather than committed disciples of Jesus. From the other direction, a number of members are engaged in reaching out to the community and beyond through acts of service. While noble and often sacrificial, this engagement can degenerate into a delivery of goods and services without resulting in personal engagement in the lives of others. In many ways, those who serve can remain distant from those who are being served.

A need existed within the church and in my own ministry to reclaim our call to connect more relationally with others. This project sought to help us connect through the particular practice of welcoming strangers. As we did so, we increasingly recognized that the wonderful work of institutional ministries and our network of partnerships have not been without their drawbacks. Through faithfully contributing to organizations and institutions, we have run the risk of outsourcing the responsibility for ministry and missions.[2] As Rowan Greer points out: "to the degree that the Church's work becomes merely institutional, it ceases to be Christian."[3] We need to learn again to live and give ourselves, both personally and corporately, for the sake of others that we might be God's people for the sake of the world. The church has the opportunity of ministering to longtime residents and newcomers, breaking down barriers through the practice of hospitality.

The purpose of this ministry intervention was to form participants into effective practitioners of the ministry of hospitality. The goal was that participants in this project would better see others through God's love and take time to give themselves to others, motivated by what God has done. As a result, participants would increasingly express to the people they encounter every day the welcoming love of God as a daily and natural practice—to those both inside and outside our congregation. As Christine Pohl points out, "the contemporary church hungers for models of a more authentic Christian life in which glimpses of the kingdom can be seen and the promise of the kingdom is embodied. More than words and ideas, the world needs living pictures of what a life of hospitality could look like."[4]

The God Who Welcomes the Stranger

God's people in every generation have been called to respond appropriately to the hospitality of a gracious God. Throughout the Scriptures, the hospitality of God is evident, as is the call to receive and share in the practice of hospitality. God's hospitality is expressed clearly in the coming, ministry, and teaching of Jesus. In an inconceivable move, the Lord came and dwelt among us in flesh in order to reconcile and restore us to the communion God intended for us.[5] The Incarnation depicts a radical and voluntary impoverishment of God on our behalf,[6] so that we could be welcomed into the kingdom of God.[7] As a result, Marjorie Thompson asks, "Could there be any hospitality to match that of the Host of Heaven?"[8] This supreme act of hospitality demonstrates an unimaginable and unfathomable act of welcome to those undeserving, radically dissimilar, and alienated from the Lord.

Furthermore, the entire ministry of Jesus embodied the hospitality of God. Jesus reached out to the poor, the powerless, the disreputable, and the outcasts.[9] His guest list included prostitutes, tax collectors, and sinners. Though these acts of welcome annoyed those who considered themselves to be "insiders," such hospitality reflected the hospitality of God, who welcomes the undeserving and provides a banquet for those in desperate need.[10] From the particular examples and summary statements related to the ministry of Jesus, to the miraculous feedings, face-to-face encounters, and numerous invitations he extended, the ministry of Jesus was marked by this radical welcome. "For Jesus, hospitality is fundamental to the very being of God."[11] Its purpose is nothing less than the transformation of the world.[12] As Jesus proclaimed and lived out the hospitality of God in such simple yet personal ways, not only were lives transformed, but a new community was being formed, and a new world was being created.

The God Who Enjoins People to be People of Welcome

Because God is a God of welcome, those who have been created in the Divine image are capable of reflecting hospitality.[13] Those who have been called to be imitators of God are enjoined to extend God's welcome. To be Christian is to be a people of welcome, participating in the life of God.

The Old Testament is filled with instruction regarding the responsibilities of extending hospitality. Hospitality is a command,[14] a responsibility,[15] and a test of piety.[16] Hospitality in the Old Testament is rooted in the character and activity of God as experienced by God's people. Only those who have experienced God's hospitality and recognized to some extent the depth of it are able to extend that welcome to others.

In the New Testament, those who benefit from God's hospitality are expected to practice hospitality toward one another and the stranger.[17] Mortimer Arias identifies hospitality as a distinctive mark of Christians and Christian communities.[18] Jesus sought to instill this spirit into his disciples through both his instruction and example. His disciples were taught to take the lowest place of service, to become servants of all, to deny themselves, and to love their enemies.

Hospitality is such a vital notion that several Scriptures indicate that we most fully extend welcome to God by welcoming others.[19] Hospitality facilitates meeting and receiving holy presence.[20] When one welcomes the stranger, one may be entertaining angels or perhaps even God.[21] This understanding of hospitality motivates Christian service.

Theological Implications

In the Western world, hospitality has become an increasingly institutional or commercial concept. Agencies, organizations, places of lodging and eating abound, "but genuine welcomes are rare."[22] What seems to have been highly regarded in biblical times is at risk of disappearing.[23] The need exists for the church to rediscover and implement practices that will express the welcome of God to others.

Hospitality as Response to God's Welcome

Pohl argues that hospitality begins with an awareness of God's grace and generosity. Hospitality is not first and foremost a duty or responsibility; rather, it is a response of gratitude and love for God's welcome of us. The hospitality we offer reflects and extends the hospitality of God.[24] As a result of God's hospitality, God's people share their homes, their resources, their lives, and their hearts with others primarily because we have received unimaginable and unmerited grace.[25] The more clearly we see ourselves as having been strangers to God, the more we see our reason for being hospitable toward others.[26] Only to the degree that we recognize the magnitude of God's welcome will we be able to extend that welcome to others.

Hospitality as Resistance

If the purpose of hospitality is the transformation of the world, it begins by resisting a number of current cultural trends toward individualism, exclusivism, isolationism, and self-protection. The practice of hospitality challenges the prevalent notion of individualism in our culture. Our modern individualism and focus on individual rights tends to create "a society of self-interested individuals and eventually, a society of strangers."[27] In this culture of pervasive selfishness, hospitality to the stranger provides the necessary means by which God's people can resist the fragmentation that results from an excessive individualism.[28] Elizabeth Newman writes, "Even though we live in a fallen world of competition and hoarding, this is not the place we are called to dwell."[29] Christian hospitality consists of receiving and sharing God's plenitude. It involves looking not only to our own interests, but also to the interests of others.[30] It is rooted not in practicality but in grace.[31] Confidence in the generosity and goodness of God as gracious host enables us to trust that God will provide what we need and free us to share through hospitality.[32]

In addition to resisting individualism, hospitality serves as a means by which God's people resist exclusivism and isolationism. God's people walk a delicate balance between living in the world and for the world without becoming like the world. Perhaps one of the greatest challenges the church of North America faces is the tendency of being exclusive or isolationist. The practice of hospitality challenges and stretches us toward an ever-widening circle of concern.[33] While the church must always diligently maintain a distinction from the world, the teaching and example of Jesus challenges the church to resist sectarian ways.

Hospitality to the stranger leads to a resistance to the tendency toward self-protection; to engage in the practice of hospitality requires vulnerability. Those who practice hospitality must open themselves up to risk rejection and the possibility of failure.[34] They must open themselves up to hurt and abuse. Brendan Byrne writes that Jesus comes offering the hospitality of God but is met with rejection and inhospitality. Even so, "rejection does not have the last word: it too, can be drawn into God's saving plan and made to further, rather than restrict, the outreach of grace."[35]

Hospitality is a movement of resistance that seeks to stand against our natural tendencies and the pressures of our culture to participate more fully in the life of God. Hospitality challenges our tendency toward selfishness, breaks us out of our isolation, and makes us vulnerable to those around us. Welcoming the stranger is disruptive and dangerous.[36] But Thompson reminds us that while there is risk to extending hospitality, there is also risk in refusing hospitality. We may miss God.[37]

Hospitality as a New Way of Thinking and Seeing

If hospitality is a response to God's welcome and resistance to the pressures experienced in this world, of what does hospitality consist? Hospitality involves seeing others and thinking differently about them. As W. Paul Jones points out, "hospitality as action is the spontaneous consequence of hospitality as disposition."[38] That means that our disposition toward others is not to be determined by another's appearance, behavior, or any other mark of societal acceptability. It is to be determined by the conviction that every human being bears the image of God, which establishes a fundamental worth and dignity that cannot be undermined by wrongdoing or need.[39] Hospitality means recognizing the value of all people no matter who they are and, consequently, being moved to provide practical care to those in need.[40] True hospitality calls for a conversion, a new way of thinking so that we see people through the eyes of God.[41] This is best accomplished when we recognize Jesus in every stranger. Allowing ourselves to see others as Jesus does, we are empowered to be agents of God's kindness to them and love them as Jesus does.[42]

Pohl characterizes a willful blindness to see others in their need and ongoing misery as a form of wickedness marked by spiritual deadness, greed, and disrespect for human life.[43] Byrne provides a specific illustration by pointing out that in the story of the rich man and Lazarus, the guilt of the rich man is found not in overt forms of wickedness but in the simple fact that "his luxury so absorbed him that he did not notice—and not noticing sealed his fate."[44] In addition, Arthur Sutherland argues that in the parable of the sheep and the goats in Matthew 25, the failure in hospitality stemmed not from an unwillingness to help or because the help needed was too demanding or demeaning. Their only protest was that they did not see.[45]

The parable of Matthew 25 also illustrates something of those who did minister to those in need. They did so without any conscious note of the magnitude of their acts. In the same way, Jesus did not go out looking for someone to help, rather as he was going, Jesus saw. Sutherland notes that this casualness goes against much of what is called Christian hospitality today. Programs, organizations, and partnerships have merit but can easily institutionalize care. When that happens, our ability to see the stranger easily erodes. Instead, hospitality is to be personal, natural, and unforced.[46] Henri Nouwen points out that hospitality is not merely receiving a stranger into our house or extending some form of help but is a fundamental attitude toward our fellow human being.[47]

For those who see the stranger as the presence of Christ in our midst, Michele Hershberger writes that the expression of hospitality ought to be approached not as ministry *to* someone but *with* someone.[48] This also expresses the mutuality and dignity that is found in hospitality. Newman points out that simply providing goods and services is not hospitality since there is no reciprocity. Hospitality acknowledges that the one receiving also has gifts to give, that the guest can also be a host.[49] Amy Oden explains the dynamics of hospitality: "One gives, yet receives. The one who receives actually gives. The host finds herself or himself blessed, receiving so much more than giving. The guest or stranger becomes the blessing, giving so much more than receiving."[50] For this type of sharing to occur, hospitality demands that guests be accepted as they are without agendas, unconditionally, with an ear to hear God through them.[51] When that happens, the gifts that human beings need most—care, friendship, and love—can be exchanged. In hospitality, we are at the same time both host and guest; for the recognition of Jesus in the stranger leads us to see people differently, respond differently to their needs, and approach them expecting an encounter with God.

Hospitality as the Creation of Space

Hospitality not only consists of a new way of thinking about and seeing others, it consists of a willingness to create space in our lives. Gerrit Dawson points out how many Christians have difficulty these days engaging in the practice of hospitality, not because their cupboards are bare of food and drink, but because their schedules are too full.[52] Our culture is marked by a prevalent and consuming busyness. Life becomes defined by events on a calendar, not by people with whom we can share God's grace.[53] As a result, hospitality involves the creation of space in our lives into which people are welcomed, a space where unless the invitation is given, the stranger would not feel free to enter.[54] As a result, hospitality requires an openness of heart and a generosity of time and resources.[55] It is only within such space that one can cross boundaries into the establishment of relationship, and it is only as people get to know one another that they begin to appreciate their human and spiritual common ground.[56]

The life of Jesus was about space. Jesus created space for time with the Father and time for others. The Gospels often portray Jesus not only withdrawing for times of solitude but also continually eating and drinking with others and sharing his life with those around him.[57] Time with others was a natural part of the life and ministry of Jesus. He was always about the Father's business, the business of people. Jesus took time for people who were often marginalized and forgotten by the larger society. To walk in his steps, Christians today must make time for others. Therefore, hospitality is "the powerful value of being *with* people, connecting with their lives and helping them to become established in a network of relations."[58] Since within these relationships, change and empowerment can happen.

The creation of space also consists of accepting others in such a way that we resist the temptation toward manipulation by allowing the stranger to remain other. "Hospitality is the welcoming of the other in his or her otherness."[59] The success of hospitality is not measured by end results, but by the degree to which one becomes available to another.[60] Thompson points out that welcome involves the creation of a free and friendly space for the guest. For the practice of hospitality, the creation of space demands humility so that we accept people as they are and do not require them to be just like us.[61] However, this does not mean that hospitality is conducted without convictions, for as Newman points out, "Christian hospitality disappears when the distinction between church and the world is collapsed."[62] But it does mean that guests experience a safe place to be and express themselves. The creation of space is a necessary prerequisite for welcoming the stranger.

Hospitality as Love in Action

Hospitality involves thinking differently about others and making space in our lives for them, but hospitality is more than just being friendly; it is love in action. The practice of hospitality may consist of any act of love, ranging from providing a cup of cold water to the sacrifice of oneself for another.[63] Its expressions are as varied as the needs experienced by people. Hospitality may include the meeting of physical needs but may also consist of meeting social needs of respect and acceptance.[64] Some people simply need to know that someone cares.[65] Though many may be able to purchase the things they need, the gift of welcome remains crucial because of our need for a network of relationships that give us a place in the world.[66] This is not something technology, money, programs, or structures can accomplish. It is up to individual people and the larger community of faith to demonstrate someone cares.

The most common and vivid example of the redemptive circle of hospitality is the shared meal. Shannon Jung points out that eating together is one antidote to excessive individualism, for it expresses our basic equality in that we all have common needs, experiences, and humanity that transcend our differences. Sharing a meal together also serves as a means of recognition and of conveying dignity upon another, particularly as we create space for one another. "Sharing food is the simplest way, the most natural way to begin the act of building up a relationship where deeper sharing becomes possible."[67] But a meal can be more than social and relational. When people eat together, in a mysterious way, God is present as well.[68] Through the shared meal, the kingdom of God can be illustrated and enacted. According to John Koenig, the kingdom of God often breaks in through shared meals and other occasions when the stranger is welcomed.[69]

Hospitality as Embodiment of the Kingdom of God

According to Hampton Morgan, hospitality is often depicted as a paradigm of the kingdom of God. "A wayward son is welcomed with robes, feasting and celebration by the father who has waited for his return (Luke 15). The king opens his wedding feast to guests previously uninvited when those with invitations spurn his hospitality (Matt 22). Jesus describes a God who welcomes outsiders to join the feast, even seating them in the place of honor (Luke 14:7-11)."[70] In the teachings of Jesus the reign of God was social and relational. His acts of inclusion and recognition were signs of his coming reign.[71] Jesus came bearing good news. The kingdom of God is marked by a radical inclusiveness in that all are invited.[72] "The kingdom of God is a place that makes it possible for the poor, the outcasts, the strangers to have life and dignity. The kingdom of God is a realm of hospitality,"[73] a hospitality that challenges the world's patterns of domination and exclusion, not through coercion, but by the power of compassionate and unconditional care.[74]

If the kingdom of God is a realm of hospitality, the practice of hospitality is an enactment of the gospel. "God by nature recruits outsiders to be partners in providence, makes a home among them, and through them enriches the world."[75] Participation in the kingdom of God "demands a life of peaceful resistance to oppressive structures in order to befriend the disenfranchised."[76] Koenig goes on to write: "The Spirit speaks within us, assuring us of our own welcome by God (Rom. 8:15–17), but it also calls us forward, leading us into new frontiers of hospitality."[77] Through these acts of inclusion and respect, however small, social relations can be powerfully reframed and welcome can be experienced.[78] Though many practices of hospitality may be regarded by society as of little consequence, from the perspective of the gospel, these practices become "a manifestation of God's Kingdom."[79]

The Ministry Intervention

The design of this ministry intervention sought to lead participants to embrace the spirit and engage in the practice of hospitality. The intervention was designed to shape how the participants see and treat others so that they might extend God's welcome to strangers. Hospitality is a skill and a gift, but it is also a practice that flourishes as skills are developed, as virtues are nurtured, and as particular settings are cultivated.[80] This intervention sought to shape the virtues and cultivate the practices necessary for the practice of hospitality.

The ministry intervention consisted of eight sessions. Sessions one through seven were roughly one hour long while session eight was extended in order to gather feedback from participants and consider future possibilities. Sessions two through six began with a short practice of "slowing."[81] Participants were asked to enter into a period of silence for the purposes of detachment from the concerns and preoccupations of life so that we might be fully present to one another and the Lord.

The intervention sessions used a model extracted from Pohl's *Making Room* and were arranged to move participants from a growing recognition of the presence of God in the stranger to an increasing engagement in the personal practice of hospitality. Each step of increasing engagement was intended to bring increased risk and vulnerability.

Most sessions included *lectio divina*[82] from a variety of texts. Also, the group spent time in reflection and reporting to deepen understanding through contemplation and communal discussion. Finally, weekly assignments alternated between practices of reflection and practices of engagement to give a balance and rhythm to the project.

The sessions were held in my home, allowing me to model hospitality. Because hospitality involves vulnerability, I sought to model this vulnerability by opening myself up to possible criticism regarding the cleanliness and condition of the church parsonage as well as a possible critique of what was prepared and served. The goal was to form a more hospitable community by understanding, observing, receiving, and practicing acts of hospitality.

Ministry Participants

I sought to enlist between eight and twelve volunteers who would be willing to participate. I chose to use volunteers because they already possessed some of the self-initiative necessary for the fulfillment of this commitment. To use volunteers also made it available to anyone interested and provided opportunity for greater diversity. An open invitation to participate was communicated through the church bulletin and from the pulpit. A preliminary meeting was held to clarify the nature of the project, how it would work, the benefits expected for participants and the church, as well as what would be required of those who would participate.

Description of the Project Sessions

Session one was entitled "An Invitation to Participate in Hospitality." The session began with the experience of welcome and refreshments at our home. Next, I presented a general introduction to the theology of Christian hospitality. We discussed the fear and uncertainty that often accompanies an encounter with strangers. We acknowledged our tendency to stay within our comfort zones, evident in the sitting in familiar seats and relating to a familiar crowd. After a discussion of the gospel as an expression of God's welcome to us, we were challenged to see the community around us, acknowledge God's love for all people, and work to extend God's welcome to others whether they ever came to our church or not. This was followed by *lectio divina* using Luke 14:15–24. Prior to closing the session, participants were divided into three groups. Each group was asked to read a different section containing eight chapters in the gospel of Luke: group one read chapters 1–8; group two read chapters 9–16; group three read chapters 17–24. As they read their assigned chapters during the week, they were asked to identify and record the times Jesus expressed God's hospitality to others in word or deed. I asked participants to look for times Jesus recognized and valued people and/or met a need. The session was closed with prayer.

Session two was entitled "Recognizing Jesus in Every Stranger, Part A." We began the session together by engaging in the practice of slowing. We then began a period of reporting and reflecting. I wrote the chapters in Luke as a timeline on butcher paper and recorded on it the instances Jesus practiced hospitality as identified by the participants. Participants discussed what they found and looked for patterns in the events. The group discussed the prominent examples of Jesus expressing God's invitation or welcome. This time of reporting and reflecting was followed by *lectio divina* on Matthew 25:31–46. Prior to closing the session, participants were asked to read Matthew 25:31–46 each day the following week. They were also asked to spend twenty minutes sitting on an outside bench at the local grocery store, recording how many strangers they saw. They were asked to do this exercise at a time when a number of people would be shopping. We closed this session with prayer and fellowship over refreshments.

Session three was entitled "Recognizing Jesus in Every Stranger, Part B." The session began with the practice of slowing followed by a period of reporting and reflecting. The group was asked to respond to the following questions related to the assignment: How many strangers did you observe? What did you find to be surprising? What went through your mind as strangers passed by? What feelings did you experience? How did your daily Scripture reading shape your perception of the strangers you saw? Was there any engagement with strangers? The average number of strangers observed was thirty-six, just under two per minute. Most saw at least twice as many that they did not know as people they did know. Those who had lived in this small town most of their lives were surprised at how many people they did not know. The period of reporting and reflection was followed by *lectio divina* on Genesis 18:1–8. Through the reading, participants observed both a hurried preparation for the strangers as well as an unhurried availability to them. The group noted that God was present in the stranger, and we discussed the reciprocal nature of hospitality, that those who extend relationship or welcome to others are often the ones who are the most deeply blessed. Prior to closing the session, a compiled list of the times members had identified Jesus practicing hospitality in Luke was distributed. As the weekly assignment, participants were asked to reread each of the instances identified, with an eye to *how* Jesus demonstrated hospitality and *to whom* his hospitality was extended. Casual conversations over refreshments followed a closing prayer.

Session four was entitled "Communicating Welcome, Part A." The session began with the practice of slowing. Members then discussed their lists of to whom Jesus expressed hospitality from their readings in Luke. They were asked to plot a dot for each instance on a bulls-eye on butcher paper according to the following characteristics: followers of Jesus in the center circle; Jews in the first ring; unclean, sinners and Gentiles in the second ring; and enemies in the outer ring. Areas that may have included multiple persons from overlapping groups were plotted in multiple areas. The following question was considered: Who were the main recipients of Jesus' hospitality? Identifying the recipients and focusing on Jesus' hospitality was one of the most eye-opening activities for our group. We found more instances in which Jesus extended hospitality to the unclean, sinners, and Gentiles than to followers and Jews combined. We related the practices of Jesus to our own tendencies and found we have a long way to go in walking in the steps of Jesus. On a separate sheet of butcher paper, they were then asked to identify and list how Jesus practiced hospitality as described in Luke. The following questions were considered: What does practicing hospitality require? What did it require of Jesus? What forms might hospitality take today? The period of reporting and reflecting was followed by *lectio divina* on Luke 14:7–14. Discussion centered on developing a spirit of humility as well as a disposition of selfless and compassionate inclusion. Prior to closing the session, the participants were assigned to read Luke 14:7–14 each day and plan and implement a means by which they could practice hospitality toward someone they normally would not. They were asked to make their time together a matter of prayer, praying as they extend an invitation to the other, praying for the other on the day they got together, welcoming the other with joy, praying again for the other as they left, and expressing appreciation following their time together. Participants were given great freedom regarding what they did, but they were asked to be sure the time spent was an unhurried event so that they could listen and share in the lives of their guests. Following prayer, participants enjoyed a time of refreshments and fellowship.

Session five was entitled "Communicating Welcome, Part B." After the practice of slowing, participants engaged in reporting and reflection related to the assignment to extend hospitality to someone they normally would not. They were asked to respond to the following questions: What did you find to be difficult, surprising, or enriching about the assignment? How did you find yourself most stretched? Did you sense the presence and activity of God in any way? Many acknowledged that this was a stretch for them, to reach outside of comfort zones, to overcome their fears, to find time to get together with others, to cross boundaries of difference, and simply to identify another to whom God would have them reach out. The intentionality of the assignment helped make them more sensitive. The period of reporting and reflection was followed by *lectio divina* on Deuteronomy 10:14–22. The following week's assignment asked participants to engage in the practice of solitude by giving God time and space that is not in competition with activities, demands, people, or television. Participants were asked to take fifteen minutes each day for quiet prayer, contemplation, or meditation for the purpose of becoming untangled from a life of hurriedness and becoming available to God. The session closed with prayer and fellowship.

Session six was entitled, "Recognizing One Another in Shared Meals, Part A." Following the practice of slowing, participants were asked to report and reflect on the practice of solitude. They were asked to respond to the following questions: What did you find difficult, surprising, or enriching in the practice of solitude? How did you find yourself most stretched? How did you sense the presence and activity of God? Though some members of the group found the practice natural, others acknowledged a difficulty in focusing, finding time, being disciplined, and hearing from God. The period of reporting and reflecting was followed by *lectio divina* on Acts 11:1–18. In this passage, participants noted not only the change in Peter's perspective toward Gentiles and the barriers overcome, but also that it began with an act of solitude. Peter was up on the roof praying. For this week's assignment, participants were asked to read Acts 11:1–18 daily. They were also asked to invite a person or family they do not know well to our celebration meal to be held during the final session. They were encouraged to stretch themselves by inviting guests who were different from themselves. Participants were asked to continue to invite others until someone agreed to come. The session was closed with prayer, and a brief time of fellowship and refreshments followed.

Session seven was entitled "Recognizing One Another in Shared Meals, Part B." Following a period of slowing, participants were asked to report and reflect in response to the following questions: What did you find to be difficult, surprising, or enriching about the assignment? How did you feel as you approached others with an invitation? How did you feel after extending the invitation? Due to scheduling conflicts and acknowledged procrastination, some struggled to find a guest who would be willing to come. For most, it was a bit difficult to extend the invitation, but once it was offered, many were surprised by the reception they received, and several found it to be much easier than they had expected. They were overcoming their fears and apprehensions and making themselves vulnerable. The reporting and reflection was followed by *lectio divina* on 1 Kings 17:7–16. We considered the rest of the story in the raising of the widow's son, noting the dynamic interchange between two different people who were a blessing to one another because God was present. The week's assignment was to pray daily for the final session together. Participants were also asked to pray for the guests who had agreed to come, any concerns they may have in their lives, and for an availability to practice hospitality toward them and the other guests who would be present. A small token was given to participants as a tangible reminder to pray regularly. Following a closing prayer, we enjoyed refreshments.

Session eight was entitled "A Celebration Meal." The final session began in our home as participants and guests arrived. I had purchased barbeque and participants had brought the sides and dessert. When everyone had arrived, I offered a welcome and blessing for the fellowship meal. Though some guests canceled prior to the meal, the group was diverse, as guests were from different ethnicities, economic classes, church backgrounds, and moral values. Participants demonstrated a tremendous willingness to express hospitality across lines of potential division through their invitations and through their welcoming of others during the meal. Following the meal and the departure of our guests, participants drove to the church, where we had a time of reporting and reflection. Participants were asked the following questions: What did you find to be difficult, surprising, or enriching in this intervention? How did you find yourself most stretched? How did you sense the presence and activity of God? What was not helpful? The group was then asked to address the question of how to move forward. Participants read Hebrews 13:2 together and considered the following questions: What do you hear in this verse? How can we continue and expand upon the practice of hospitality individually? Corporately?

Conclusion

The group was open, sharing their experiences and insights as well as their struggles. This openness created an atmosphere of welcome in which people could be vulnerable within the group and encouraged a willingness to try new things. The group's intentionality and accountability created a motivation and commitment in the participants. The intervention was a timely and helpful process that connected with the congregation's context. Participants noted comfort zones and ruts both in their individual lives and in the church, indicating how comfortable we can become in isolation from the people to whom God has sent us.

Through the process, members were also encouraged to participate in a number of spiritual disciplines. Many members were introduced to the disciplines of slowing, solitude, and *lectio divina* for the first time. While many of the participants were already practicing their own spiritual disciplines, the specific disciplines introduced seemed to enhance their own practices and provided a name for some disciplines a few members had already done somewhat naturally. These practices appeared effective in deepening the participants' relationship with God as well as a means of enhancing their understanding of hospitality.

In addition to introducing participants to a number of new spiritual disciplines, the assignments themselves seemed effective in guiding people toward a more hospitable spirit. The assignments of contemplation had an impact on the way participants saw and thought about the strangers among us. Some indicated that they had become less judgmental and more willing to reach out. The assignments of engagement led us to put our thoughts into action and become practitioners of hospitality. The group was challenged to make time to do some things they would not normally do, and members had time to reflect upon and internalize what they discovered and what they sensed God was saying to them. In addition, the variety of assignments caused different members to be stretched in different ways. The assignments also held the participants accountable to the group for the purposes of spending time with others and with God. One of the most enriching aspects of the process was the participatory method of learning. Members of the group learned not from a teacher or a prepared lesson but from doing, sharing, and reading. The open process of *lectio divina*, reporting and reflecting, and prayer enhanced the participants' theological reflection on the practice of hospitality.

While open and participatory, the intervention also had a strong biblical foundation. Though not intended to be a Bible study, about a third of our time together was spent reading and sharing in the word of God. The *lectio divina* firmly grounded the project in God's word, and the passages discussed brought out a range of issues related to the practice of hospitality.

While no two congregations are alike, the intervention has a number of potential benefits for any congregation. People everywhere live in need of welcome, and God's people, wherever we may be, are called to extend the welcome we have received from God. This group process can create a deeper spirit of partnership and a common focus for the church. It invites the church to change, to look outward, and extend God's love to others; particularly those not like themselves. Participation in this process can create a new perspective of church, a new way of living in society and, ultimately, a new world. The practice of hospitality can enable a church to embody the kingdom of God.

———————————————

1. Jerry Bob Shields, "Welcoming the Stranger at First Baptist Church, Colorado City, Texas" (DMin thesis, ACU, 2009).

2. Christine D. Pohl, *Making Room: Recovering Hospitality as a Christian Tradition* (Grand Rapids: Eerdmans, 1999), 7, 45–47.

3. Rowan A. Greer, *Broken Lights and Mended Lives: Theology and Common Life in the Early Church* (University Park, PA: Pennsylvania State University Press, 1986), 137.

4. Pohl, *Making Room*, 10.

5. Marjorie J. Thompson, *Soul Feast: An Invitation to the Christian Spiritual Life* (Louisville: Westminster John Knox, 2005), 130.

6. Lucien Richard, *Living the Hospitality of God* (New York: Paulist, 2000), 56.

7. Pohl, *Making Room*, 29.

8. Thompson, *Soul Feast*, 131.

9. Richard, *Living the Hospitality*, 57.

10. Pohl, *Making Room*, 16.

11. Arthur Sutherland, *I Was a Stranger: A Christian Theology of Hospitality* (Nashville: Abingdon, 2006), 79.

12. John Koenig, *New Testament Hospitality: Partnership with Strangers as Promise and Mission* (Philadelphia: Fortress, 1985), 29.

13. Thompson, *Soul Feast*, 129.

14. Exod. 22:21–24, 23:9; Lev. 19:9–10, 33–34; 23:22; Deut. 10:14–22; 14:27–29; 24:17–22; 26:12–13; Jer. 22:2–3; Ezek. 47:21–23.

15. Num. 9:14; 15:14–16; 15:26, 29–30; Deut. 1:16–17; 16:13–14.

16. V. H. Kooy, "Hospitality," *The Interpreter's Dictionary of the Bible*, vol. 2, ed. Emory Stevens Bucke (New York: Abingdon, 1962), 654. He argues that the Old Testament portrays

the practice of hospitality as a demonstration of piety in Job 31:32–33 and Isa. 58:6–7 and the lack of hospitality as a failure of piety in Ezek. 22:6–8, 29–31.

17. Christine D. Pohl, "Responding to Strangers: Insights from the Christian Tradition," *Studies in Christian Ethics* 19:1 (2006): 98. See Matt. 25:31–46; Luke 12:41–48; Rom. 12:13; Phil. 2:29–30; Col. 4:10; Heb. 13:2; 1 Pet. 4:9–10; 3 John 7–8.

18. Mortimer Arias, "Centripetal Mission, or Evangelization by Hospitality," in *The Study of Evangelism: Exploring a Missional Practice of the Church*, ed. Paul W. Chilcote and Laceye C. Warner (Grand Rapids: Eerdmans, 2008), 424.

19. Gen. 18; Matt. 18:5; 25:31–36; Mark 9:37–38; Luke 9:48.

20. Thompson, *Soul Feast*, 127.

21. Darryl Tippens, *Pilgrim Heart: The Way of Jesus in Everyday Life* (Abilene, TX: Leafwood, 2006), 54.

22. Koenig, *New Testament Hospitality*, 2.

23. Hampton Morgan Jr., "Remember to Show Hospitality: A Sign of Grace in a Graceless Time," *International Review of Mission* 87:347 (Oct. 1998): 535.

24. Pohl, *Making Room*, 172.

25. Tippens, *Pilgrim Heart*, 63.

26. Sutherland, *I Was a Stranger*, 26.

27. Elizabeth Newman, *Untamed Hospitality: Welcoming God and Other Strangers* (Grand Rapids: Brazos, 2007), 139.

28. Richard, *Living the Hospitality*, 20.

29. Newman, *Untamed Hospitality*, 101. See also: Christine Pohl, "Practicing Hospitality in the Face of Complicated Wickedness," *Wesleyan Theological Journal* 42:1 (Spring 2007): 13.

30. Phil. 2:4.

31. W. Paul Jones, "Hospitality Within and Without," *Weavings* 9 (Feb. 1994): 8.

32. Newman, *Untamed Hospitality*, 81.

33. Christopher P. Vogt, "Fostering a Catholic Commitment to the Common Good: An Approach Rooted in Virtue Ethics," *Theological Studies* 68:2 (June 2007): 410.

34. Pohl, *Making Room*, 14.

35. Brendan Byrne, *The Hospitality of God: A Reading of Luke's Gospel* (Collegeville, MN: Liturgical Press, 2000), 53.

36. Amy G. Oden, "God's Radical Welcome: A Path of Hospitality Marked by More Than Cookies," *Mutuality* 15:1 (Spring 2008): 9.

37. Thompson, *Soul Feast*, 135.

38. Jones, "*Hospitality Within*," 9.

39. Pohl, "Responding to Strangers," 86.

40. Pohl, *Making Room*, 33.

41. Michele Hershberger, *A Christian View of Hospitality: Expecting Surprises* (Scottsdale, PA: Herald, 1999), 61.

42. Ibid., 91.

43. Pohl, "Practicing Hospitality," 12.

44. Byrne, *Hospitality of God*, 137.

45. Sutherland, *I Was a Stranger*, 78.

46. Ibid., 78–79.

47. Henri J. M. Nouwen, *Reaching Out: The Three Movements of the Spiritual Life* (Garden City, NY: Image, 1986), 67.

48. Hershberger, *Christian View of Hospitality*, 29.

49. Newman, *Untamed Hospitality*, 92.

50. Amy Oden, *And You Welcomed Me: A Sourcebook on Hospitality in Early Christianity*, (Nashville: Abingdon, 2001), 133.

51. Hershberger, *Christian View of Hospitality*, 30.

52. Gerrit S. Dawson, "Feasts in the Desert and Other Unlikely Places," *Weavings* 9 (Feb. 1994): 34.

53. Morgan, "Remember to Show Hospitality," 539.

54. Pohl, *Making Room*, 39.

55. Ibid., 13.

56. Pohl, "Practicing Hospitality," 27.

57. Thomas R. Hawkins, *Sharing the Search: A Theology of Christian Hospitality*, (Nashville: The Upper Room, 1987), 48.

58. Pohl, "Practicing Hospitality," 29.

59. Robert Vosloo, "Identity, Otherness and the Triune God: Theological Groundwork for a Christian Ethic of Hospitality" in *Journal of Theology for South Africa* 119 (July 2004): 71.

60. Oden, *You Welcomed Me*, 109. Oden goes on to write: "The practices of hospitality are independent of their outcomes. One lives hospitably without any guarantee of a payoff. The sick person may die, the stranger may misuse the resources shared, the hospitality offered may not be honored. Desire for a particular consequence of hospitality must be released," 147.

61. Thompson, *Soul Feast*, 134.

62. Newman, *Untamed Hospitality*, 41.

63. Matt. 10:42; John 15:13.

64. Oden, *You Welcomed Me*, 14.

65. Christine D. Pohl, "Hospitality from the Edge: The Significance of Marginality in the Practice of Welcome," in *Annual of the Society of Christian Ethics* 1995 (Georgetown University Press): 121.

66. Pohl, "Responding to Strangers," 83.

67. Shannon L. Jung, *Sharing Food: Christian Practices for Enjoyment* (Minneapolis: Fortress, 2006), 45.

68. Walter T. McCree, "The Covenant Meal in the Old Testament," *Journal of Biblical Literature* 45:1–2 (1926): 128.

69. Koenig, *New Testament Hospitality*, 124–25.

70. Morgan, "Remember to Show Hospitality," 536.

71. Hawkins, *Sharing the Search*, 51.

72. Richard, *Living the Hospitality*, 41.

73. Ibid., 43.

74. Thomas E. Reynolds, "Welcoming Without Reserve: A Case in Christian Hospitality," *Theology Today* 63:2 (2006): 200.

75. Koenig, *New Testament Hospitality*, 126.

76. Jirair S. Tashjian, "Whatever Happened to Friendship and Hospitality in the Parables of Jesus?" (paper presented at the 41st Annual Meeting of the Wesleyan Theological Society, Kansas City, MO, March 2006).

77. Koenig, *New Testament Hospitality*, 134.

78. Oden, *You Welcomed Me*, 14.

79. Newman, *Untamed Hospitality*, 174.

80. Pohl, *Making Room*, 9.

81. I followed a variation of "Spiritual Exercise 1" under "Slowing" as described by Adele Ahlberg Calhoun, *Spiritual Disciplines Handbook: Practices That Transform Us* (Downers Grove, IL: InterVarsity, 2005), 80.

82. Eugene Peterson, *Eat This Book: A Conversation in the Art of Spiritual Reading* (Grand Rapids: Eerdmans, 2006), 90–91.

CHAPTER 9

A Gospel Large Enough to Unite a Diverse People

DAN BOUCHELLE[1]

For over a century, the Central Church of Christ in Amarillo, Texas, has been one of the largest and most prestigious churches of its fellowship in the Texas Panhandle. Central was a church of over a thousand in weekly attendance before the final quarter of the twentieth century began. At its height, in the mid-eighties, Central averaged almost two thousand people in worship attendance when churches of that size were rare in any fellowship. Large staffs, budgets, and programs were the norm.

In its heyday, Central invested significantly in prime radio spots that promoted its slogan, "The Exciting Central Church of Christ." It had a program for every need and a minister for every subgroup. In these years, Central grew primarily by absorbing Church of Christ members who moved into Amarillo from the small towns in the Texas Panhandle and by recruiting members from other churches in town to its superior programs and warm grace orientation at a time when other churches were mired in a contentious legalism.

Things began to change in the late 1980s as the religious and social landscape in Amarillo shifted. Excessive building indebtedness and an economic downturn pushed Central into a financial crisis in the late '80s, as people moved out of Amarillo in large numbers. In addition, there were more grace-oriented Churches of Christ not asking for money so often. New seeker-churches that catered to market tastes of those with a Church of Christ background better than Central arose in the developing area of town. Central began to lose members to booming non-denominational mega-churches. As sectarianism receded among Churches of Christ, Central found itself in a larger "market" of churches where it could not dominate. As new growth and money moved away from downtown, many churches relocated, taking some of Central's members with them.

After a long period of slow decline, the elders at Central decided it was time for a change in direction and in the pulpit. However, the pulpit transition went badly, and their preacher of twenty-five years joined a splinter group that formed a new church in southwest Amarillo and took hundreds of members. The glory of the past was gone, and no one seemed to know what direction to take.

At this time, the leaders of Central began to take a serious look at the location of their property, history, and context as a means of seeking a new vision. Central's facilities are located in the historic downtown area. The property is surrounded by need on all sides. Amarillo is an increasingly diverse city. Racial, cultural, and economic diversity had expanded and churches catered to increasingly homogeneous niche markets. Most of the large and growing churches targeted the privileged classes in southwest Amarillo. Against this trend, the leaders at Central felt called to remain downtown to minister to the poor who lived near downtown and the wealthy professionals who worked downtown.

During the days of the "Exciting Central Church of Christ," Central developed a reputation as a "country-club" church for the privileged. For at least half a century, the members of Central stepped over their opulent building's neighborhood to worship. The people who lived downtown were not disposed to come to Central for anything—even a handout. Central was off-putting to people of humble means.

Central's leadership was comprised of professionals comfortable with complex programs. They were forward thinking and open to new ideas. However, a quick-fix, programmatic approach would not work with Central's new vision because the challenges it created were rooted too deeply in the beliefs and habits of the church for surface programs to be effective. If Central was going to see the new vision become a reality, it had to rethink gospel and church.

The core concept of Central's vision was the belief that "God has put us in a position to demonstrate the unifying power of the gospel." This new vision called for the church to be God's agent of reconciliation in four distinct ways:

1. Our mission is to work toward reconciling God and humanity in Christ.
2. Our mission extends to helping families live reconciled lives of Christlike love.
3. Our mission also extends toward reconciling the various factions of the body of Christ.

4. Our final mission is to reconcile the various racial, cultural, and socio-economic factions of humanity in Christ.

Central recognized God put them in a position to minister to the neediest people in Amarillo. Central's vision was based on the model of Jesus, who was known for going to the people who were in most need and least able to help themselves.

The Communal Eschatological Aspect of the Gospel

In order for Central to cross social barriers, it needed a conceptual foundation that could not only support such diversity but drive it. That foundation was readily available in theological vision of Scripture.

The Bible begins with a description of God creating a world designed to function in perfect harmony with itself and with God. Genesis shows how carefully God planned for every part of creation to work together. Then God created human beings in God's own image, in part at least to enjoy fellowship with the Divine. Prior to their rebellion, Adam and Eve lived in perfect harmony with God and each other. The text gives no indication of tension, conflict, or any separation in God's newly created world.

The unity of creation began to break down when humanity decided they could not trust their creator. Eve acted alone in an effort to become "like God, knowing good and evil" (Gen. 3:5 RSV). As she attempted to elevate herself, she rejected her rightful God. While Adam joined his wife in rebellion, their common transgression did not unite them but set them against each other. Sin entered the world as a violation of trust between God and humanity. Immediately, humans turned on each other. Adam blamed Eve, and they hid their nakedness from each other and hid from God also. Everyone was alone.

With the entry of sin, the intended harmony of God's world was destroyed. The stratification of humanity into classes was part of the curse God placed upon a fallen world. God told Eve her desire would be for her husband, but he would rule over her. Human beings would now engage in a perpetual power struggle in place of the peace God designed. Subjugation and separation were the new order. Harmony and community became difficult, as is demonstrated in the subsequent stories. The first two men born on the earth had a deadly conflict. Soon, all humanity was in conflict and God grieved that he made humanity. Even the extreme judgment of the flood could not purge the earth of the disruptive power of humanity's rebellion. As a result, God separated humanity into competing groups by confusing their language at Babel to limit the evil they could do if they worked together in their fallen state. This separation into competing tribes and nations was a tragic necessity in a world where humans would be gods. The dream of a unified humanity seemed lost.

God responded to this hopeless world by calling Abraham for a special mission. Abraham and his descendants were set apart as God's instrument to bless all nations. God's action through Israel was not merely for the benefit of one nation, but to use a nation, descended from Abraham, as priests to serve all nations. Yet, God did not form them into a nation until after they had become slaves in Egypt, where they suffered the full weight of poverty, oppression, and segregation. There, God appeared, reaffirmed the calling and covenant to Israel, and gave Israel the specific purpose of revealing God's nature and power to all nations.

In the books of Moses, God routinely instructed Israel to be graciously inclusive within an exclusive loyalty to God. They were the priestly nation ministering to all others in God's name. They were commanded to take in aliens and strangers and demonstrate compassion to the weak and poor because they were once aliens and slaves in Egypt and God rescued them. The Psalms routinely declare that the Lord reigns over all the earth, which is a clear universal claim. God demonstrated his universal concern through oracles to many nations in the prophets. These same prophets collectively described a future of peace when all nations would stream to Jerusalem to worship the Lord, and the Lord would be recognized as King of all the earth. The prophets anticipated a day when God would act decisively to unite creation again under God's reign in a world of peace and sufficiency for all. For the prophets, God would make Israel the center of the world, where all nations would come to worship God together in a unified voice.

When Jesus appeared in the New Testament Gospels, he claimed to be the long-anticipated fulfillment of these promises and dreams. Jesus' message was inherently communal and global. He preached the "good news of the kingdom of God" and invited all people to enter it regardless of their social or religious standing. Luke in particular indicates his message was "good news to the poor." Human societies may stratify themselves into social classes with differing levels of honor and access to power and resources, but the kingdom of God is not stratified, and social-class distinctions are to be ignored or inverted. Christians serve a Lord who came as a servant to all and taught the greatest should be the least.

After his resurrection, Jesus sent his followers to make disciples of all nations. In Acts, they went from Jerusalem to the international capital of the Gentile world, gathering up people of all nationalities as they proceeded to Rome. God was ending the separation of human beings into competing nations—each speaking a distinct language. On the day of Pentecost, as the kingdom was preached in every language represented, Jesus was hailed as the universal Lord and Christ.

While Paul did not typically use the distinctly Jewish language of the "kingdom of God" in his Gentile mission, he did describe the activity of God in universal language. For Paul, the gospel was God's effort to reconcile all things through Christ. In Christ's death and resurrection, God not only bridged the gap with rebellious humanity, but broke down the barriers between all groupings of humanity. Paul refers to the church as a new creation in the line of Jesus—the second Adam. In the new creation, there are no racial, socio-economic, or gender divisions but all are one in Christ. God's goal for the gospel is for all humanity to join in one voice in unified praise of their one God. In Revelation, people from every nation, race, tribe, and language come together to worship God in the New Jerusalem. Jesus is King of kings and Lord of lords, and all the nations serve him in unison.

The gospel is an inherently relational message rooted in the story of God's saving activity. From creation to the climactic events of Jesus' life, death, resurrection, and beyond the present day into the future, the God of Scripture works to restore God's broken creation. The gospel, or good news, is connected to the entire story of creation, rebellion, and restoration of God's world through Christ. It is a story as big as creation itself and as small as any creature that inhabits God's world. The good news is that in Christ God has begun to reconcile all things in the universe and restore the world that rejected the Holy and fell into the current broken state of conflict, competition, and exploitation.

There is no way to reduce this story to an individualistic message of making Jesus our "personal Lord and Savior" without severe distortion. Regrettably, American churches have privatized the gospel in order to cater to a narcissistic culture of the supreme individual. As a result, the church has almost forgotten the gospel is about the reign of God over the people of God rather than a way to receive a private salvation in heaven when this life is over. White, middle class, individualistic, American churches tend to miss many social implications of the gospel, which challenge the alienating structures of this age. As a result, evangelistic campaigns among the poor have rarely been successful because the message has focused on saving individuals for a remote "heaven" without developing an understanding of how God is actively working to advance God's kingdom in the present world. A more communal understanding of the gospel is essential for churches to cross social barriers.

The foundation for the good news of the kingdom of God is the relational, or triune, nature of God. God has always lived in a community, and through God's saving activity in Christ, God forms a new community called church. Since God is fundamentally relational, the church must also be relational. The gospel does not exist to serve the purposes of the church; rather the church is God's instrument and witness of the gospel reconciliation. Life in Christ is not merely a matter of individual experience or personal legal standing. Rather, life in Christ means becoming part of Christ's body and mission.

The gospel is rooted in and driven by an eschatological view of God's mission for the church. For us to see churches break racial and social-class barriers, we will have to build more on the message of Jesus. Jesus proclaimed, "The time has come, . . . The kingdom of God is near. Repent and believe the good news" (Mark 1:14–15 NIV 1984). The kingdom of God is a theme that has virtually disappeared from evangelistic preaching and has been replaced with variations on a "plan of salvation."

Rather than presenting the gospel as a message about individual salvation, we need to present the gospel as an announcement of God's kingdom breaking into our disordered world. The church is not a loose association of individuals with a personal salvation and little rationale for meaningful community. Rather, the church is the agent of God's emerging kingdom that witnesses to God's ongoing activity by word, deed, or sign. The church becomes the living demonstration of what the gospel is designed to produce. While the church speaks prophetically to the world about issues of righteousness and justice, the purpose of the church is not to transform this world as much as to be an alternative future world in the midst of a world passing away.

The assembling of diverse people from all the earth into a single people of God is an essential eschatological sign that the kingdom of God has broken into our world. The nature of the church to transcend social barriers is not an end in itself, but a means to a larger end—testifying to the reality of the kingdom of God among us. Jesus' concept of the kingdom lays waste to all exclusive groupings of humanity.

Proclaiming the gospel cannot be reduced to offering acquittal from individual guilt, but must also include announcing and extending the reign of God over the principalities and powers of this corrupt world. This gospel deconstructs the status symbols of our world, which serve the interests of the powerful. Then the gospel builds a new community in midst of this same world. Sin is not just a matter of individual guilt needing expiation. It is a collective force, which destroys all relationships and breaks down God's intended harmony for all creation. It not only breaks the relationship between an individual person and God, but breaks all the relationships humans have with each other, and breaks the relationship humans have with their environment. Sin is woven into the entire fabric of human life.

The gospel sets people free from a distorted social order and announces the strongholds of power in this world have been broken through the death and resurrection of Christ. By the power of God's Spirit, the church is called to live out transformed social relationships that cross the barriers characteristic of this world. This common life is a sign of God's judgment on these barriers and God's acceptance of all classes of people. God intends for the church to demonstrate the ability to unite the full range of humanity. "Separate but equal" approaches to human diversity in the church may be more successful for numerical church growth, but they fall far short of the vision of the church held in Scripture. A healthy understanding of the gospel cannot stand without this eschatological foundation so evident in Jesus' preaching. The gospel is not just about being prepared to go to heaven if Jesus comes today or when we die. The gospel is about living out the future as God's people today.

The gospel is not just a message of forgiveness for individual guilt, but an invitation to become part of the people of God or kingdom of God. Evangelism necessitates explaining what God is doing in history and helping people become partners in his saving activity. Evangelism is the good news that through Christ, God is offering a covenant relationship to all, even and most particularly, to the poor and marginalized. This is why Jesus intentionally began his ministry at the periphery of society among the poor, the oppressed, the sinners, and the outcasts. He began at the outside, in Galilee, and moved toward the center of power in Jerusalem, where he was rejected and killed by the powerful insiders. Jesus' strategy demonstrated the radical inclusiveness of the reign of God. In his death on the cross, Jesus experienced the rejection of the powerful and the suffering of humanity as God's judgment on the fallen order of the old world. This message is indeed good news for the poor.

The Gospel as Multifaceted Event

If we are going to change the nature of evangelism, we must think deeply about the gospel. One of the reasons the gospel resists reduction to a simplistic, canned message is that it is fundamentally an event, or set of related events, rather than a set of propositional truths. Something happened. God's son came in human form, lived among us, and was rejected by his own people, condemned to death by a Roman governor, crucified, buried, and raised from the dead.

While the word "gospel" unifies the New Testament, it does so through a wide variety of images. The gospel is a multifaceted event that cannot be captured by any one image or metaphor. The New Testament does not attempt to do so. Each of the four Gospels tells the same story. They each spend a disproportionate time on the events of the final week of Jesus' life, but none offers a theory of atonement.

Paul says his message is "Christ and him crucified" (1 Cor. 2:2). He summarizes the gospel in 1 Corinthians 15:3–5: "Christ died for our sins according to the Scriptures, that he was buried, that he was raised on the third day according to the Scriptures, and that he appeared" (NIV). Yet, nowhere does Paul give a single explanation of the atonement. He offers no theories about how the atonement works. He offers only a series of images or metaphors: reconciliation, justification, propitiation, and redemption.

Throughout the New Testament, a variety of images and metaphors reveals some aspect of the meaning of salvation, but there is no single explanation of the meaning. The events surrounding the cross defy simple codification because the gospel is not a set of abstract concepts to be affirmed intellectually or confessed verbally. Rather, the gospel is an event. It is news. Something happened. God has acted to save the world. The gospel declares that a new reality now exists and invites people to live within the new reality. The gospel expresses itself primarily in story, dialogue, or drama rather than abstract propositions.

Because the gospel is an event, news, a story, or drama rather than a set of propositions, the gospel can be understood in a myriad of ways. Just as physical objects appear different from various angles, so events look different depending on one's location or experience. All understandings of the gospel are, at least in part, dependent on the hearer's context. What all images of the gospel have in common—what binds them together—is that they all are rooted in the same story. God has acted in the life, death, and resurrection of Jesus of Nazareth to save humanity and create a new state of affairs. This new reality inspires hope and demands a response.

However, the flexibility of the gospel does not permit it to take on just any meaning. The gospel has a prevailing common logic rooted in the narrative of the cross and resurrection of Jesus. In the words of Mark Love, "the gospel not only says something; it wants to behave in a certain way."[2] The gospel is primarily a story to be lived out in community. As the church lives out the gospel story in appropriate ways in various cultures and contexts, it communicates and validates the gospel.

No culture-free expression of the gospel exists. The gospel must be incarnated within a particular human situation, and it will of necessity take on certain linguistic and cultural features for its environment. Because the gospel must be translated in part into the receiver's language and culture, the church always reduces the gospel somewhat in its efforts to tell the story.[3] However, the reduction can be overcome in part by presenting multiple metaphors of the gospel in the process of evangelism.

The multidimensional nature of the gospel stands in sharp contrast to the rigid, familiar presentations of the "plan of salvation" in evangelical churches. Uniform, propositional messages, designed to yield individual decisions for Christ, do not take advantage of the richness of the gospel. These static formulaic presentations, focused exclusively on the removal of individual guilt by accepting a "personal Lord and Savior," neglect the story of God's kingdom and ignore the story of the hearers. They assume everyone will hear the good news the same way. Yet if a person does not already have a sense of condemnation for personal guilt, the message of forgiveness of sin may not sound like good news. It may sound like a punch in the face.

Because of a narrow understanding of the gospel, many evangelistic approaches start with bad news: "you are a guilty, condemned sinner." While this message may be true, it is not good news. In a postmodern world where a large percentage of the population does not believe in moral absolutes, we are not choosing a wise strategy if we continue to present the gospel in this way only. Most believers will not practice evangelism if it must start by condemning their friends and neighbors rather than offering them hope.

Perhaps the greatest barrier to overcome in reawakening the church to a deeper understanding of the gospel is the dominance of penal substitution atonement theory. For a vast percentage of Christians, this is not one theory or metaphor of salvation among many. It is the whole enchilada.

The typical setting for this metaphor is an American courtroom. God is the judge. Each person appears alone as defendant. We are each guilty of individual sins and must give a justification to the judge. Satan is the prosecuting attorney who reviews the damning evidence of our guilt and demands we be sentenced to hell as the only just course. Then Jesus, acting as our defense attorney, in a brilliant, if confusing, legal maneuver, convinces the judge to allow him to take the guilty party's place. Jesus is then condemned and dies on the cross to pay the individual debt to justice, and the sinner goes free, acquitted though actually guilty in practice.

The solution for sin in this metaphor is purely legal. While it is rooted in the New Testament concept of justification and while there are legal overtones to that metaphor in Scripture, this way of explaining salvation has massive weaknesses that need supplementing with other metaphors. It provides little motivation for righteous living beyond the ritual acceptance of forgiveness. It in no way addresses larger social-ethical issues. It is open to gross misunderstandings such as "Jesus suffered so I will not have to." It calls no one to take up a cross and follow Jesus.

This suffering-free view of salvation eliminates the aspect of the cross that speaks most profoundly to people whose life experience involves suffering, poverty, and oppression. The penal substitution theory provides little rationale for the existence of the church. Why do we need it other than as an aid to our personal spiritual life? The penal substitution model provides no rationale for relationships that cross social barriers. This shrunken gospel has no rationale for any community—much less a community that breaks down the social barriers of our world. It is preoccupied with the afterlife status of the individual hearer rather than the larger story of what God is doing.

If our only understanding of salvation is penal substitution, white, middle-class believers may feel the need to share the good news with a homeless man or black woman so that they can have their sins forgiven. However, once the white, middle-class believers have convinced poor or minority people to receive Jesus through the sinner's prayer or accepting baptism, they have little reason for an ongoing relationship.

Given the American preoccupation with the individual and with assigning blame, penal substitution can still be one effective way to explain the gospel in our culture. The New Testament does talk about salvation as justification. Instead of abandoning substitutionary language, we need to add other salvation images from Scripture. Substitution is too prevalent in the Bible—Old and New Testament—to ignore. However, this one picture of the gospel is woefully inadequate to produce churches that live out the gospel in meaningful ways. We will not likely see multi-social-class churches or even significant evangelism of the poor, suffering, and oppressed in America unless we learn more complete ways of telling the good news.

Project Intervention

David Watson suggests that there are four key questions we must ask as we form our presentation of the gospel:

1. What is the gospel?
2. What is our context?
3. What makes the gospel good news in this context?
4. How does this contextual response to the gospel further illumine its good news?[4]

The first two questions have been answered above. In order to answer the remaining questions, I developed a series of nine brief narratives rich with images and metaphors of salvation. Each narrative draws on a different picture of God's saving work in Christ. They are rooted in the language and narratives of the New Testament, but they are written in simple, contemporary English for easy understanding. Each has a strong communal dimension. Each takes about three minutes to present orally. They take about twenty-four minutes to present in all. The nine narratives are:

1. The End-Time Banquet (theme: table fellowship with outsiders)
2. Legion (theme: Jesus' power over the evil forces that alienate the lost)
3. Slaves Set Free (theme: redemption/ransom)
4. Coming Home (theme: reconciliation/forgiveness)
5. Sacrifice (theme: propitiation/expiation)
6. The Victorious Christ (theme: Christ's defeat of principalities and powers)
7. The New Creation (theme: new creation)
8. Cleansing/Washing (theme: purification/sanctification)
9. New Birth (theme: regeneration)[5]

I presented these narratives to thirteen people from Central's various ministries to the poor. Seven of the interviewees were homeless at the time of the interview, and the remaining six had some type of personal shelter though they had been homeless on occasion. None of the people I interviewed had been baptized though one was planning to soon and two were baptized shortly after the interview. I subsequently presented the same narratives to a focus group at the Salvation Army to validate the information gathered from individual interviews.

After reading the stories, I asked the interviewees to respond to two questions: Which of these stories sound like good news to you? Why?

Interview Responses

As expected, the responses to the interviews were greatly varied. Some stories had appeal to many people, and some had little or none. However, I was surprised that most of the stories received about the same amount of support and no one story stood out significantly. As expected, people's personal experiences were the dominant factor in determining why they heard a certain story as good news. Yet I was occasionally surprised at how the interviewees made the connections between the images and narratives and their own lives. I won't give raw numbers in this abbreviated account, but I will share some overall reactions and themes that emerged.

As I listened to the responses of the interviewees, I began to realize that each story had unique qualities that made it appear to be good news to some people. Most of the time, the appeal of the image or story was obvious and expected. At other times it was surprising what characteristics made a story sound like good news to an individual. It is also possible that the stories with the greatest appeal were simply better stories. It may not have been the image itself that appealed to someone in each instance; rather, the quality of the artistic rendering of an image likely impacted the responses.

"Cleansing/Washing" was the story heard as good news most often. Some were attracted to the image of physical cleanliness. Several homeless individuals mentioned liking the image because it is difficult to stay clean when you have no home in which to wash your body or clothes. One man talked of washing in pools, rivers, lakes, or anywhere he found water. The reason interviewees cited most often for liking the "Cleansing/Washing" story was the image of Jesus jumping into the pool of sewage with the people. They liked the idea that Jesus is willing to condescend to be with people caught in filth. This radical action by Jesus demonstrates he will accept people where they are even if their lives are unappealing.

"Coming Home" also resonated with interviewees for a variety of reasons. The two prevailing reasons cited were the images of a reconciled family and the theme of forgiveness. Many interviewees had experienced alienation from their family and longed for a seemingly impossible reunion.

"New Birth" also sounded like a word of hope because it tells the story of someone who is able to start life over. This story speaks to many people who feel a sense of responsibility for the difficulty of their lives. The majority of people who said "New Birth" was good news associated it with a conversion experience in their own lives.

"New Creation" was the story with the widest variety of reasons for its appeal. Some liked the image of a new world in which bad things do not happen to people and there is peace. Others were drawn to the lush pastoral images of the new world or the idea of being a new creature.

For the "End-Time Banquet" metaphor, the freedom from judgment and criticism was appealing. Poor people are often rejected by the rest of society, which makes them feel trapped in hopelessness.

The appeal of the "Victorious Christ" is primarily rooted in its image of Jesus defeating the devil. This idea inspires hope and a sense of peace.

I was surprised regarding the reasons "Slaves Set Free" appealed to people. One woman was attracted to God adopting slaves because she had experienced adoption in her family. Another said she felt her mother had sold her into slavery. Her mother had allowed her brother to sexually molest her as a child in exchange for his financial support to the family. Another woman was attracted to Jesus' motive for saving slaves: he wanted to make the slaves his family. Others saw in this story a hope for release from generational curses. Several liked the story because it reminded them of when they were released from incarceration.

"Legion" had limited appeal to people in my study and "Sacrifice" did not sound like good news to anyone interviewed. In fact, one woman expressed a strong dislike for this image because it involved the killing of animals. She brought her dog to the interview and was horrified at the image of animal sacrifice.

In each case, each story had almost as many reasons for appealing to people as there were people who heard it as good news. The stories most closely tied to actual scriptural texts, "Legion" and "Sacrifice," also appeared least appealing to the poor in the study. The stories that translated images into more contemporary contexts, such as "Cleansing/Washing," had greater appeal.

Themes

Personal Experience

The most important theme surfaced by the interviews was the influence of personal experience. All those interviewed explained their choices primarily in terms of their own life story, not their social class. Beyond this, it often appeared unnamed personal experience was behind particular selections. This was the most constant theme of the interviews. It occurred in every case. Because human experience is greatly varied, the images of salvation that appear as good news also vary. One man said it well, "They are all good news, really," he said, "it's just those four jumped out at me because they talked about my experience."

Individualistic Interpretation

Another theme, less pronounced, was the tendency to interpret communal stories from an individualistic point of view. For example one man liked the story of "New Creation" but seemed to miss the idea of a renewed world. Rather he liked the idea of being a new individual creature. This tendency should not be surprising in light of the individualistic bias of our culture. It could also be a function of the isolation of the poor I interviewed. All those who demonstrated this tendency were men who lived alone and were often homeless. Their lives were extremely individualistic. They had virtually no community. The individualistic impulse implies we cannot trust the communal aspect of images and narratives to work on their own as we present the gospel. For the relational aspect of images to register with some people, we must point it out overtly.

Nonrational Appeal of Images

While most people could explain the reasons they were attracted to a certain image, some could not. I also noticed a tendency to avoid obvious connections between certain stories and the lives of the people who said they found them to be good news. One woman had a husband in his last year of a twenty-year prison sentence. They were still married and she eagerly looked forward to his imminent release. She identified "Slaves Set Free" as good news but did not verbalize any connection with her incarcerated husband.

Our rational legacy in western culture probably causes us to overlook the power of images to function apart from rational explanation. We cannot control how images will connect to the lives of people who hear our teaching—regardless of how well those images are set within stories or rational discourses. This is the power of images and metaphors and explains much of the beauty and power of God's revelation and God's divine action in a diversity of images.

Hunger for Relationships and Acceptance

Virtually all the people I interviewed live in isolated conditions. What relationships they have are generally short-term and surface level. They are mostly disconnected from their family, if they have any family at all. Repeatedly, the people I interviewed demonstrated a longing for connection to other people that stood in sharp contrast with the isolation of their day-to-day existence. They responded to different communal images, but it was typically the communal dimension of the images that made the stories appealing. This communal appeal is ironic in light of the interviewees' tendency, mentioned above, to interpret communal images individualistically. The interviewees seem to hunger for community but do not think communally or have the life skills to live in healthy relationships within a community.

Conclusions

The data from my research lead me to several conclusions. The first and most prominent is that evangelism of the poor, like all evangelism, needs to start with listening rather than speaking. The poor are not all alike. They are incredibly diverse. People find themselves in a state of poverty for a wide variety of reasons. Some were born in generational poverty and have never known anything else. Some are poor because of bad choices. Some have lived in the middle class most of their lives, but are now in poverty because of tragic circumstances beyond their control. They come from every people group in our globalized world. Few generalizations about the poor are accurate.

The diversity among the poor means there is no one image or metaphor of salvation that will sound like good news to all, or even most, of them. In order to know which images of salvation will sound like good news to any individual, we will do well to hear the story of the person we are trying to reach. To learn that story requires both the formation of a significant relationship between the person who wishes to communicate the good news of Jesus and the person who may hear that good news. Presenters of good news must first earn the trust of those with whom they wish to share good news. Having gained trust, the presenter of good news needs to listen to the story of the other person in sufficient depth to have some idea how the hearer has experienced the brokenness of the world. In this case, I knew all of the people I was interviewing because I was with them on a regular basis. Personal relationships put the evangelist in a better position to know which images of salvation might speak a word of good news to a particular person.

Too often, gospel presentations roll off an assembly line like a one-size-fits-all garment. Yet the New Testament does not present a one-size-fits-all message. It presents a series of image clusters of salvation, which speak to the full range of human need and hurt. We cannot speak good news until we know how people have experienced the bad news. We must begin with a relationship that involves listening.

Second, the gospel must retain its incarnational nature. Jesus came as a particular human at a particular time and place. He interacted with real people in real situations. He touched them, ate with them, and attended their weddings and banquets. He spoke words of hope to the daily hurts and needs of the people around him in a particular language. He saved the world, not through a great idea or simple concept, but through action—through events that have unending significance. The saving actions of Jesus speak a word of hope to every human situation. Yet, words must be combined with action on behalf of people in need by those who have embraced the way of Jesus.

The New Testament writers drew points of connection between the events of the gospel and the situations of the readers of their documents. No place in the New Testament gives a definitive summary of the gospel. Modern rational attempts to summarize the gospel into a single word weaken the gospel's ability to function as genuine good news to many people. No one image of salvation will connect with every person.

It was a foolish move on the part of the church to allow the single image of justification, interpreted through penal substitutionary atonement theory, to eclipse the other images of salvation. None of the images in my study, even the powerful images of cleansing and washing, were good news to every person in the study. Most images connected with half of the people or less. We should take note of the full diversity of ways the New Testament presents good news and take full advantage of this richness in our proclamation of the good news.

Third, as valuable as it is to know the story of an individual candidate for evangelism, we cannot always predict which images or metaphors any individual will hear as good news. While there is often a connection between the story of an individual and the images of salvation that sound like good news to him or her, sometimes the connection is not obvious or even understood by the individual. Thus, even after listening to a person's story, evangelistic approaches need to present a variety of images of the saving work of God. We should not overestimate our ability to forecast how another person will hear good news.

It is no accident that most of the Bible is narrative and little of the Bible is in the form of analytical discourse. None of the Bible is removed from actual life situations. It is all set within a larger narrative framework. While we will at times need to do some teaching in the form of analytical discourse, the majority of our efforts to communicate the gospel should be deeply rooted in the images and narratives of the gospel, which transcend the limits of rational discourse. These narratives can, and should, be rooted in the biblical story, but they need to be accessible to people who live in a contemporary society. Images such as sacrificial animals and demonic exorcism will likely have a limited appeal in a contemporary western setting, regardless of how biblical they may be. That will not be true in other parts of our world or with certain recent immigrants. The value of such images will likely remain hidden for most people in the West until they are trained in the faith and biblical backgrounds.

Fourth, I learned to stress the communal nature of the images of salvation. Our culture is so biased toward individualistic thinking that people easily miss the communal dimensions of any salvation image. Even though the people in the study demonstrated a strong desire for relationships and community, they still had a tendency to interpret the salvation narratives individualistically. If our gospel presentations are to provide a rationale for meaningful community across social barriers, we must make that relational aspect of the gospel images explicit. We will have to draw attention to it and reiterate it throughout our communication, especially among the poor, who often live in or near physical and emotional isolation.

We cannot merely talk about a communal message; we must demonstrate it in the life and ministry of the church. The poor must see the church acting as community and not merely talking about the importance of community. The church must overcome the bias of the poor that they are unwanted and unclean in the eyes of the church. When they feel loved and welcome, the communal nature of the gospel presentations will be more understandable and, more importantly, will have greater validity.

Finally, it is not sufficient for any church to present a communal gospel to the poor alone. Even if the poor have a rationale for relationships that can cross social-class barriers, they will not become part of a community that does not welcome them with open arms. The greater burden will almost certainly be to develop a greater understanding of the communal dimensions of the gospel in the church itself.

Implications

First, churches that intend to cross social-class barriers need to develop an evangelism curriculum and train their members to listen to the stories of people we seek to convert. One way to do this might be to train them to interview people in a manner similar to this research project. Furthermore, we need to develop an evangelism curriculum flexible enough that it can adjust to fit different types of people with different types of stories. It needs to incorporate a wide variety of salvation images to support whichever primary image we present to any individual. This effort will involve developing people more than developing teaching materials. It will require our people to develop good listening skills, judgment, insight, and skills in sharing their faith. It will not be possible to do evangelism in this fashion by handing people a set of simplified lesson plans. The greatest challenge will be to develop good discernment and relational abilities in members rather than to pass on a large amount of information. The images and narratives necessary for this work are easily comprehended and easily shared.

Second, church leaders will have to spend effort in the pulpit, Bible classes, small groups, and other teaching opportunities reacquainting the church with the gospel in its many dimensions. The leadership will have to perform a systemic and comprehensive analysis of how the gospel is currently being taught through the ministries of the church. Then a strategic effort to expand the church's understanding of the gospel can follow. In particular, the church will need to learn to understand and live out the communal aspects of the gospel. The church is probably as prone to read the communal images of the gospel individualistically as were the people interviewed in this study. To overcome the individualistic perspective of our culture, we will have to teach the church to see the communal meaning of the gospel. We will also need to teach the church relational life skills to demonstrate the gospel.

Third, the preaching, education, and outreach ministries of the church will need to work in close cooperation. The church cannot do evangelism as described here if it functions as a set of isolated departments. Rather, the various ministry leaders must work together to form a teaching strategy that spans the width and breadth of the entire church. From the earliest childhood classes through the ministry to senior citizens, every group and subgroup in the church will need to be trained to hear and speak a multi-dimensional gospel.

If the theological reflections presented in this chapter are correct, the ability of the church to cross social-class barriers is critical to both the mission and validity of the gospel. The formation of diverse congregations is not an optional matter. Rather, the truth of the gospel is at stake in the nature of the fellowship of the community of faith. The Bible claims the cross of Christ has torn down the barriers between races, social classes, cultures, and genders. Is that true? Is it true in experience or only in theory? If the church does not demonstrate the truth of this claim, how can we preach it?

During the nine years I worked with the Central Church, we sought to implement the insights of this project in innumerable ways and we saw real change and felt real resistance. Some abandoned our congregation while simultaneously commending our vision as laudable but "not for us." We went from being a homogeneous congregation uncomfortable in its own neighborhood to being the only church in the city where millionaires and homeless people worshiped together and knew each other by name. The depth of those relationships was not often deep, but it was real. To this day, it is still possible for people to hide out in restricted enclaves of "their own kind," but that is not the norm and it is recognized to be incompatible with the values of the church. While the Central church did not break down all social barriers, it did become socio-economically diverse. I am proud of what God did among us as we came to understand the more communal nature of the gospel and expanded our faith vocabulary and practice.

---

1. Dan Bouchelle, "Presenting the Gospel to the Poor in a Multi-Social-Class Congregation" (DMin thesis, ACU, 2004).

2. Mark Love, "Preaching and Evangelism, Lecture 2: Living the Story in Community," lecture, Hazelip Biblical Preaching Seminar, Lipscomb University, Nashville, May 12–14, 2003, sound cassette.

3. Darrell Guder, *The Continuing Conversion of the Church* (Grand Rapids: Eerdmans, 2000), 98.

4. David L. Watson, "Christ All in All: The Recovery of the Gospel for Evangelism in the United States," in *The Church Between Gospel and Culture: The Emerging Mission in North America*, ed. George R. Hunsberger and Craig Van Gelder (Grand Rapids: Eerdmans, 1997), 188–97.

5. While I am not including the narratives here, I will gladly supply them to anyone who desires to see them. You can contact me at dan.bouchelle@mrnet.org.

CHAPTER 10

Ministering to Undocumented Immigrants

STEPHEN AUSTIN[1]

On the pedestal of the Statue of Liberty are these words: "Give me your tired, your poor . . . send these, the homeless, tempest-tossed to me . . . ." For much of its history, the United States has given immigrants a "golden door" to escape from hopeless lives and re-invent themselves, and the nation has largely benefited from their contributions. However, in the last several decades, the golden door has slammed shut for most immigrants wishing to come legally to the United States, resulting in millions of immigrants arriving or staying illegally, many of whom are Hispanic. The political climate of growing hostility toward undocumented immigrants and the debate about their perceived impact on the economy has created suspicion, fear, and resentment among many citizens, on local and national levels.[2]

In 1998, I came face-to-face with this issue when invited to serve as the bilingual minister at the Impact Houston Church of Christ in Houston, Texas. Houston was the fourth-largest city in the United States, with millions of Hispanics, including many undocumented ones. Impact was an inner-city congregation of around 450, about equal parts Hispanic, African American, and Anglo. Impact drew members from the first, third, fourth, fifth, and sixth wards of Houston. These communities reflected two of the community categories which Ray Bakke describes as a "slum."[3] Impact's intentional location in the heart of Houston placed it squarely in the middle of the usual cauldron of inner-city problems—drugs, prostitution, gangs, theft, and violence. In many areas, housing was horrible and overcrowding the norm. Inner-city schools often did not provide a high-quality learning experience, resulting in poor literacy and inadequate education. Poverty ran rampant, not only among the homeless, but also in thousands of homes.

I spent most of my time working with the Hispanic group and functioned as a bridge between Spanish and English groups of all kinds, translating in bilingual services, ministers' and elders' meetings, youth activities, and inter-church activities in Houston. About 80 percent of our Hispanic members first arrived at Impact through our benevolence ministry, and many were undocumented. I eventually talked to hundreds of undocumented families, both at Impact and in their homes, about their background, their successes, and their most pressing needs. I visited their children's schools, accompanied them to doctor's appointments and government offices, spoke to their landlords, and even translated for a few of them in court appearances.

While the lack of legal documents complicates many aspects of their daily lives, the most pressing daily need of the undocumented is work.[4] A job with an adequate salary is the main attraction for immigrants coming to the United States. They not only provide for their families here but often send money to needy family members back home. Work also grants the worker and his family the dignity and self-respect necessary for emotional stability and health, tending to produce better-adjusted families, safer and more stable neighborhoods, and less crime and violence. The typical undocumented family also needs help occasionally with food, clothing, and of course housing. Acquiring a proper house is nearly impossible without steady work. Landlords often abuse undocumented renters because they know the family does not want to risk detection by getting any kind of official help.

The U.S. government does guarantee emergency medical assistance to undocumented immigrants, as well as Medicaid to those children of undocumented immigrants born here.[5] However, these families must either tolerate or improvise treatment for non-emergency illnesses. The government also guarantees public education for children of undocumented immigrants through high school, though the Hispanic dropout rate is 41 percent.[6] Poor English, reading, computer, or technology-related skills hamper the adjustment and daily functioning of many undocumented people.

As might be expected, undocumented immigrants face many of the problems associated with poverty. In his book *La Vida*, Oscar Lewis coined the phrase "culture of poverty" to describe a lifestyle or mindset that leads to being trapped in a poverty cycle, which results in resisting opportunities to escape. He detected over seventy characteristics of this mindset that occurred on four levels—the larger society, the local community, the family, and the individual.[7]

In general, people living in a culture of poverty are dominated by a "present-time orientation," which results in little desire to defer gratification or plan for the future. Often attitudes of resignation and fatalism are strong. Moreover, people in poverty distrust most authorities, particularly the government and police, and are even cynical about structures or practices of religious institutions.[8] They do not join organizations such as labor unions or political parties, and make little use of banks, hospitals, department stores, museums, or art galleries. They tend to trust and rely on their family and close friends, though this trust is not always well placed. Families in a culture of poverty suffer from a high incidence of abandoning wives and children, and spousal or child abuse is a grim problem. Children face an early initiation into sex, whether through their own choice or molestation, and teenage pregnancies are common.[9] In spite of the matriarchal center of the family and frequent absence of a steady father figure, there is a widespread belief in male superiority.[10]

All families, regardless of social class or setting, experience emotional or relationship difficulties at some point. The mother and father can fight, separate, or divorce; a daughter can get pregnant out of wedlock; a son can rebel; and complications can arise at school. A poverty-ridden, unstable situation produces some of these problems and exacerbates all of them. Therefore, the family also needs access to various kinds of counseling services—marital, parental, AIDS, pregnancy, abortion, and others.

Finally, undocumented families in particular struggle with various emotional and spiritual issues related to separation from their families and life as strangers in a foreign country. They go through waves of culture shock and homesickness, as any travelers do. They try to learn the written and unwritten rules which govern every aspect of their lives. They grapple with the questions of where they belong, whether they should return to their home countries, and how best to take care of their families wherever they are. They worry about their children, especially those born in the United States, who are considered third-culture children, fully belonging neither to their parents' culture nor to American culture.[11] All of these needs collide to produce a complex, difficult, confusing life for undocumented immigrants.

How Can (Should) a Christian Respond?

The immigration issue, previously a faceless debate, came to life as I met hundreds of real people with real concerns. Their daily lives were often bitter struggles filled with prejudice, injustice, suspicion, uncertainty, poverty, and fear. I found that the vast majority were likeable, hard-working, gifted, good-humored people whom I admired. They were not trying to mistreat or steal from anyone. They just wanted to survive and give their children a chance to have a future. I felt a real empathy for them, since I desired the same for my family.

At the same time, I also understood the real concerns of people taken advantage of by the undocumented. It is unfair for immigrants to vandalize property and steal from families or towns located on the United States' southern border. It is unjust for emergency health care, births, and education to be subsidized by tax payers who have no say over the millions of families and children who benefit from these services, often for free. It is frightening to feel invaded by a small minority who commit crimes of various kinds. It is frustrating to have to pay for imprisoning or deporting them.

How should I respond to this tension? I wanted to show these undocumented families Christ's compassion and mercy—and yet at the same time I was concerned that in helping them, I would act inappropriately or even break the law. I began to investigate how the church could respond biblically, legally, and wisely to this unavoidable issue.

"Love the Alien as Yourself, for You Were Aliens . . ."

Old Testament authors use several different words to describe foreigners. The word I will focus on is the Hebrew word *ger*, which translates as 'sojourner' or 'alien.' It refers to people of foreign origin who make their home in Israel. Although not of Hebrew descent, they are permanent members of the Hebrew community and demonstrate loyalty to Israel.[12] The Lord continually reminded the Israelites of their alien status in other countries, and of the spiritual reality that God owns everything, including the land and the people.[13] Key figures in Israel's history at one time or another were considered aliens, such as Abraham, Moses, Ruth, and Rahab. In these cases, the alien identity was eventually overshadowed by the importance of becoming part of the people of God. Numbers 15:15 summarizes the overall state of God's heart toward the alien, "The community is to have the same rules for you and for the alien living among you; this is a lasting ordinance for the generations to come. You and the alien shall be the same before the Lord (NIV)."

God provided for the material needs of the alien. The Israelites were to leave the gleanings of their fields for the aliens to gather, and part of the tithes the Israelites gave were to go to the alien, the fatherless, and the widow.[14] The alien could participate in Israelite celebrations such as Passover and the Day of Atonement.[15] The alien was privileged to hear the same reading of the law as the Israelites.[16] In case of accidental murder, the alien could run to the cities of refuge.[17] The employer was not to take advantage of the alien in any way. Judges were to mete out justice impartially to the native-born and alien alike.[18] In summary, the law tended to include aliens, treating them with kindness, rather than harshly excluding them. God made laws against alien customs, not the alien.[19]

This attitude sets the stage for New Testament teachings on the relationship between Jew and Gentile, and between the people of God (the church) and the people of the world. Regardless of national origin, the people of God share a common status as aliens and strangers on earth. Their primary citizenship is in the kingdom of God.[20] The borders God sees are not those located on a changing earthly map, but rather those separating the kingdom of light from the kingdom of darkness, those separating believers in Jesus from unbelievers. The ultimate identity of the church is tied to God, not to a place. Jesus declared that he would preach the good news to the poor and release the oppressed.[21] The top priority of the church, therefore, should be to proclaim the gospel to the marginalized. Jesus sharply rebuked and condemned to hell those who did not invite the stranger in.[22] Moreover, Jesus says in John 20:21, "As the Father has sent me, I am sending you" (NIV). In the same way, the church must incarnate and personify God's love and concern for all people.[23] When the church comes to the aid of the poor, the undocumented, or the helpless, God is using people to assist in God's restoration of the creation. Although a variety of problems inundate the undocumented immigrant, God provides plentiful, assorted resources to meet those needs.[24] However, the church must responsibly administer the gifts it possesses. As Floyd McClung points out, the church's involvement must include a commitment to rebuilding social, familial, educational, medical, and economic systems.[25]

Theology and Practice Today

Does the situation of undocumented immigrants today exactly parallel that of the alien or sojourner in the Bible? In the Old Testament, no law existed declaring a person to be illegal or legal, whereas the United States has specific laws. Even if undocumented people obeyed this country's law in daily living, their presence would still be illegal according to immigration law.

In the later stages of this project, when several focus groups reviewed how biblical teaching impacts action, one man who is a documented Hispanic cited the story of Joseph going to Egypt. When Jacob and all the family arrived, the Pharaoh received them as honored guests and gave them the best of the land. Later, a new Pharaoh forgot who they were and what Joseph had done for Egypt and subjected them to oppressive slavery. This Hispanic leader drew a parallel between that story and the Hispanic peoples who had come to America long before many other groups, helped established the country, contributed immensely to the culture, and who now are not welcome.

The undocumented Hispanic focus group correctly stressed the importance of giving compassion and aid to undocumented families, citing Matthew 25:31–46. The Kingwood elders and ministers focus group accurately highlighted the need to obey the law, citing Romans 13:1–7. Both groups focused on what one might expect; both groups were right; both benefited from honestly examining the viewpoint and experiences of the other.

Principles of Empowerment

Though many organizations provide help to needy people, the way in which they do so can be damaging to the recipients. Our goal at Impact was not just to give away aid of various kinds, but to empower the recipients to take charge of their lives. Following this line, David Ellwood suggests what he calls four value tenets of the American people: individuals should have a valuable choice about what they will or will not do; work should be rewarded; families' unity and health should be rewarded; and all should be integrated into the community.[26] Amy Sherman adds that there must be a shift from commodity-based benevolence to mercy. "When relief is merely a band-aid that alleviates the symptoms of poverty but fails to address its root causes, then it is illegitimate." Sherman notes that commodity-based ministry allows one to hold the poor at arm's length, whereas relational, holistic ministry is much less clinical and sterile.[27]

In establishing a truly merciful and practical ministry, the most important step is for us to bring people into a relationship with God so that he may restore them first spiritually and then proceed to renew every aspect of their lives. In *Restorers of Hope*, Sherman speaks of a commitment to a distinctively Christian mercy ministry that emphasizes God's love in word (proclamation, evangelism, discipleship) and deed (meeting people's physical, social, and emotional needs).[28]

The second step is to invite people to share the responsibility in finding and implementing a solution to their problems. For example, in the New Focus ministry of Allendale, Michigan, if a needy mother calls asking for help with her electric bill, the receptionist tells her that the church has a group of people who would be willing to sit down and talk with her about some financial manage- ment principles and that she will receive a free bag of groceries just for coming. If the mother is interested enough to come, she receives the groceries and more information and is given a further choice as to whether she wants to continue in the program. Betsy Dekker, the director of New Focus, states that they believe eco- nomic problems are often God's way of applying pressure to families to transform their lives to conform to God's will. Thus, if New Focus fails to consider God's purpose in applying that pressure and eliminates it by prematurely resolving the economic need, it could be working against God and against the best interests of the people.[29]

Marvin Olasky points out that in early American history, those who gave material aid without requiring even the smallest return were considered as much a threat to true compassion as those who turned their backs on their neighbors. He notes that many groups utilized work tests to determine whether people truly desired to help as much as be helped. Often, when faced with chopping wood in exchange for a meal, supposedly starving people found their appetites surpris- ingly diminished.[30]

Aiding these families also requires sacrificial giving of money, time, resources, and energy. Ronald Sider preaches the obligation of responsible churches and governments to live and give sacrificially. He mentions various forms of giving, from graduated tithes to communal living to voluntary poverty. He asserts that God is on the side of the poor and that Christians who would imitate God must seek ways to help others sacrificially.[31] Sherman discusses three groups of 'restorers' who choose to involve themselves more deeply in the lives of those whom they help. The 'settlers' move into the community they serve and put down roots in order to work side by side with their neighbors. The 'gardeners' are people or churches that do not live in the actual neighborhood they serve, but who view that neighborhood as extensions of their churches. They participate in the neighborhoods and feel ownership in them, work alongside community leaders, and introduce additional tools and resources from outside the targeted community. The 'shepherds' provide people with pasture—places of safe refuge, nurture, and instruction.[32]

The final step is to help the undocumented families affiliate—to build relationships and integrate the poor and needy into the community.[33] Robert Linthicum says that some churches choose to be the church in the community—the church is present, as a fortress, but does not attach itself to or identify with the community. Some opt to be the church to the community—the church assumes a savior mentality, deciding itself what the community needs and doing ministry to the community. Eventually burnout comes, and the programs die because they were never a project of the people. The most effective churches act with the community—the church assumes a partner mentality, allowing the people of the community to instruct it as it identifies with them.[34] John Kretzmann and John McKnight espouse the principle of asset-based community development—determining what capacities, skills, and assets are already present in the community before searching for any outside resources. This focuses internally by concentrating on the agenda-building and problem-solving capacities of local residents, associations, and institutions. It is relationship driven, building and rebuilding the relationships between and among local residents, associations, and institutions.[35]

Scattered Band-Aids or Holistic, Integrated Help?

At Impact, one of the first practical questions I faced had to do with which kinds of aid were legal and which were illegal. Romans 13:1–7 urges obedience to the government and the law, an exhortation we intended to honor. At the same time, we kept in mind Acts 5:29, realizing that in certain instances God's law and human law might conflict.

We quickly discovered that we could legally help the undocumented in these ways: teaching about Jesus; giving food and clothing; providing transportation within town; translation; individual, family, and marital counseling; and helping find free health care and free legal advice regarding visas or papers. We could also direct them to places where they could be temporarily employed, legally. We encouraged them to be legally self-employed (lawn care, making and selling tamales, etc.). We showed them how to get an ITIN (a tax-identification number) with the IRS and encouraged them to pay taxes on the money they earned.

After we began to work with families, this unsettling question struck: Even if the aid itself was permitted, was I legally obligated to inform the authorities that many of those we helped were undocumented? I found that I was not; in fact, the minister's position is much the same as that of the lawyer's or the licensed counselor's, who by law cannot reveal what their clients have told them in confidence. The law does not require that ministers (or even policemen!) report undocumented people.[36]

We refused to help with other kinds of activities: buying or giving money to buy false papers, drivers' licenses, or Social Security cards; giving false references, such as letters lying about people being members of the church; hiring people to work on a permanent basis without legal papers, or recommending that others do so; hiring workers on a temporary, random basis (which is legal) but then taking advantage of them; or transporting or paying for people to be transported across international borders. In general, though all knew their presence here was illegal, our policy was to encourage them to live legally in every way possible—i.e., not adding more illegal activities such as driving without a license or insurance or using false documents.

We were happy to provide these kinds of aid to many families legally. It was immediate and gratifying, and demonstrated Christ's love and concern for them. As mentioned, many people became members at Impact partly through these contacts and help. However, while some families required only this kind of Band-Aid, others needed more, and we needed to relate to them in a different way. They lived from emergency to emergency, always on the edge of relational collapse or financial disaster. They were mired in the microscopic details of each second, having no big-picture view, no healthy processes, and no integrated long-term plan to establish a balanced, Christian personal and family life. To the extent that we let ourselves be dragged into this microscopic, emergency-response mode, we were only helping temporarily and perpetuating the cycle.

Our goal was to develop a biblical, holistic, integrated model—not only considering the present emergency but also the long-term view, not only one small aspect of their lives but also how the facets of their lives worked together. In developing this model, we sought the involvement of various experts or groups. Four of the experts were directors of national or local agencies with goals and experiences similar to those of Impact. Another was a respected Christian financial consultant and certified public accountant. Also there was a noted author in the field of urban ministry and equipping programs. The last group was the ministry team at Impact, a tri-racial group with widely different backgrounds, a shared heart for ministry, and expertise regarding the Impact setting, culture, history, ministry, and theology.[37]

We also asked for guidance and evaluation from three focus groups: one group comprised of eight undocumented Hispanics who were members at Impact; one group of six documented Hispanics, also members; and the ministers and elders of the Kingwood Church of Christ. Many of their ideas, improvements, and evaluations are included in the following model.

Developing the Model

Selecting the Families

How do we choose the families whom we want to help? We start by praying, keeping our eyes and hearts open, and asking the Lord for agreement among us regarding possible families. At first, they likely will be families known to Impact members for some time, and perhaps they will be members themselves. Though not a primary criterion, how close they live to Impact, and how accessible they are geographically to the members of the helping team, is a factor.

If we have been in their homes, and know their needs, desires, and lifestyles, we can be more certain that they truly need our help. We will have already developed a certain level of trust with them, which is important if they will be making themselves vulnerable by granting us deep access to their lives, and giving us permission to challenge them in what will seem like risky or paradigm-changing ways.

As we get more experience, it is possible to increase the number of families helped, and also take families relatively unknown to us through referrals from other churches or agencies; however, Sherman declares that helping a small number of families more extensively and long-term is more effective than helping a large number of families with a scattered, short-term, shotgun approach.[38]

Assessing the Families

Once the families are selected, we then begin assessing their situation. Church ministers and members who have worked extensively with such families conduct the intake interviews at first; in time, they can train other members. We adapted a profile form similar to that used by most programs and social workers, which obtains information relating to the personal data of the family or individual, their history, their arrival in the United States, their educational status, special skills or experience, and problem areas. To some extent, the assessment also examines the family system, its dynamics, and its functioning.

Depending on the family or situation, this intake interview can be broken up into an interview and then a follow-up visit to the family's home. Lower levels of literacy may pose a problem for some families attempting to read and fill out the form. A helpful tactic could be for the interviewers to ask questions and write down the answers. Though the goal is to obtain as much useful information as possible, it is important to avoid overload or intimidation.

In addition, many undocumented families have a natural fear or distrust of authorities. The families may believe that if they give too much information, it would put them at risk for detection by U.S. immigration services and eventual deportation. The families need to be assured that all information given is confidential and will not be used to harm them.

Selecting and Orienting the Mentors

Once the initial intake is completed, we have a fairly good idea of which type of help or resources may be needed. The next step is to select a mentor or group of mentors who will be involved with the family for the next several months. Impact uses its members and network of contacts in area churches and organizations to shoulder-tap people who are competent in providing the various kinds of aid required. We tailor the makeup of the mentor team to the family's needs and, if possible, their personality. We also can provide a translator if needed. Of course, a core requirement of any mentor is demonstrating the heart of Christ to serve willingly and humbly. We do not want to be or even be seen as dictatorial, patronizing, or unfeeling.

Assuming that the mentors are well-qualified in their own fields, we ask them to participate in at least four training sessions concerning the biblical teaching about undocumented people, the culture of poverty, the daily life of an undocumented person, and principles of empowerment. Jack Roland states that the first goal of the mentors should be to establish warm, sensitive relationships with the families they serve and gain credibility to offer advice tailored to the families' assets and needs. He also recommends periodic debriefing meetings with the mentors to monitor how they are responding mentally, physically, and socially. The families themselves can also help the mentors debrief as they learn.

Kit Danley stresses the importance of the mentors understanding cultural differences. Sherman counsels building mentor teams that feature a mix of personalities in order to respond to various people and situations. Anna Babin highlights the importance of specific job descriptions for all mentors—roles, hours, responsibilities, and paperwork—so that later evaluations could be specific and efficient. Danley also warns of the dangers of mentor burnout. In order to give the mentors a different perspective, she poses the questions, "If this family were your neighbors, how would you be a friend to them? How would you know when you've taken on too much?"

The Initial Counseling Session

Before the first counseling session with the family, each mentor receives and studies a copy of the intake interview done with the family to facilitate knowledge of background information and development of a tentative strategy to speak with them. Impact helps the mentor(s) set up the initial meeting with the family, which serves as a welcoming, assessment, and covenant session.

During this stage, the primary goal is to set a friendly, positive atmosphere, and begin to develop a working relationship among the family and the team helping them. The team strives to find common points of interest, background, or experience. The mentors need to know something about the culture of the family's country of origin, their education, their race, and why the family came to this country. Each family is unique in its struggles, gifts, and opportunities, and should be treated as such. During this first meeting, Danley also advises giving a brief description of what the church can and cannot do for the family in order to avoid unrealistic expectations on their part.

Dekker suggests that a good opening question for this session might be, "Are you satisfied with your life situation right now personally?" If they are not, they need to believe that God can change them and ask that God to do so. Then the mentor asks the follow-up question, "Do you want to be a part of what is happening here?" Using the intake interview data, the mentors acquire any information lacking about the family's background or current situation. The family and the mentors confirm the specific needs of the family in the areas of work, finances, food, clothing, housing, medical care, transportation, and counseling. The undocumented focus group for this project divided these needs into two tiers: the first included emergency needs, such as food, lodging, work, medical services, and spiritual care; the second tier, also important but not as urgent, encompassed documents, education, counseling, legal aid, transportation, child care, and financial services.

Identifying and Assembling the Resources to Help

Impact has developed and maintains a list of resources, people, agencies, churches, or church members to provide multiple kinds of aid. Resources available include the following description of the types of resources which may also be available in your community.[39]

Regarding work, if an undocumented immigrant has no contacts, the best place to begin in Houston is at Casa Juan Diego, a Catholic benevolence center that chooses to minister primarily to undocumented people.[40] In conjunction with GANO/CARECEN, Casa Juan Diego administers a job cooperative in which undocumented people can register, pay one dollar annually, and receive a photograph identification card, which they can then use as identification when looking for sporadic labor. The employer pays the cooperative; the cooperative gives the entire wage to the worker; and the transaction is legal. Apart from such organizations, undocumented men must rely on scattered odd jobs garnered from friends, families, or other frequently fruitless contacts.

Such cooperatives are needed for undocumented women, but far less available. Even if jobs are occasionally granted, child care poses a daunting challenge, since family or friends may not be close, or they may be unreliable.

Many jobs require some knowledge of technology, advanced education, or specialized skills. A large number of undocumented workers are blue-collar, possessing limited education and skills. For these people, several agencies offer classes and special training, ranging from GED, ESL, and literacy programs to computer education or classes in basic cooking, sewing, and car repair.

In the area of finances, the family in need can enroll in programs designed specifically to teach all the basic concepts of budgeting, saving, debt retirement, investing, and financial planning in general, such as the New Focus program in Allendale, Michigan.[41]

The two basic needs of food and clothing are available at most of the churches and agencies already mentioned.[42] The primary challenge associated with distributing these commodities involves training volunteers. Olasky notes that the volunteers are susceptible to compassion fatigue—a weariness and reluctance to help when their generosity is abused or serves no purpose. For their part, the recipients are susceptible to what could be called the Lazarus syndrome, if they perceive themselves as the beggar and the volunteer/church/ organization as the rich man. Desperation, anger, cynicism, and resentment can mount.[43]

Most landlords are reluctant to rent accommodations to the undocumented, given the unstable nature of undocumented peoples' lives.[44] Churches are able to coordinate housing options. Likewise, transportation is often difficult to obtain, but most individuals learn to utilize available resources. Many churches and agencies give out tokens or bus passes.

In Houston, Harris County offers the gold medical card to anyone who meets basic requirements, although county officials now demand more documents than before. This card provides basic medical care in certain hospitals or clinics. Harris County does provide emergency medical assistance for anyone. Some agencies or hospitals also furnish prescribed drugs. Most undocumented immigrants can secure counseling (e.g., marital, parental, AIDS, pregnancy, abortion, adoption, and legal issues). Many agencies provide these services to everyone in group or individual settings.[45]

Developing a Strategy—Together

The mentors next invite the families to generate various solutions for their challenges, and select the most appropriate response to each need. The mentors' most valuable contribution at this point, perhaps, is to broaden the horizons for the family, to help them dream, to affirm their potential and encourage them to be positive. Since a chief characteristic of the culture of poverty is fatalism—believing nothing one does can change his or her future—here the mentor can help abolish self-defeating attitudes.

It is crucial at this point for the families to take a large role in deciding which goals and methods will be utilized. Goals which are imposed on the families by mentors, however well-meaning, will often not be met. Together the mentors and the family set SMART goals (Specific, Measurable, Attainable, Results-oriented, and Time-limited) for the response to each need. If several families have approximately the same needs, they might come together to set similar goals and encourage each other to meet those goals.

Making a Covenant

The mentors and family construct a covenant that includes several key features: a suitable meeting schedule for the mentors and family, clearly delineated responsibilities corresponding to the mentors and the family, specified rewards or incentives the family will receive according to their progress, services the family will offer in return for help given them, and a target date for evaluation.

This step of covenanting may seem too formal or inappropriate, especially if the literacy level of the family is poor. However, a tangible reminder of the goals, methods, and responsibilities for each person involved can motivate them to achieve their part. The more specific and clear such a pact, the more useful it is for all. After the family and the mentor sign the covenant, they may choose to exchange a physical symbol of the covenant, to be placed in a prominent location in their homes as a reminder.

Fulfilling the Covenant

In addition to the various scheduled meetings between the family and the mentors, the church can also designate one or more of its ministers and/or members (who have a relationship with the family) to have a weekly meeting together. The goal of the weekly meeting is to encourage the family to continue in the program by inquiring about progress, sharing timely, applicable biblical principles, and praying for all aspects of the family's life.

Dekker highlights the difference between a controlling, authoritarian environment and a caring, affirming one, as the families set goals and begin the difficult daily struggle to achieve them. These are significant, risky, untried changes in many cases, and the best attitude for mentors and helpers to take is a non-anxious, loving, even humorous one, as they share the presence of Christ in them with the family.

At the previously-decided time, the mentors and family will compare the results achieved to the established SMART goals. The mentors also are evaluated, not just the family. The families and mentors should celebrate each positive step taken, perhaps even with small incentives and prizes such as gum, soap, food, coupons, or even paying a bill. Danley suggested using a scale of one to ten to reflect the progress of the families compared to where they began. The mentors define success not only in terms of accomplished goals, but also in terms of transformed lives—both the family's and the mentors'.

Depending on the results of the evaluation, the cycle can repeat, with renewed needs assessment, goal-setting, and covenanting, or the mentors and family can choose to terminate the intervention.

Conclusion

I regret that we didn't have time to utilize this holistic model within the time frame of the project thesis with at least two or three families, and report on that. An earnest implementation of all facets of this would have taken at least a year, if not longer. I do believe that this is a valid model, which with implementation and adaptation can serve undocumented families in a holistic, biblical, and healthy fashion.

However, we did apply almost all aspects of this program separately as we aided hundreds of families during my time at Impact. In that process, I benefited from what I learned about the biblical teaching, the insights about the culture of poverty, and the principles of empowerment. I was able to share much of this with my fellow ministers, members of the church, undocumented families, and groups of Christians in other forums such as mission seminars and lectureships.

The U.S. Hispanic population, both documented and undocumented, will only increase in future years.[46] The church must be ready to respond biblically, legally, and wisely. Biblically, we must demonstrate the compassion of Christ and be creative and persistent in how we apply scriptural principles. We must also be wise, helping without patronizing, crippling, or ignoring others in need.

Legally, we must stay up to date on current immigration laws, and perhaps work for fairer ones. Richard Land, president of the Ethics and Religious Liberty Commission for the Southern Baptist Convention, has developed a challenging proposal for a new immigration law which could at the same time help secure the U.S. southern border and give immigrants a fair chance to acquire papers legally, pay any fines owed for being in the U.S. illegally, get a background check, and learn English.[47]

Whether through this proposal or another, a healthy goal is for the undocumented to become documented citizens with the right and obligation to earn a living and pay taxes to help contribute to a society from which they have benefited. I give the final word in this essay to Daniel Rodriguez, missions professor at Pepperdine University, from a class at the 2010 Pepperdine Lectures, "The most important thing for Christians in the undocumented immigrant debate is how you enter the debate—as a Christian, not as a taxpayer or homeowner or American. In a thousand years it won't matter if we're American, but it will matter if we're Christian."

---

1. Stephen Austin, "'Love the Alien as Yourself, For You Were Aliens:' Developing a Model for the Impact Church of Christ's Response to the Needs of Undocumented Hispanic Persons" (DMin thesis, ACU, 2000).

2. George Vernez and Kevin F. McCarthy, *The Cost of Immigration to Taxpayers: Analytical and Policy Issues* (Santa Monica, CA: RAND, 1996), accessed August 20, 1999, http://www.rand.org/content/dam/rand/pubs/monograph_reports/2007/MR705.pdf. Other works germane to this include ones such as Douglas Groll,"Proposition 187: Catalyst for Reflection on Our Immigrant Identity as Impetus for Mission," Concordia Journal 22 (April 1996); and Yolanda Pupo-Ortiz,"The Real Issue," Christian Social Action 6 (September 1993): 31–32.

3. Ray Bakke and Jim Hart, Urban Christianity (Downers Grove, IL: InterVarsity, 1987), 109.

4. The author has written a fictional account of the daily life of a typical immigrant, a composite picture based on hundreds of people's experiences. If you would like to receive this or other documents referenced in this chapter, you may write to him at slaustin@cebridge.net.

5. "Personal Responsibility and Work Opportunity Reconciliation Act of 1996," Title IV of Pub. L. No. 104-193, 110 Stat. 2105 (1996).

6. Richard Fry, "Hispanics, High School Dropouts and the GED," Pew Hispanic Center report, May 13, 2010, http://www.pewhispanic.org/files/reports/122.pdf.

7. Oscar Lewis, La Vida: A Puerto Rican Family in the Culture of Poverty—San Juan and New York (New York: Random House, 1966), 43–45.

8. Ibid., 45.

9. Ibid., 48.

10. Ibid., 49.

11. The DREAM Act, which stands for Development, Relief, and Education for Alien Minors (http://dreamact.info/) focuses on the plight of the children brought to the United States by undocumented immigrants. In most cases these children were young when they arrived with their parents. They often have no memories of or connections to their lives in their countries of origin. They have built their lives here and know this culture. They have no legal documents and find it difficult to get jobs or attend college. They did not choose to come, yet must deal with the consequences of their parents' decisions.

12. George Buchanan Gray, *A Critical and Exegetical Commentary on Numbers*, International Critical Commentary, ed. S. R. Driver, A. Plummer, and C. A. Briggs (Edinburgh: T & T Clark, 1956), 175; Ronald E. Clements, Exodus, Cambridge Bible Commentary, ed. P. R. Ackroyd and A. R. C. Leaney (Cambridge: Cambridge University Press, 1972), 125.

13. Deut. 23:7; Lev. 25:23. See Erhard S. Gerstenberger, *Leviticus: A Commentary*, The Old Testament Library, ed. James May (Louisville: John Knox Press, 1996), 283; Gordon J. Wenham, *The Book of Leviticus*, New International Commentary on the Old Testament, ed. R. K. Harrison (Grand Rapids: Eerdmans, 1979), 320.

14. Ps. 146:9; Deut. 10:18; Lev 19:9–10; Deut. 26:12.

15. Exod. 12:48; Lev. 16:29. To take part in the Passover, the alien was to circumcise all the males in the household.

16. Josh. 8:33.

17. Josh. 20:9.

18. Deut. 1:16.

19. U. Cassuto, *A Commentary on the Book of Exodus*, trans. Israel Abrahams (Jerusalem: Magnum Press, 1997), 291.

20. Phil. 3:19–20; Heb. 11:13b–16; 1 Pet. 2:11.

21. Luke 4:18–19.

22. Matt. 25:41–42.

23. Ps. 12:5.

24. Luke 12:48; 1 Cor. 12:1–30; Eph. 4:11–16; Rom. 12:3-8.

25. Floyd McClung, *Seeing the City with the Eyes of God* (New York: Revell, 1991), 114.

26. David T. Ellwood, *Poor Support: Poverty in the American Family* (New York: Basic Books, 1988), 44.

27. Amy Sherman, *Establishing a Church-Based Welfare-to-Work Mentoring Ministry* (New York: Center for Civic Innovation, 1996), 6.

28. Amy L. Sherman, *Restorers of Hope* (Wheaton, IL: Crossway, 1997), 137–156.

29. Betsy Dekker, interview by the author, July 29, 1999, New Focus, Allendale, MI.

30. Marvin Olasky, *The Tragedy of American Compassion* (Washington: Regnery, 1992), 8–9.

31. Ronald Sider, *Rich Christians in an Age of Hunger* (Dallas: Word, 1990), 61, 151–161.

32. Sherman, *Restorers*, 23–27; Olasky, *Tragedy*, 197–98.

33. Olasky, *Tragedy*, 102.

34. Robert C. Linthicum, *Empowering the Poor*, ed. Bryant L. Myers (Monrovia, CA: MARC, 1991), 21–23.

35. John Kretzmann and John McKnight, *Building Communities from the Inside Out* (Chicago: ACTA, 1995), 5–8.

36. This was confirmed to us by Omar Velez, the director of GANO/CARECEN, in an interview by the author, June 29, 1999, in Houston; and also by Mark Zwick, director of Casa Juan Diego, Houston, in an interview with the author on May 27, 1999.

37. Anna Babin, director of the Associated Catholic Charities in Houston, Texas; Kit Danley, director of Neighborhood Ministries in Phoenix, Arizona; Sherrie Santos, director of Neighbors Plus in Holland, Michigan; Amy Sherman, author and also director of urban ministries at Trinity Presbyterian Church in Charlottesville, Virginia; Jack Roland, CPA and financial consultant in Kingwood, Texas; Betsy Dekker, director of New Focus in Allendale, Michigan; and the Impact Church of Christ ministry team (Paul Woodward, Ron Sellers, Alejandro Arango, Charlie Middlebrook, Les Rose, Doug Williams, Brian Mashburn).

38. Sherman, *Restorers*, 163.

39. Other resources include: YMCA International, especially the refugee and immigration department; Rudy Orosco in Pasadena, California, at the Harambi Family Center; Noel Castellano, a leader in Latin Christian community development and a member of the Christian Community Development Association. Also, the local bilingual or Hispanic support groups such as Alcoholics Anonymous, Parents Anonymous, or Narcotics Anonymous as possible sources for Hispanic counselors.

40. In many cities, the Catholic Church has a distinguished history of service to the poor and social justice. Associated Catholic Charities offers a wide selection of useful resources.

41. For more information about New Focus see their website at www.newfocus.org.

42. In Houston, such programs include Target Hunger; Wesley Baptist; the Women, Infant, and Children program; West End Baptist; Fletcher Baptist; GANO/CARECEN; Gulf Coast Community Center; Heights Outreach; the Hester House; Bear Creek Assistance Ministries; Cypress Assistance Ministries; Associated Catholic Charities; and Casa Juan Diego.

43. Olasky, *Tragedy*, 65.

44. Some places that either provide housing on-site or help find or fund it are the Salvation Army, Casa Juan Diego, Bear Creek Ministries, Guadalupe Social Services, Gulf Coast Community Services, Search, and the Wesley Community Center.

45. Such agencies include Associated Catholic Charities, Guadalupe Social Services, Casa Juan Diego, and GANO/CARECEN.

46. The Pew Research Center, http://www.pewhispanic.org/.

47. "The Immigration Dinner Party," moderated by Jake Silverstein, *Texas Monthly*, November 2010, online edition, http://www.texasmonthly.com/story/immigration-dinner-party.

CHAPTER 11

Bridging the Generational Gap

JONATHAN W. CAMP[1]

The White Station Church of Christ exhibits warmth and hospitality. Yet, a generation gap within the congregation reveals a deeper issue. Here is a snapshot of a typical Sunday morning: I arrive with my wife and three-year-old at 8:15 for the contemporary service in the Family Life Center. We park our minivan in the north parking lot, where mostly families with young children park, because that lot is closest to the contemporary service, which is in the same building that houses children's worship and children's classes. On the other side of the campus lies a larger parking lot, where a mostly older group arrives for the traditional service at 8:30 in the auditorium.

The contrast between the two services is similar to other congregations that have separate traditional and contemporary services. On the one hand, the traditional service takes place in the auditorium, where worshipers are seated in pews. This service incorporates mostly standard hymns, keeps to a fairly consistent order of worship, and is led by a veteran worship leader who has served White Station since the 1970s and who, amid other duties, currently leads the senior adult ministry. In Robert Wuthnow's terms, this assembly exudes the ethos of a "spirituality of dwelling."[2] The contemporary service, on the other hand, is housed in a multi-purpose room with folding chairs. This service incorporates newer songs, often varies the order of worship, allows innovation in observing communion, contains a few worshipers who clap or raise hands, and is led by a twentysomething worship leader who also serves the college student ministry. This service reflects the ethos of a "spirituality of seeking."[3] Although both services contain age diversity, it is clear that the average age of worshipers in the traditional service is much older than that in the contemporary service, an observation confirmed by other church members.

After services, my wife and I walk through the children's wing to take our three-year-old to his class and then enter our classroom, where mostly adults under forty are gathered. Designed to provide the basic relationship opportunities in the congregation, the Bible classes are mostly divided along generational lines. After classes, we and the other class members gather our children, converse with each other, and sometimes go to lunch together; many of us never even enter the auditorium building on a Sunday morning. Therefore, from the time we arrive on the church property until the time we leave, many adults under forty have few opportunities to interact and build relationships with adults over sixty-five. Even our literal pathways on the campus rarely intersect with those of the older generation.

After almost a year of active membership, it occurred to me that I was forming few relationships with members over fifty, even though the twelve-hundred-member congregation had a significant number of senior members. At the same time, I was hearing a constant refrain from members of the congregation—a kind of unwritten slogan—that went something like this: "In our fifty years of existence, we have never had a church split." The focus of the DMin project came into view when I realized that the congregation had no need to formally split; in a sense, it already had, along generational lines. Thus, the project crystalized around the problem of bridging the generation gap at White Station. How could authentic, inter-generational interaction be encouraged? In 2006, I led an inter-generational planning group through an eight-week process to bridge the generation gap at the White Station Church of Christ, in Memphis, Tennessee, a project based on Paul's "household" (*oikos*) metaphor in Ephesians 2.

A Multigenerational Congregation

White Station served as an ideal setting for this project to bridge the generation gap, because of its remarkable age diversity. Many congregations today minister specifically to one age group or another, resulting in lopsided age distributions. White Station contains a roughly equal distribution of four distinct generations. In addition, at the time of the project, White Station was one of the few congregations that had four distinct generations represented in the eldership, with a forty-seven-year age difference between the oldest and youngest elder. And yet, it was difficult to experience this multigenerational richness. Efforts at congregational renewal had contributed significantly to new growth, especially among younger families. Yet many of the strategies designed to promote renewal, such as age-defined Bible classes and ministries, had further promoted a generation gap in the congregation. To a degree, two separate congregations met on Sunday mornings on the White Station campus, forming a happy, but not necessarily healthy, equilibrium.[4] The purpose of my project was not to merge the different generations so that their respective distinctions and identities disappeared, but to invite members of different generations to discuss openly with each other their vision for the church. With the help of the intergenerational planning group, we established some common ground for authentic conversation across the generational gap, and Ephesians 2 served as our starting place.

A Theology for Generational Bridge-Building

The theological foundation for this project takes into account the nature and challenge of intergenerational communication. Early in the twentieth century, German sociologist Karl Mannheim suggested that those belonging to the same generation possess a "common location in the social and historical process" that predisposes "certain definite modes of behaviour, feeling, and thought."[5] The "problem of the generations," according to Mannheim, is that sharing the same generational "social location" also likely "excludes a large number of possible modes of thought, experience, feeling, and action, and restricts the range of self-expression open to the individual to certain circumscribed possibilities."[6] Different generations possess different lenses through which they make meaning in the world, lenses influenced by a certain Zeitgeist, or "spirit of the epoch," during which a generation comes of age.[7] As a result, generations struggle to understand each other. While generations possess unique visions of the world, their strengths are underappreciated by other generations whose members struggle to see beyond the weaknesses they perceive in generations other than their own. Bridging the generation gap is possible only when members of different generations cultivate an ability to understand and appreciate generational difference. An appreciation of the household (*oikos*) metaphor in Ephesians 2, and how it is cultivated through epistemic humility and narrative imagination, expands the possibilities for how congregations might promote that ability.

The Church as Oikos

The use of the word "household," or *oikos*, in Ephesians 2 occurs within the context of the central message of Ephesians: God has adopted the Gentiles through the reconciling work of Christ, who destroys the wall of hostility between Jew and Gentile (Eph. 1:5; 2:11–18). Prior to their inclusion, we read that the Gentiles were once "dead through the trespasses and sins" (2:1 NRSV), "aliens from the commonwealth of Israel, and strangers to the covenants of promise, having no hope and without God in the world" (2:12 NRSV). In Christ, however, God has reconciled Jew and Gentile into "one new humanity" (2:15), having "access in one Spirit to the Father" (2:18 NRSV). This message of Gentile inclusion into God's family is the mystery given by special revelation to the writer (3:5) to urge the Christians in Ephesus to make "every effort to maintain the unity of the Spirit in the bond of peace" (4:3 NRSV). The letter concludes with specific instructions on how to "lead a life worthy of the calling" that the Gentiles have received (4:1 NRSV). It is in this context that the household theme most prominently occurs, in Ephesians 2:19-22:

> So then you are no longer strangers and aliens, but you are citizens with the saints and also members of the household [*oikos*] of God, built upon the foundation of the apostles and prophets, with Christ Jesus himself as the cornerstone. In him the whole structure is joined together and grows into a holy temple in the Lord; in whom you also are built together spiritually into a dwelling place for God. (NRSV)

The use of *oikos* reveals both the nature and purpose of God's unifying work in Christ. First, the *oikos* of God welcomes all humankind.[8] To the devout Jew, the divide between Jew and Gentile was more than ethnic or cultural. The "nations" were outside of God's covenant with Israel. The separation was bound up with the historic faith of Israel. Therefore, the adoption of the Gentiles as coheirs with Israel reveals God's salvific intention for the world. God calls the church to participate not only in the ministry of reconciliation between individuals and God, but reconciliation between peoples. The gospel is not a matter of individual atonement, but essentially the interruption of God's kingdom to the dismantling of whatever societal structures that interrupt the harmony of God's creation, whether racism, class, nationalism, sexism, or ageism. In God's new economy in Christ, we are intimately joined together with God and each other, and our individual destiny is interwoven with the whole of God's creation. An ecclesiology based upon *oikos* contrasts strikingly with popular church-growth strategies that rely on and appeal to preexisting interest groups for their success. Such strategies hinder the formation of familial bonds because they reify existing lines of separation in the church. Just as young and old are isolated from each other in modern society, they are likely to remain isolated in a congregation that follows the market model for numeric growth. Rather than offering reconciliation to a fragmented world, popular church-growth strategies often fall short of reflecting the essential nature of the gospel.[9] Whatever the makeup of the local community in which they reside, members of a congregation who nurture a self-understanding as God's *oikos* will recognize that the wall of separation is indeed broken; they may now embrace the other as sister and brother.[10]

Second, the church as *oikos* serves as a public sign of God's creation of "one new humanity." It is important to note here how the *oikos* metaphor shifts from a familial relationship in verse 19 to a temple-building image in verses 20–22.[11] In the ancient world, a temple represented a particular deity's presence in the city. God manifests God's presence in the world by means of a temple constituted by the reconciliation of Jews and Gentiles, two groups previously considered irreconcilable. Just as "the Church is always an event of public manifestation,"[12] this *oikos*-temple publicly manifests God's ultimate purpose in reconciling to Godself the whole world in all of its diversity. The church as *oikos* thus serves as a sign pointing beyond itself to God's purpose to unite the world. Consequently, efforts to bring unity to churches are not just to improve the health of the congregation or to enrich members' experience of that congregation. At stake is that congregation's faithful, public witness to the gospel of reconciliation. When a congregation welcomes intergenerational diversity it proclaims to the surrounding community a rejection of contemporary America's cruel idolatry of youth. Such a congregation points the surrounding community beyond itself to the eschatological purposes of God reflected in the final prophecy of the Old Testament: "He will turn the hearts of parents to their children and the hearts of children to their parents" (Mal. 4:6 NRSV). When conceived as a sign of God's ultimate purposes for the world, bridging the generation gap takes on a missional posture of love for the surrounding community.

Third, the church as *oikos* indicates that the church is a work in progress, an ideal to which we ever must strive. Even though the foundation and the building of *oikos* has begun, it yet "grows into a holy temple in the Lord . . . a dwelling place for God" (Eph. 2:21–22 NRSV). The building is constructed upon the foundation of God's past work in Christ and is empowered by God's continued work in the Spirit. The reconciled Jews and Gentiles, empowered by the Spirit, participate with God in the transformation of the *oikos* into nothing less than the glorious temple of God through which God is manifest to the world. To achieve God's mission in the world, God invites and empowers people to unite in mutual love, and thereby coconstruct God's dwelling place. Therefore, since God's *oikos* is yet unfinished, it becomes incumbent upon members of God's household to ask ourselves, what kind of house are we building together? Are we building a house in which only a select few have a privileged place? Are we building a house designed to cater to specific interest groups?

Building God's Oikos *through Epistemic Humility and Narrative Imagination*

As many have acknowledged, the generations do not speak well with each other.[13] Generations typically react against what they see to be weaknesses in the other generations. In congregations, win-lose struggles often result from generational misunderstandings and unwillingness to see the world from a perspective other than that of one's own generational cohort. Because communication is constitutive of the social worlds we inhabit, we must take responsibility for the kind of household we are building.[14] Essential communication tools include epistemic humility and narrative imagination.

Just as no individual possesses all the truth, no particular community, including generational cohorts, possesses all of the truth by itself. Like pieces of a "shattered mirror," we must connect with other pieces so that we not mistake our piece for the whole.[15] We connect in order to see a more complete picture of what is going on in the world. To appreciate the truth-forming benefits of generational diversity, members of a generation must understand that their generational formation is a reaction to the excesses or lapses of the previous generation and that their own weaknesses and limitations will provoke a reaction in the succeeding generation. This kind of reflexivity, or critical self-awareness, is essential to cultivating epistemic humility[16] because it produces an attitude of openness to different perspectives, fostering the growth of edifying intergenerational relationships. Yet, improving intergenerational communication has as its goal more than solely building relationships as ends in themselves. When a multigenerational congregation embodies intergenerational cooperation and discernment, it can better function as a public community of discernment for the sake of the world. The church can thus instantiate a pattern of intergenerational cooperation that can inform other contexts in which generational diversity poses challenges, such as in business, education, and local government.

Cultivating a narrative imagination is also essential for improving intergenerational communication, because it is through stories that we can fully enter into the life of another.[17] Listening attentively to stories allows us better understand how a belief or action is formed in a community other than our own. In this way, stories generate empathy. In congregations, disagreements and misunderstandings between generations fester when no vehicle exists for sharing narrative reasons for a given belief or action. But when different generations gather to exchange stories, faulty attributions and negative stereotypes recede. For example, during my DMin project, the leadership of White Station held a church-wide meeting to discuss coming plans to build an outreach center on the campus of White Station. Several elderly members expressed concern over what would happen to the magnolia trees on the west side of the church property. Younger and newer members, such as myself, likely had no context for understanding why these magnolia trees were a concern. Why would they (the older members) be more concerned about trees than with outreach to the community? Such unfair stereotypes were corrected through the older members' stories of their voluntary involvement in developing the church property. The trees carried memories, and the stories enabled younger members like me to imagine why they would be valued. This vignette convinced me that the method for my DMin project would benefit from inviting younger and older members of White Station to share their stories.

Method

The purpose of this project was to equip members of an intergenerational planning group to provide recommendations for bridging the generation gap at White Station. My equipping strategy included content transmission and focused discussion to guide the process. Convinced that the generation gap is in large part a communication gap, I wanted to invite members of two different generations together to engage in honest and transparent communication about values and visions for the church. And yet, I wanted the interactions to proceed from a positive emotional climate; the method of Appreciative Inquiry (AI) proved to be extremely helpful in this regard. A research approach arising from organizational development, AI seeks long-term organizational change through processes that focus on what the organization is already doing right and building upon that, rather than focusing problems that seek to provide a "quick fix" for identified weaknesses.[18] Accordingly, I sought to elicit group members' memories, stories, and ideas of congregational unity, for these reflect the hope of White Station and could thus serve to promote more lasting organizational change.

The project involved eight one-hour planning sessions intended to provide (1) a theological foundation for generational bridge building, and (2) recommendations for bridging the generation gap at White Station, to be submitted to the leadership team and the elder administration committee. The project sessions also incorporated asset-mapping exercises, a practical extension of Appreciative Inquiry.[19] Such an organization-affirming approach to planning allowed the participants to recognize the strengths of the generation that founded the congregation, and appreciate how these strengths would be key to positive organizational change.[20]

Participants

Co-Facilitator

Earl Manning, one of the elders at White Station and a member of the Silent generation, served as a cofacilitator for this project. It was crucial to the success of the project to recruit a coteacher from an older generation for three reasons. First, since I was new to White Station and because of the separation of generations that exists in the White Station ministry context, I had little if any rapport or relationship access with a large number of members above the age of sixty-five. Manning, who had recently celebrated his seventieth birthday and who was active in the life and leadership of the congregation, lent credibility to the project for his generation, which greatly helped with recruiting older participants for this study. Second, it made sense for a project on bridging the generation gap to be facilitated by a younger and an older member. Because Manning and I had already established a good personal relationship, we intended our relationship to model to the planning-group members the kind of bridge building our project was designed to promote. Third, Manning already embodied many of the qualities of a bridge builder. He and his wife both attended the Crosswalk class, which was composed mainly of adults under forty. As a regular member of this class, I had perceived in Manning a unique ability to interact meaningfully with members of my generation. In addition, Manning expressed to me on numerous occasions that he was troubled by the generation gap at White Station and that he appreciated this project.

Planning group

Manning and I recruited fifteen White Station members to participate in this study. Nine participants were from the Silent generation (born mid-1920s to mid-1940s), and six members were from Generation X (born mid-1960s to early-1980s). I chose to include these two generations because (1) Gen Xers are rapidly coming into church leadership while the Silents are still a part of the leadership, and (2) without any generational overlap, the gap that exists between these two generations is more pronounced. The group included three elders, comprised of two Silents and one Gen Xer (1965). To ensure that this project had investment from the leadership team, a ministerial staff member attended most of the project sessions as a project monitor. The planning group consisted of roughly equal numbers of men and women. Criteria for selection in the group included (1) an interest in serving as a generational bridge builder, (2) perceived ability for intergenerational communication, and (3) active involvement in the life of the congregation.

Description of the Project Sessions

The eight one-hour sessions took place during the regularly scheduled Wednesday assemblies in the fall of 2006. During the first five sessions, Manning and I co-presented a theology of generational bridge building, and the remaining three sessions were devoted to exercises designed to produce the recommendations.

Session one, entitled "Bridge Builders Wanted," introduced the project. Manning opened the session with a welcome and prayer, as he did for each session that he attended. I then invited planning-group members to state their name, their length of time at White Station, and one sentence that they thought defined their generation. I wrote down their responses to the last question to share in a later session. I then described in detail the nature of the project and completed the informed consent process. Finally, I introduced the topic of White Station as a multigenerational congregation, elaborated on the challenge of intergenerational communication, and issued an invitation to become a generational bridge builder. We closed with a reading of Ephesians 2:19–22, followed by a prayer.

Session two, entitled "Approaching the Gap," began with an ice-breaker exercise, reading humorous quotations about the generations. Next, I spelled out some of the assumptions guiding the study. In the main body of teaching, I introduced the *oikos* metaphor in Ephesians 2 and discussed how it grounds a theology of generational bridge building. Next, I read through the generational "self-descriptions" that I had recorded from participants' responses the previous week and led a discussion about what patterns they were seeing in their responses (See Table 1).

I then provided a definition of a generation. To conclude, Manning and I each shared what it was like growing up in our respective generation eras. The purpose of this last exercise was to illustrate the vast cultural differences between the worlds into which the Silents and Xers were born and to illustrate the power of story-telling to bridge the generation gap. The session thus represented an effort to cultivate a narrative imagination, essential to shaping appreciation of cultural difference.

Table 12.1. Generational "Self-Descriptions"

Silents (b. 1925–1945)	Xers (b. 1965–1983)
Committed to institutions	Thirst for information
Responsible	Technologically savvy
Cautious (sometimes overly cautious)	Wants things "my way"
Emphasize "credentials"	Wants things "right now"
Hard working	Critical thinkers (at times too much)
Patriotic	Question authority
Spiritually minded	Be our own advocate
Not risk takers (rely on "tried and true")	Lack of brand loyalty
Brand loyalty	Entitled
Extension of Brokaw's "Greatest Generation"	Spiritual, but not religious
Caring	Pessimistic
Very trusting	Spiritually seeking
Handshake is sufficient	Emphasis on relationships
Team players	Desiring authenticity
Respectful of authority	
Cooperative	

Session three was an extension of session two and was therefore entitled "Approaching the Gap, Part 2." In this session, I reviewed the previous week and led another reading of Ephesians 2:19–22, our key text. Next, I invited participants to share a story in which they had experienced a generation gap, and a story in which they had bridged that gap. The bulk of the session was dedicated to teaching the generational theory of William Strauss and Neil Howe as represented in Carl Eeman's *Generations of Faith*.[21] I closed the session by leading a discussion on how much of what we observe about a generation is a reaction to the generation that preceded it.

In session four, entitled "Building God's Household," I began by leading a discussion about the current place of "family" language in church. I then discussed family imagery in Scripture, and Manning read and commented briefly on Old Testament images of the generations coming together, from Psalm 78:1–11, Zechariah 8:1–5, and Malachi 4:5–6. Next, I provided a more developed interpretation of Ephesians 2:19–22, further emphasizing the *oikos* metaphor and its importance to our project to bridge the generation gap. I concluded the session with group discussion on the following questions: (1) What kind of household are we building at White Station? (2) What specific practices could White Station adopt to build a household that honors God and welcomes all?

Session five, entitled "Bridging the Communication Gap," emphasized the agency of the bridge builder as a communicator. I discussed how each generation, as a unique culture, possesses its preferred forms of communication, which often clash with other generations' preferred forms. For this session, I had written a hypothetical case study, "What to Do with Reserve Church Funds?" which is provided below. We read the case and discussed how the issue of stewardship is a likely site for different generational perspectives to clash because the concept of stewardship may carry different connotations to each generation. I concluded the session by listing and explaining Gil Rendle's four principles for resolving generational conflict: (1) Move to the balcony, (2) work descriptively, (3) seek common space, and (4) install civility.[22]

CASE STUDY

"What to Do with Reserve Church Funds?"

A five-hundred-member congregation in the South received a charitable donation of $50,000 from the estate of a long-term member who recently passed away. Neither the member who had died nor her family gave any indication as to how the funds were to be used. They only asked the church leaders to use the money as they saw fit. Before making a decision, the church leaders sought input from the finance committee, an eleven-member body composed of both older and younger members. The finance committee could not reach a consensus on how the money should be used. Frustrated by the committee's inability to resolve the conflict, the elders set the money aside into a reserve account until they could reach a decision for its ultimate use. Three years later, the money was still in the reserve account.

The congregation is fifty years old, situated in a middle-class community, and has had a history of stability. The congregation owns its building, is well-staffed, and contributes generously to mission work and benevolence. The congregation is fairly middle of the road when it comes to fellowship-wide issues of doctrine and practice.

In the late 1990s, a minister resigned after thirty years in the pulpit. Then the leaders hired a dynamic, thirty-five-year-old preacher who encouraged many of the younger adults to get involved in the life of the congregation through teaching, serving on various committees, and outreach. The rapid influx of young and new members into the various committees generated some intergenerational conflict, especially with the worship committee.

Encouraged by the new preacher, the younger members on the committee wanted to form a worship team, hire a full-time worship leader, and cultivate more expressive forms of worship (i.e., applause and raising hands). The older members on the committee, however, were upset by these suggestions and blamed the new preacher for "stirring up trouble." The elders sought to mediate, but the new preacher was unwilling to wait out the storm. After eighteen months, he resigned to plant a new church, taking with him forty members, almost all of them younger than age forty. This split, even though not detrimental to the future of the established congregation, still caused much pain. Some of the conflict was eased with the hiring of another preacher, this one in his late forties. Certain uneasiness between the older and younger generations persisted, however.

When the elders informed the finance committee about the $50,000 gift, the chairperson immediately called a meeting to discuss the use of the money. It quickly became clear that a conflict would ensue. Six of the older committee members, all of whom had served on the committee twenty-plus years, wanted to use the money to fund an interest-bearing reserve account, anticipating that the money would be needed in three to five years for building renovations, repavement of the parking lot, and staff salary raises.

The remaining five members, all under forty-five, objected to putting the money into the bank. They agreed that the most faithful stewardship of the money would be to use it immediately—"What good can it do in a bank?" they asked. They argued for using the money to hire an associate minister who, among other responsibilities, would lead worship.

The older group thought the reasoning of the younger group was unsound, and driven by an agenda to introduce "innovations" in worship. If they wanted to use the $50,000 for the first-year salary of a new minister, where would the money come from for the second year, and third, and so on? The younger group responded that if it was God's will to have a new minister, then God would provide the funding after the first year. The older group claimed that it would be more faithful stewardship to put the money into a secure account so it could be used when it was really needed.

Even with two more meetings, the finance committee failed to reach a consensus. Old feelings from the previous conflict surfaced, and the committee entered into a win-lose style of conflict. The younger members complained that the older members on the committee were "stuck in their old ways" and "old fuddy-duddies" when it comes to money. The older members saw the younger members on the committee as fiscally "irresponsible" and as having an agenda to change the church. They were greatly concerned about the financial future of the congregation in the hands of this younger generation.

Questions:

1. How would you describe the different views of stewardship in this case? How are these views shaped in terms of a generation's culture and formative years?
2. Would some form of compromise have been a good solution to the use of the excess funds? Why or why not?
3. As inter-generational bridge builders, what would you do to mediate this particular conflict?

The remaining three sessions involved discussions to develop recommendations for bridging the generation gap at White Station. In session six, entitled "Beginning to Dream," I opened by asking the group to share what themes had emerged during the previous sessions that stimulated their interest in bridging the generation gap. For most of the session, I arranged for the Silents and Xers to break up into separate small groups to conduct Rendle and Alice Mann's "Favorite Hymn Exercise."[23] The group members shared their favorite hymn, and then the two groups discussed the following questions: (1) What do these hymns teach us about the nature of God? (2) What do these hymns teach us about human nature? and (3) What do these hymns teach us about the mission of the church? Then the two groups, representing two different generations, came together to discuss their findings. As a mode of Appreciative Inquiry, this exercise was designed to tease out each generation's unique way of seeing God, humanity, and the church in such a way that framed differences as complementary strengths. I concluded the session by emphasizing how our complementary theology was richer because it embraced diverse generational perspectives and how this intergenerational theology would serve as an invaluable foundation for our recommendations. Of all the activities I led, the Favorite Hymn Exercise was, in my opinion, the most influential to the group, leading to a collective aha moment.

Sessions seven and eight were similar in that they were mostly directed toward drafting a document containing the planning group's recommendations for bridging the generation gap. In session seven, I summarized the results from the Favorite Hymn Exercise and then invited participants to brainstorm in response to the question, How can we promote intergenerational fellowship at White Station in a way that reflects the congregation's strengths and dreams? I wrote their responses on a whiteboard while another participant took careful notes, which she later typed and sent to me electronically. Session eight, the final planning session, was devoted to organizing and clarifying what we had discussed in the previous brainstorming session. Again, I wrote the group members' responses on the whiteboard while another member took notes. Following the last session, I composed a draft of a document entitled "Recommendations for Bridging the Generation Gap at the Church of Christ at White Station" to present in the final focus-group evaluation.

Conclusion

The tangible outcome of this project was the composition of a document entitled "Recommendations for Bridging the Generation Gap at the Church of Christ at White Station," submitted to the elder administration committee in February 2007. This document reflected planning group members' three key perspectives on how the cultivation of intergenerational understanding and respect experienced by the group can be promoted within the larger congregation: (1) The planning group sessions must be replicated in other small groups; (2) intergenerational relationships will form only through gradual, organic process; and (3) efforts to bridge the generation gap in the congregation will benefit the other programs of the congregation. When I moved away from Memphis in the summer of 2007, a Sunday morning class had taken the lead with following through on the recommendations.

But yesterday's recommendations are soon forgotten in the constant struggle to meet the complex needs of a large congregation. For that reason, the intangible outcomes in the lives of the planning group members, I believe, may achieve a more lasting impact. My project field notes along with a focus-group evaluation with the planning group revealed a perceived improvement in understanding and respect between the two generations, mainly through the erosion of generational stereotypes and a renewed appreciation to listen to each other's stories.

Implications for Ministry

This project yielded at least three implications that may be generalized to other Doctor of Ministry projects or general ministry interventions. First, selection of an adequate planning group was critical to the success of this project. I chose three criteria for selection: The planning group members had to be (1) a member of either Generation X or the Silent generation, (2) actively involved in the life of the congregation, and (3) already demonstrating some interest and skills in bridging the generation gap. A large portion of my time developing this project was spent on the phone or at a restaurant, talking with potential group members or soliciting advice from key members regarding who should be selected. This project hinged upon recruiting both younger and older participants. Because I did not know many of the older members of White Station, a symptom of the problem I sought to address in the project, I recruited Earl Manning, an elder and representative of the Silent generation, to cofacilitate this project. With Manning's endorsement and heavy involvement, the project gained credibility with several older key members who think highly of Manning and were thus willing to participate. Ironically, I was initially concerned that the project would not draw enough older members, when in fact we ended up with more Silents than Xers in the planning group. Without the involvement of this particular group of participants, I doubt the project would have fared as well.

Second, the success of this project depended on the emotional investment of planning-group members. A Doctor of Ministry project will fail if participants perceive it to be a dry, academic exercise. For a ministry intervention to be effective, people must be excited about it. This project demanded a substantial commitment from the participants for several weeks. Yet they were willing to put forth the effort because they were committed to the goal of the project. Accordingly, the outcome of this project was not only a document containing the planning group's recommendations but also the formation of a group of both younger and older White Station members convinced of the need to bridge the generation gap, genuinely excited about promoting intergenerational fellowship within the congregation, and equipped to model such fellowship before others. I suspect that the unplanned effect of this group will have greater impact on the culture of White Station than the written recommendations produced by the group.

Third, this project was successful because it met a perceived need in the life of the congregation. Not being on White Station's ministry staff, I was in an unusual position to lead this Doctor of Ministry project. I knew that as a new White Station member, and lay member at that, it would be necessary to select a topic that would meet a perceived need among the church leaders. In consultation with the leadership team on a variety of project topics, we agreed elders would be more likely to invest in a project to bridge the generation gap precisely because they recognized it to be an unaddressed challenge. Throughout the process of preparing this project, I did not need to persuade others of the problem of a generation gap; it was already on many of the planning-group members' minds. That the church leaders and the planning-group members lent their enthusiastic support to this project and invested in me as both a newcomer and non-staff member is evidence that the project touched a chord in the life of the congregation.

---

1. Jonathan W. Camp, "Bridging the Generational Gap at the White Station Church of Christ" (DMin thesis, ACU, 2007).

2. Robert Wuthnow, *After Heaven: Spirituality in America since the 1950s* (Berkeley, CA: University of California Press, 1998), 3–8. Wuthnow argues that religion in America has changed in the last half century from a "spirituality of dwelling," or a traditional spirituality of inhabiting sacred places, to a "spirituality of seeking," characterized by a negotiation of more fleeting, partial, and competing glimpses of the sacred.

3. Ibid., 6–8.

4. Gil Rendle, "The Illusion of Congregational 'Happiness'" in *Conflict Management in Congregations*, ed. David B. Lott (Herndon, VA: Alban Institute, 2001), 83–94.

5. Karl Mannheim, "The Problem of Generations," in *Essays on the Sociology of Knowledge*, ed. and trans. Paul Kecskemeti (London: Routledge & Kegan, 1964), 291.

6. Ibid.

7. Ibid., 313.

8. Markus Barth, Ephesians: *Introduction, Translation, and Commentary on Chapters 1–3*, Anchor Bible (Garden City, NY: Doubleday, 1974), 321.

9. David Matzko McCarthy, "Generational Conflict: Continuity and Change," in *Growing Old in Christ*, ed. Stanley Hauerwas, et al. (Grand Rapids: Eerdmans, 2003), 242.

10. Pheme Perkins, *Ephesians*, Abingdon New Testament Commentaries (Nashville: Abingdon, 1997), 78.

11. Barth, *Ephesians*, 270.

12. Markus Barth, *The Broken Wall: A Study of the Epistle to the Ephesians* (Chicago: Judson, 1959), 114.

13. E.g., Gil Rendle, *Multigenerational Congregations: Meeting the Leadership Challenge* (Herndon, VA: Alban, 2001), 109–112.

14. W. Barnett Pearce, *Communication and the Human Condition* (Carbondale, IL: Southern Illinois University, 1989), 17–25.

15. Kwame Anthony Appiah, *Cosmopolitanism: Ethics in a World of Strangers* (New York: Norton, 2006), 5.

16. Frederick D. Aquino, *Communities of Informed Judgment: Newman's Illative Sense and Accounts of Rationality* (Washington, DC: The Catholic University of America Press, 2004), 100–117.

17. Kwame Anthony Appiah, *The Ethics of Identity* (Princeton, NJ: Princeton University Press, 2005), 258, argues that "the basic human capacity to grasp stories, even strange stories, is also what links us, powerfully, to others, even strange others."

18. David L. Cooperrider and Suresh Srivastva, "Appreciative Inquiry into Organizational Life," in R. Woodman and W. Pasmore, eds. *Research in Organizational Change and Development*, vol. 1 (Greenwich, CT: JAI, 1987), 129–69; For applying appreciative inquiry in congregational settings see Mark Lau Branson, *Memories, Hopes, and Conversations: Appreciative Inquiry and Congregational Change* (Herndon, VA: Alban Institute, 2004).

19. John P. Kretzmann and John L. McKnight, *Building Communities from the Inside Out: A Path toward Finding and Mobilizing a Community's Assets* (Chicago: ACTA, 1993).

20. Similarly, Gil Rendle and Alice Mann, *Holy Conversations: Strategic Planning as a Spiritual Practice for Congregations* (Herndon, VA: Alban Institute, 2003), 121–23, argue that the unique congregational culture of shared meaning, rituals, and symbols provides the "tool kit" by which change is enacted in a congregation.

21. Carl G. Eeman, *Generations of Faith: A Congregational Atlas* (Herndon, VA: Alban, 2002).

22. Rendle, *Multigenerational Congregations*.

23. Rendle and Mann, *Holy Conversations*, 260–61.

CHAPTER 12

Collaborative Preaching

ALLEN BURRIS[1]

The Mitchell Church of Christ is a typical church. Our congregation's identity is rooted in the Stone-Campbell heritage. Like others in our heritage, we have wrestled with who we are and how we should present ourselves to the world around us. While being rooted in our tradition, we are more open and inclusive than we used to be, but still value biblical teaching deeply.

Over the years, I have been concerned about the effectiveness of preaching, often wondering how much of the sermon people heard. I often questioned what I did and how I did it. Is there anything I could do to improve the hearing of the sermon? Is there anything the listener could do? The second question prompted me to pursue how those who hear the Sunday morning sermon are unprepared to hear its message. They have not read, meditated, or prayed about the preaching text. I therefore focused on the disciplines of reading, meditating, and praying because these three disciplines are connected with my sermon preparation, and the congregation is familiar with them.

I also realized that the congregation has not discussed the text with the preacher or with other members of the congregation. If there is no contact or collaboration between the preacher and the congregation in preparation, then the sermon is primarily a disconnected monologue. It is not a communal interaction. If the preacher alone prepares the sermon, then preaching can be perceived, accurately, as a dogmatic monologue instead of a communal interaction. If the congregation does not participate in preparation, then the opportunity for the message to be heard effectively is diminished. If the preparation is not communal, then there is no opportunity for preparation on the part of the hearer.

The project's purpose is predicated on the belief that hearing of the sermon will be improved by participation in sermon preparation with the preacher through a reflective conversation regarding the preaching text. If there is a greater connection among the preaching text, the preacher, and the members of the church who hear the text, Sunday morning preaching will be transformed from an individual monologue to a communal interaction. If church members receive the biblical text in advance with reflective questions, suggested prayers, and meditations, and study the text with the preacher, then they will hear the sermon more effectively. Subsequently, they will retain more of the sermon content and have a greater opportunity to practice what was preached. The result will be spiritual transformation. The process, I believe, will allow the Spirit of God to do God's transformative work individually and communally.

Listener-Centered Preaching

From the days of Fred Craddock, much has been written that seeks to improve preaching by considering the listeners of sermons. The "New Homiletic" states that the sermon belongs to the hearers also, not the preacher alone. The hearers of the sermon are invited to complete the sermon with their thoughts and applications.[2]

Some have sought a solution to the ineffectiveness of preaching by emphasizing "preaching as the church's language."[3] In the context of the worship assembly, the church remembers its story and talks to itself, finding distinct language about God and the world, preparing itself to enter the world as a witness. Therefore, preachers must be a part of a communal conversation with the hearers. As preachers participate in the conversation, they need to acknowledge the mission of the church, assisting it in finding the right words to speak to the world.

Wesley Allen presents a "conversational ecclesiology," stating that the church is "a community of theological conversation."[4] He proposes that preachers participate in a matrix of conversations consisting of different contexts: personal, sociohistorical, theological, congregational, and liturgical.[5] The preacher is one of many conversation partners. Preachers have a privileged voice, however, because they are invited by the congregation to present a monologue to the church.[6] Thus, the preacher, through multiple conversations, is helping the church find the right language to speak. As the people listen to the sermon, they should hear their thoughts and ideas expressed in new ways, with new words.

In 2001–2002, Christian Theological Seminary in Indianapolis, funded by the Lilly Endowment, conducted an extensive study of how people listen to sermons. Researchers discussed with more than 260 lay people, in twenty-eight diverse congregations, the elements of preaching that engage or disengage congregations. Essentially the researchers approached the participants with a request: "Teach us how you listen to sermons so that we can help ministers become more effective preachers." The study asked specific questions derived from Aristotle's three categories of rhetoric: *ethos*, *logos*, and *pathos*. *Ethos* involves the listener's perception of the preacher's character, personality, and trustworthiness during the preaching event. *Logos* is concerned about the content of the sermon. *Pathos* involves the role of feelings stirred during the preaching.[7]

The study discovered that people listen to sermons primarily through one of the three rhetorical categories. The researchers found that twenty percent of people listen to sermons primarily through the category of *pathos*. The listening categories of *ethos* and *logos* were evenly divided among the remaining participants, each receiving 40 percent. An examination of the study helps preachers gain insight into those who listen to their sermons each week. It does not, however, help hearers hear the sermon more effectively. Its primary focus is creating a greater awareness of how people listen to the sermons preachers present. Preachers should be aware of these findings, making sure that all of the categories are represented in sermons on a regular basis. In this way, they will better connect with their audiences.

While one cure for ineffective sermons involves the preacher's listening to listeners to better understand their needs, another cure is to invite the listener to actively participate in sermon preparation. John McClure and Lucy Rose suggest inviting church members and others to a roundtable discussion as a part of sermon preparation. McClure advocates collaborative preaching. He suggests convening a "preaching roundtable," which he describes as a sermon "brainstorming group."[8] The preacher and hearers work together to create face-to-face relationships based on the idea of Christian *koinonia* (partnership). These relationships are rooted in deep respect for the other person. People in these relationships strive, as McClure characterizes it, to "come to terms" with one another.[9] The preacher listens to others and learns from them. The goal of collaboration with the congregation is for

> the biblical interpretations and theological insights of the congregation to find voice in the pulpit. When used over a period of time, collaborative preaching empowers members of the congregation to claim as their own the ideas, forms of religious experience, and theological vision articulated from the pulpit. Preaching, therefore, becomes a focal point for congregational self-leadership and mission.[10]

From this roundtable group, Rose observes that a "conversational preaching" style will emerge. Conversational preaching has five characteristics: communal, non-hierarchal, personal, inclusive, and scriptural.[11] It is concerned with the formation, development, and edification of the church. These, according to conversational preaching, are not the sole responsibility of the preacher. Rather, through participation at the roundtable, the church takes responsibility for its own formation and reformation. The goal each week is to gather the community of faith around the Word in order to foster and refocus its central conversations. Preaching in the roundtable church is focused on mutual edification, orientation, clarification, encouragement, discrimination and direction-finding.[12] Rose is concerned that the voices of the marginalized be heard at the roundtable: "the silenced, disenfranchised, the poor, and women."[13]

Another form of collaborative preaching involves sharing the preaching text with the congregation. David Schlafer proposes a collaborative approach to preparation, in which the congregants have the preaching text, with reflective questions, in advance. If the church comes to the worship assembly ready to listen through having read the text and reflected on the questions, then, even if the preaching seems impoverished, the hearer will still receive a "nourishing meal from God." He believes, however, impoverished sermons are less likely in a collaborative process. Preaching, along with hearing, will improve as a result of collaboration.[14] He calls this collaborative approach "ideal," but he questions how it could be accomplished each week. He does not propose a weekly dialogue between the preacher and the hearers, but he describes a time when such a dialogue took place at a seminar. The result was an improved preaching experience for the preacher and the hearers.

> The intensity of everyone's participation in the sermon was palpable. While the organizational development, images, and sentence constructions were my own, the meaning had come forth from the shared dialogue of the community. Furthermore, when articulated in the sermon, the meaning re-engaged us all with more depth and power than it probably could have if each one of us had come to the sermon independently.[15]

The work of Schlafer is similar to what Clyde Reid proposed several years earlier.[16] Reid was concerned that those sitting in the pews perceived preaching as "barren" and "sterile". The pulpit was "empty" in the sense that communication was failing due to a lack of relevant preaching; there was "no message heard, no results seen, and no power felt."[17] One corrective, Reid suggests, is collaborative conversations regarding the preaching text. Reid believes that pre-sermon Bible study groups move sermons from a monological to a dialogical experience. He cites several models for accomplishing this move. These models involve groups meeting to discuss the preaching text in advance of the sermon. Some of the models are similar to the project presented in this chapter but none are identical.

Not everyone agrees with a dialogical or collaborative approach to preaching. Some critics believe it is overly anthropocentric and a threat to the authority of God. Paul Scott Wilson is concerned about the teachings of McClure, Rose, and others.[18] He identifies them as a new school of homiletics that he calls "radical postmodern." His concern about the radical postmodern school is that they "leave God out of the discussion."[19] Specifically, according to Wilson, the radical postmodern school avoids hierarchy, deconstructs authorities, minimizes transcendence, represents an ethic that diminishes God, and implies that theology is a metaphor without a metaphysical meaning.[20]

In a paper presented to the Academy of Homiletics, Joseph Webb responded to Wilson's criticism.[21] Webb questions Wilson's Barthian idea that the preacher's voice represents the voice of God and that something "miraculous" happens during the presentation of the sermon. Webb believes that such a hierarchal approach to preaching often results in sermons that never "come down" to provide answers to the questions and needs of "real life." He admits beginning his theology from "below," in immanence, concentrating on the struggles of human existence. From there he works his way "back up" to understanding God's will.[22]

Somewhere between the views represented by Wilson and Webb, I believe in the power of God to bring transformation in the lives of people, and I believe the Scriptures have authority over individuals and the church. These thoughts should be brought to the collaborative conversation and articulated. In addition, the conversation needs to include the admission of real-life struggles that humans experience as a part of their existence. The conversation should continue until there is an understanding of how the text applies to the struggles of human existence. After the conversation is finished, the sermon should be prepared carefully. When the sermon is presented to the church, it is the message of God that must be heard and understood by people who are living "down below." The sermon acknowledges the anthropological situation and offers a theological response.

The literature discussed thus far has the common goal of improving preaching and improving the hearing of sermons. The primary focus may be on the performance of preachers, but their performance improvement seems to be motivated by an improved hearing of the sermon. The theology behind the methodology mentioned above is diverse, varied, and debated, but the goal seems to be the same: improved preaching and improved hearing.

I believe effective hearing, which results in spiritual transformation, is crucial to salvation. God has chosen sound as his most typical way of communicating with humans. The speaking of words is the form of sound that God uses most frequently to make the message known.[23] "God can do whatever God wants, but according to the Bible, God ordinarily chooses to accomplish the work of salvation through the spoken word."[24]

> God is received through hearing; hearing is more important than seeing. Hearing draws us out of ourselves in ways that gazing, inspecting, and looking do not. We have more control over our eyes, which we can quickly and completely close, than our ears, which are vulnerable to loud sounds even when we cover them with our hands. Words can reach deep inside us in ways we find hard to resist.[25]

God speaks and expects creation to hear.

A failure to hear the message of God results in self-centeredness, or self-righteousness. "We can become mired in an inward dialogue that distracts us from the world outside. We need to hear an external sound to save us from the temptation of turning our life into a monologue."[26] A monological life is focused on personal achievements. It is self-centered and unacceptable to God.

Paul argues this in Romans 10, especially in verses 14–17. Paul carefully explains to his fellow Jews that the Gentiles attained righteousness through faith, which comes from hearing "the word of Christ." Through the work of Christ, believing Gentiles are now experiencing the righteousness of God; they are God's children, justified and saved. There now is no distinction between Jews and Gentiles. "The same Lord is Lord of all and is generous to all who call on him. For 'Everyone who calls on the name of the Lord shall be saved'" (Rom. 10:12–13 NRSV).

Following this great statement of God's desire to save people, Paul poses a few rhetorical questions, followed by a powerful statement:

> But how are they to call on one in whom they have not believed? And how are they to believe in one of whom they have never heard? And how are they to hear without someone to proclaim him? And how are they to proclaim him unless they are sent? As it is written, "How beautiful are the feet of those who bring good news!" But not all have obeyed the good news; for Isaiah says, "Lord, who has believed our message?" So faith comes from what is heard, and what is heard comes through the word of Christ.[27]

Salvation results when people call on the name of the Lord. This call originates in hearts that believe the message they have heard; the call is a response of faith. Belief in God comes when people are in contact with preachers who are sent, ultimately, from God and who proclaim a message of Christ. The key to connecting proclamation and salvation is hearing. Faith comes from hearing the word of Christ, the gospel of Christ, the "word of faith."

Romans 10:14–17, in the broader context, emphasizes the importance of preaching and hearing. From the days of the prophets, public proclamation has been a centerpiece of God's plan of salvation. God speaks, using human voices. God has chosen hearing to be a vital part of the means by which salvation is received and sustained. Faith comes from hearing. People must hear God, as they hear the proclamation of God's word in the voice of humans.

Hearing is much more than a physical act. The Hebrew (*sama*) and Greek (*akouo*) words for "hearing" include processing what is heard and then responding with obedience. "Hearing leads to a process of internalization and enactment or performance."[28] It is important that preachers seek ways to improve the hearing of God's word. Hearing the word preached provides an encounter with God. It provides an opportunity for faith and transformation. The word must be heard effectively for these things to take place. The preacher seeks to establish a communion between what is proclaimed and the listener. "When those listeners let themselves be addressed by the proclamation, they are opening up their deepest interiors; a spiritual giving of themselves or—in the negative case—a closing off and resistance takes place."[29]

How can preachers foster a better hearing of God's word? How can they create an environment in which listeners open their deepest interiors? How can preachers create a disposition of active, attentive hearing? Preachers must have a good, healthy relationship with God. They must believe that they are called by God to preach and believe that their spiritual gifts are utilized best in preaching. Preachers must listen to God as they study the preaching text, praying for guidance and humility. Preachers have privileged positions in the collaborative process because of their call, gift, training, and role. They choose the texts, put the finishing touches on the sermons, choose the ways to present the texts, and select illustrations. Humility must be present at all times; collaborative preaching will not work without it.

As preachers seek to improve the hearers' reception of the message, they need to share with the congregation the text that will be preached. The congregation should receive, along with the text, reflective questions, meditations, and prayers. This process will create space for the Holy Spirit of God to do the work of transforming people into the image of Christ.

It is important for preachers to have a "matrix of conversations." They especially need to converse with those who have been reading and experiencing the preaching text that will soon be preached. Collaboration takes place as preachers listen to the participants. Not all participants will be able to exegete or fully understand the text, "but they can do theology, and they can, out of their own process of making meaning in and of the world, proclaim their perspective on/from the Christian faith authentically and meaningfully."[30]

Preachers can gain insight and understanding of the community in which they speak by listening to those who listen to them. It is important for preachers to know what the listeners think, believe, and feel. Preachers need to hear the theology of the listeners articulated by them in their own words.

In a dialogue the hearers of sermons need to hear their own words processed and purified by Scripture as a part of the collaborative process. These purified and processed words then become a part of the proclamation, as the church seeks to live out the story of God faithfully, finding the right "local" language to tell the story in their context.

A collaborative process will help the listener hear the sermon more effectively. Through the collaborative process, the listeners are familiar with the text, and they are hearing their thoughts and ideas expressed in new and fresh ways through the voice of the preacher. They will listen better and hear more effectively.

Collaborative preaching creates greater unity in the congregation. Those who participate in it will be united in thought as they consider the same biblical text all week. The participants will share with one another their experiences with the text. They likely will find common thoughts and interests coming from these experiences. Differences in thoughts and experiences will be opportunities for more dialogue and a greater knowledge of one another. Collaborative preaching cooperates with the Spirit's desire to form God's people into a community of unity and to transform them into the image of Christ. Collaborative preaching will improve the hearing of sermons, create greater unity in the congregation, and allow the Spirit of God to do the work of transformation.

My original concept of collaborative preaching utilized and expanded the ideas of McClure, Rose, Schlafer, and others. Combining thoughts and ideas from them with my own, I designed a project that gave the preaching text to a selected group of hearers in advance with reflective questions, meditations, and prayers. After the participants had had three days of experiencing the text, I met with them to discuss their thoughts, ideas, and insights. I considered the thoughts, ideas, and insights that came from the conversation in the final sermon preparation, making sermon preparation collaborative. My original project took place over seven weeks and included seven sermons that were prepared in collaboration with the study group.

The selected study group sought a good balance between theology and anthropology. We avoided anthropocentricity by acknowledging that God is supreme and has authority over all of creation. Further, we acknowledged that the Scriptures have authority over individuals and the church. From that base we acknowledged also that we live in a world in which problems and difficulties are present. We acknowledged that we are sinful people living in a sinful world. We sought open and honest conversations about our lives and the problems we face participating in the life of God. The goal of the conversation was to acknowledge our anthropological situation and find a theological response from the text.

When the sermons associated with my project were presented, I spoke with conviction and authority without silencing other voices. I avoided making preaching an act of domination, trying to remain open, approachable, and willing to learn from other saints.[31] My goal was for the sermon to be a message from God that was heard by people living in a world of problems.

The purpose of my project was to enhance the hearing of the sermon by giving the hearers the preaching text in advance. They read the text, meditated upon it, and prayed for understanding. Their individual experience with the text prepared them to sit at the table with fellow participants and the preacher. At the table, all shared in a reflective conversation regarding the text. The personal experience with the text, coupled with the communal conversation, prepared the participants to hear the sermon more effectively.

The goal of this project was to improve the hearing of those who listen to Sunday morning sermons. According to the three methods of evaluation—field notes, a preaching response questionnaire, and a visit by an independent expert—the goal was met. Those who participated in the project heard more effectively. They indicate they experienced spiritual growth.

What is the significance of this project? It demonstrates that a collaborative approach to preaching is effective. The preacher and those who participate in the collaboration of sermon preparation all benefit.

The preacher benefits as he listens to others. Many times throughout this project, participants expressed thoughts, insights, or ideas that I had not considered. Many of them were excellent; some were brilliant. These often became the catalyst for other creative thoughts and directly influenced the content of the sermon.

The preacher benefits from instant feedback. There were times during the collaborative conversation when I would express an idea that the group did not understand fully. Without the benefit of the group, I would not have known to clarify the idea before preaching it.

The preacher benefits from directly interacting with people who are living lives that represent the members who will hear the sermon. Through conversation with group members, I gained insight into what it is like to teach school, to sell, to deliver mail, to raise babies, to work in a factory, and many other activities that members of the Mitchell Church of Christ do all week. I was able to think about how a text applies to those situations because I was able to hear directly from them how the text applies to them. This often became a source of illustrations.

Preachers benefit as they are relieved from the possible perception or accusation that they are delivering a disconnected or dogmatic monologue. The word of God belongs to the community of God. There needs to be a close connection between the community and the public proclamation of God's word. Preachers certainly have privileged voices; God has called them. Even in a collaborative approach to preaching they will make decisions about what will be presented and how it will be presented, but collaboration keeps them honest and in the mainstream of communal thought. There were occasions during this project when my thoughts about the main idea of the text were not the same as those of the group. I was challenged deeply by this, and the result was a more comprehensive sermon.

Preachers benefit greatly from a collaborative approach to preaching, but they are not alone. Members of the community who are involved in collaboration also profit. They are given an opportunity to better focus on God's word. The members of my group expressed appreciation for the structure they were given in experiencing the text.

Collaborative preaching participants benefit from the process of listening and interacting with one another and with the preacher. Each Wednesday evening during this project, the thought, idea, or insight expressed by one member would lead to other thoughts, ideas, and insights expressed by other members. All profited by the group's synergy as they considered new and different ways of thinking about the text. All of this prepared the participants to hear the sermon better since the thoughts expressed in the sermon were not totally new to them.

Participants benefited from the feedback they received in the collaborative conversation. The community that formed among the group members provided a safe environment to express thoughts, ideas, and insights honestly. Through group feedback the participants learned better discernment and articulation. They gained insight into the lives of other group members. They heard about how the biblical text is applied in different situations and circumstances.

Members of the collaborative preaching community benefited from being a part of the preparation process. They felt responsible for what was preached on Sundays. They understood the significance of their role in collaborative preaching. At least once, after a lively class interaction, the group joked with me about how I would be able to make a sermon out of the large amount of material generated by the discussion.

Everyone involved in this project benefited, including the congregation that heard the sermon. Though they did not know the preaching text in advance and were not involved in any collaborative conversations, they still gained because the sermon was shaped, in part, by those who are similar to them; by those who represent them. This project allowed the Spirit of God to do the work of transformation through the use of Scripture for all who heard the sermons.

The project study group began as a diverse group of individuals, some of whom did not know each other. As a result of the project, the study group became a community in which openness, honesty, and confession were present. The Spirit of God worked to form community. The group grew closer together with each passing week. They highly valued their participation; they were eager to be with one another. They demonstrated love and patience. They were not afraid to challenge each other's thoughts or ideas, and they were not afraid to challenge my thoughts or ideas.

The study group indicated that they grew spiritually as a result of the project. There was an increased interest in the Sunday assembly, especially in the preaching. There was an increased involvement with the biblical text during the week. The group indicated that the weekly exercises and experiences with the text prepared them to hear the sermon and have a positive listening experience.

The project described above took place a few years ago. The project changed the way I preach, and the change is permanent. I cannot imagine preaching without a process of collaboration with others in the church community. I continue to do it and continue to explore ways to expand the method.

Modifications to my approach are possible. Many years ago, Clyde Reid suggested several different models of collaborative or dialogical preaching. One of these models involved small groups meeting in neighborhood homes to study the preaching text, which had been given to the group one week prior. The groups' leaders, after meeting to study the text with the group, would then meet with the preacher to discuss what they had heard during the study.[32]

Another approach is to provide the preaching text to the congregation one week before the sermon is preached. Then an invitation is given to everyone to come to a class later in the week to discuss the preaching text. The preacher gives a brief exegesis of the passage. Following the exegesis, the group divides into several groups of ten to twelve participants. Each group selects a leader who notes what is said about the text. After about forty-five minutes, the groups come back together. After they have reassembled, each leader gives a brief report of what was heard in the small group. Prayer follows these reports.[33]

As I expanded this project to the entire congregation, my first move was to invite all congregants to be involved. Experience sheets, similar to the ones used with the project study group, were inserted into the church bulletin each week. There is an example of one at the end of this chapter. The same material also was e-mailed to a church distribution group. Any congregant who wanted to be a part of a discussion regarding the preaching text was invited to attend a class that I lead on Wednesday evenings during the church's Bible class time. Our congregation provides other class options for those who choose not to participate in this method of preaching.

After the original seven-week project was over, the study group continued to meet with me. One evening a participant prayed, thanking God that he and the others had been a part of something that could help the kingdom of God. Another participant, describing his experience in the project, said, "I do not know how you can write about it or describe it, but something special has happened here. It is beyond words."

EXAMPLE EXPERIENCE SHEET

Jesus and the Practice of Thankfulness

Instructions: Find a quiet place. Take some time to quiet your heart and mind as you prepare to meet God. Ask him to help you in this experience. You may take as much time as you want to do these exercises, but try to spend at least fifteen minutes each day focusing on this text.

The Text: Mark 8:6–7 (NIV 1984)

He told the crowd to sit down on the ground. When he had taken the seven loaves and given thanks, he broke them and gave them to his disciples to set before the people, and they did so. They had a few small fish as well; he gave thanks for them also and told the disciples to distribute them.

Monday's Experience

Guide Question

How does this passage fit with the broader context?

Meditative Activity

Read the passage slowly, carefully noting each word. Sit silently for about a minute, thinking of what you just read. Do this three times. Now, imagine the scene described by the passage. What do you see? What do you hear?

Prayer

Lord, help me to think of this passage often throughout this week. Help me to see and to hear what is taking place.

Tuesday's Experience

Guide Question

What does this passage reveal about Jesus and thankfulness?

Meditative Activity

Read the passage slowly, carefully noting each word. Sit silently for about a minute. Do this three times. Focus your imagination on Jesus. Can you see Jesus? What is he doing? Why is he thankful?

Prayer

Lord, help me to see you.

Wednesday's Experience

Guide Question

What does this passage reveal about you?

Meditative Activity

Read the passage slowly, carefully noting each word. Sit silently for about a minute, thinking of what you just read. Do this three times. How is God speaking to you through this passage? How can this passage make a difference in your life?

Prayer

Lord, reveal what you want me to hear and to learn from this passage. Prepare me to discuss my experience in this evening's study group.

Thursday–Saturday's Experience

Continue to read the text daily. Reflect upon Monday through Wednesday's experiences. Reflect, also, upon the discussion that took place in Wednesday evening's reflective Bible study. Allow your thoughts and experiences to direct your prayers. Pray specifically that you will hear the Sunday sermon effectively.

---

1. Allen Burris, "Sermon Preparation for Hearers: A Collaborative Approach to Preaching in the Mitchell Church of Christ" (DMin thesis, ACU, 2006).

2. Fred Craddock, *As One without Authority* (Nashville: Abingdon, 1979), 60.

3. Richard Lischer, "Preaching as the Church's Language," in *Listening to the Word: Studies in Honor of Fred B. Craddock*, ed. Gail R. O'Day and Thomas G. Long (Nashville: Abingdon, 1993), 113–30.

4. O. Wesley Allen, *The Homiletic of All Believers: A Conversational Approach* (Louisville: Westminster John Knox, 2005), 38.

5. Ibid., 46–49.

6. Ibid., 39.

7. Four books were published about the study: John S. McClure et al., *Listening to Listeners: Homiletical Case Studies* (St. Louis: Chalice, 2004); Ronald J. Allen, *Hearing the Sermon: Relationship, Content, Feeling* (St. Louis: Chalice, 2004); Mary Alice Mulligan et al., *Believing in Preaching: What Listeners Hear in Sermons*, (St. Louis: Chalice, 2005) and Mary Alice Mulligan and Ronald J. Allen, *Make the Word Come Alive: Lessons from Laity* (St. Louis: Chalice, 2005).

8. John S. McClure, *The Roundtable Pulpit: Where Leadership and Preaching Meet* (Nashville: Abingdon, 1995), 59–72.

9. Ibid., 21.

10. Ibid., 7.

11. Lucy Atkinson Rose, *Sharing the Word: Preaching in the Roundtable Church* (Louisville: Westminster John Knox, 1997), 121.

12. Ibid., 98.

13. Ibid., 106.

14. David Schlafer, *Surviving the Sermon: A Guide to Preaching for Those Who Have to Listen* (Boston: Cowley, 1992), 100.

15. Ibid., 50.

16. Clyde Reid, *The Empty Pulpit: A Study in Preaching as Communication* (New York: Harper and Row, 1967).

17. Ibid., 9.

18. Paul Scott Wilson, *Preaching and Homiletical Theory* (St. Louis: Chalice, 2004), 137.

19. Ibid.

20. Ibid., 138–45.

21. Joseph M. Webb, "A Reply, Both Academic and Personal, to Paul Scott Wilson's 'Radical Postmodern: A Prophetic Ethics?'" in *The Academy of Homiletics: Papers of the Annual Meeting* (Memphis: Memphis Theological Seminary, 2004), 240–49. Webb is replying to a paper read by Wilson: "Radical Postmodern: A Prophetic Ethics?" in *The Academy of Homiletics: Papers of the Annual Meeting* (Memphis: Memphis Theological Seminary, 2004), 230–39.

22. Webb, "A Reply," 245.

23. Stephen H. Webb, *The Divine Voice: Christian Proclamation and the Theology of Sound* (Grand Rapids: Brazos, 2004), 145.

24. Ibid., 167.

25. Ibid., 41–42.

26. Ibid., 41.

27. Rom. 10:14–17 (NRSV).

28. Webb, *Divine Voice*, 30.

29. Hans Van Der Geest, *Presence in the Pulpit: The Impact of Personality in Preaching*, trans. Douglas W. Stott (Atlanta: John Knox, 1981), 91.

30. Allen, *Homiletic of All Believers*, 20.

31. See Charles L. Campbell, *The Word before Powers* (Louisville: Westminster John Knox, 2002), 161–64.

32. Reid, *Empty Pulpit*, 111.

33. Browne Barr, *Parish Talk Back–A Minister's Reply to the Critics of the Local Church* (New York: Abingdon, 1964), 76–78.

CHAPTER 13

Responding to Crisis

JOHN KNOX[1]

Congregational life can change instantly. In a matter of moments, a crisis event of significant proportions hurls a community of believers into a state of shock and disequilibrium. The precipitating event could be a natural disaster that causes substantial property damage and loss of life in the city that the congregation calls home. It could be an internal crisis where individuals lose their lives or face serious injuries from an accident on a church-sponsored trip, or a beloved minister dies rather unexpectedly following a sudden illness. Moral failure of a church leader is still another kind of event that can shake the spiritual moorings of congregants. In any event, one thing is certain—as a church family, their life together will never be the same.

Are believers equipped to face the unthinkable when it occurs at church? Leaders prefer not to think about such scenarios. It is not uncommon for Christians to think that churches are immune to awful events that occur in other sectors of society. When the unthinkable happens at church, members who have been affected by a traumatic event need and expect some level of spiritual guidance.

Trauma often creates a crisis of faith. Well-trained social workers and counselors offer exceptional service in the aftermath of all kinds of crisis situations, but what they have to offer is not necessarily theologically driven. Local counselors from schools, private practices, and clinics are often kind enough to offer their services following a major tragedy, but they are not necessarily providing counsel from a Christian worldview.

Is the local church ready to step in and adequately serve a community that has been traumatized by some unexpected and horrific event? Churches often have excellent resources sitting in the pews on Sunday. Christian counselors, social workers, police officers, and other public servants often comprise an important dimension of church membership. They are uniquely qualified to serve others in times of sudden calamity.

The research I did for the DMin in 2001 came from a desire to equip churches to serve effectively during such crisis events. Specifically, the project grew out of my experience as a volunteer law-enforcement chaplain. At the time, I had served in that role for twelve years. While still serving as a chaplain today, I continue to be reminded just how fast life can change. In this role, I assist police officers with death notifications stemming from suicides, homicides, fatal car crashes, and fires. I am also called to serve people who have been victims of crime and other forms of trauma. I am additionally privileged to serve the spiritual needs of the officers as they encounter human suffering in indescribable ways.

As a chaplain, I am trained in the area of Critical Incident Stress Management (CISM). I am certified to lead critical incident debriefings for emergency first responders following particularly difficult calls in which they have served. Many police and fire departments have CISM teams that are comprised of people from several different disciplines. A team of four individuals, for example, might include a chaplain, a police officer, a paramedic, and a social worker.

My background led me to question: "Why could a church not have a crisis intervention team?" A team of this nature consisting of skilled professionals from various fields could serve the church and the community alike. They, of course, could also bring a spiritual dimension to critical incident debriefings and other forms of crisis intervention. This would necessitate theological training, as well as certification in CISM.

The Fifth Street Church of Christ in Woodward, Oklahoma, provided the ministry setting for the execution of this project. Woodward is a unique community in several ways. One distinctive factor is the geographic isolation of the city. Woodward serves as the medical and shopping hub for an eighty-mile radius that includes northwest Oklahoma, southwest Kansas, and a portion of the Texas Panhandle.

At the time, the demographic make-up of the congregation was another factor that influenced the direction of the project. In studying the demographics, I discovered that approximately 10 percent of the adult members were medical professionals. Also, several individuals within the congregation worked as allied health professionals, counselors, and social workers. Another significant proportion of the church served as professional educators. Members from these three groups were interested in ministering to the community during periods of crisis.

The third factor regarding the ministry setting was the personal trauma members of the Fifth Street Church of Christ had experienced in the years leading up to the initiation of this project. In October 1998, a twenty-one-year-old member died of complications related to a brain tumor. In May 1999, members witnessed the devastation resulting from a tornado in Oklahoma City. In May 2000, one of the congregation's leaders lost his wife as a result of suicide. In September 2001, one of the elders lost his twenty-one-year-old son in a car crash.

Traditional pastoral care was provided after each of those events. But the congregation did not have the opportunity to deal with any of those traumas as a group. As a result of these events, church leaders recognized the value of being more prepared to minister to people collectively.

The final factor that drove the development of the project concerned ministry preparedness. At that time, there was not a response plan to implement in times of community crisis. A plan to minister to people in the aftermath of traumatic events did not exist. Professionals who were members of the congregation were willing to volunteer their services in a crisis event, but there were no deployment plans in place to make use of their expertise.

The project problem was the need for a theologically-oriented crisis volunteer team that would respond in times of regional crisis events. The purpose of the project was to equip a Christian crisis response team in the congregation to minister to a traumatized community in a theologically reflective manner.

A Theology of Crisis Care

The Role of Pastoral Prayer

Christian crisis workers are called to serve people who have been traumatized. Believers volunteering for such a task must be aware of the thought processes and initial faith issues going on in the minds of those dealing with tragedy. People in trauma question life's meaning and purpose. They also wonder if the God in whom they believe has an active role in the world.

Crisis workers must additionally be aware of difficulties in communicating with other Christians facing a crisis event. Traumatized individuals find it difficult to articulate a theology of suffering during the crisis event. The stress and sorrow of the moment lead to emotional responses that communicate theologically erroneous concepts. When the forces of trauma overwhelm people, the concept of God they once held does not match their understanding of God once the trauma is over. Their relationship and experience with God is no longer storybook perfect. God's nature is quickly changing in their mind.

Serving those in crisis necessitates entering the spiritual world of the traumatized person. Here are some matters to consider in that process:

1. The ultimate comfort for suffering people includes presence, help, silence, and tears.
2. Verbal expressions of encouragement should not be based on the assumption that they must answer an implicit "why."
3. Suffering is associated with feelings of guilt.
4. It is important to offer hope.
5. The ultimate goal is to help people to know God better.[2]

In addition to the powerful ministry of quiet presence, appropriately worded prayer can be one of the most valid forms of verbal communication. Such prayer must occur in a framework of pastoral presence. Effective communication with the sufferer does not have to include theological answers to all of the "why" questions being expressed. Crisis workers are called to theological reflection regarding the direction of prayer before a traumatic episode arises. Such reflection entails gaining an awareness of different types of prayer that can be offered on behalf of those who are suffering.

An awareness of the different types of petitions that are exhibited in Scripture is a starting point. One type is characterized by petitioning God for inner strength and renewal. Prayer of this nature brings inner peace, calmness, clarity of outlook, and new strength. Petitions for physical health and healing may also be fitting at times.

Lament is a distinct form of prayer that can be a viable option for the Christian crisis worker. Lament is the form of prayer that expresses to God the pain and suffering of grief. Lament expresses the irrationality of suffering and communicates the conflicting emotions being experienced.

The psalms of lament serve as a theological resource for pastoral prayer. Hicks lists three dimensions of such psalms.

1. Invocation: God is called upon to hear the prayers of his people.
2. Redemption: God is petitioned to deliver his people from their fallen situation.
3. Imprecation: The people ask God to destroy their enemies.[3]

Psalm 13 illustrates these three dimensions of lament. The psalmist repeatedly invokes the name of God (Ps. 13:1–3). The redemptive petitions call on God to notice his suffering servant, answer his pleas, and redeem him from darkness. (Ps. 13:3–4). God does not allow the enemies to rejoice over the demise of godly servants, so the imprecation is implied in the psalm. Psalms of lament often follow this structure: the psalmist laments over the situation and then offers a petition for God's help (Ps. 22:1, 11).

Pastoral prayer can follow the form of a lament during a traumatic period. The person petitioning on behalf of the traumatized individual can express in prayer the hurt and frustration that the individual no doubt is feeling. It can be a true lament in the sense that God's mercy and grace are sought out in a petitionary manner. Careful theological reflection must precede the offering of such a prayer.

In serving as a law-enforcement chaplain for twenty-two years, I have learned that victims of trauma appreciate authentic prayer. Prayers filled with predictable clichés are not helpful. An understanding of the components of lament is helpful. The one serving can cry out to God on behalf of people who have experienced the incomprehensible in their life.

A Theology of Crisis Ministry

The development of an actual theology of crisis ministry is an integral step in preparing to help those experiencing crisis. Crisis theory is a helpful tool for Christians serving traumatized individuals, but workers must consider several matters of theological relevance. As a beginning point, the crisis experience needs to be defined in theological terms. A crisis, according to secular theory, is defined as: "A temporary state of upset and disorganization, characterized chiefly as an individual's inability to cope with a particular situation using customary methods of problem solving, and by the potential for a radically positive or negative outcome."[4] Such a definition fails to include major faith issues that are an integral part of the experience.

Charles Gerkin offers a theological definition of a crisis. In a crisis, according to Gerkin, people must face their human vulnerability and finitude. Individuals in a situation of that nature confront a religious choice. Either they can defend themselves with whatever human defense is possible, or they can open themselves up to the vulnerability of an unknown future. The second option means trusting in the power and care of God.[5] The theological framework offered by Gerkin is a reminder that significant faith issues are going on in the lives of those traumatized. The implicit goal of believers responding to the crisis is to view such events in that light, so the positive outcome can be a renewed faith.

Several years ago, I served a family that lost a teenage daughter in a fatal car crash that would be characterized as a true accident. They experienced the above-mentioned vulnerability and temporary state of disorganization, along with a host of other emotions. First responders at the scene of that crash allowed their faith to inform their interactions with the family. I did follow-up pastoral care acting on behalf of the police department. One of the officers initiated follow-up visits to assist with their emotional healing. The family's church provided exceptional pastoral care in the months following that event. In all of those encounters, faith issues were a primary focus of the discussions. The tragedy is still a constant reality in the life of each family member, but they have also found a renewed faith as they continue to heal from their loss.

Karl Slaikeu describes some of the major assumptions of crisis theory that add to the framework necessary for theological reflection.

Crises have definite beginnings. The crisis is touched off by some specific event.

1. The crisis event is interpreted by the victim as a breaking point. The event may even appear minor, but it is at the end of a long list of stressful events.

2. Situational crises are accidental or unexpected. They could include the death of a loved one through a natural disaster or being the victim of a violent crime.

3. Developmental crises entail the developmental moves from one life stage to another.[6]

He does not refer specifically to the spiritual issues at hand during such crises, but the spiritual dimension is real. When a person experiences an emotional breaking point, an array of spiritual concerns begins to surface. Where is God in that situation? How is God working in my life? How much is God going to give me to deal with at this juncture in my life? Those are the kinds of questions the person in crisis asks. Those serving should be prepared for such intense faith-driven inquiries. The sudden nature of many crisis events leads to the need for interventionists to be prepared to bring a sense of calm in the immediate hours following a tragedy. A peaceful ministry of presence, appropriate prayer, and even the fitting use of Scripture can accomplish that sense of calm.

In terms of ministry priority, Jesus is frequently seen in the gospel accounts serving the needs of those experiencing situational crises. The man suffering from paralysis sought out Jesus. He experienced both physical and spiritual healing (Mk. 2:1–12). Peter reached a spiritual crisis in his life following his denial of Jesus (Mk. 14:66–72). Jesus reached out to him during this critical point in his life with a message of reassurance and redemption (John 21:15–23). The ministry of Jesus indicates that serving people experiencing crisis moments in their faith is important.

Theological Foundations for Critical Incident Stress Management

The task of the individual providing pastoral crisis intervention is to mediate hope in the midst of the apparently contradictory evidence of death and destruction. The specialized field of CISM is a valuable asset to those striving to offer good pastoral care. Critical incident debriefings and defusings can include a spiritual dimension. As a rule, the goal for these structured interventions is to provide some emotional first aid in the immediate days following a traumatic event. But the possibility exists for a theologically driven CISM model. The primary goal of such a model is to mitigate a faith crisis. A critical incident debriefing would then include spiritual reflection on matters regarding God's providence, pastoral prayer, and Scripture.

George Everly introduces the concept of pastoral intervention: the integration of religious, spiritual, and pastoral resources with the assessment and intervention strategies typically thought of as crisis intervention. He lists the following mechanisms unique to pastoral crisis intervention:

1. Scriptural education and insight
2. Individual and conjoint prayer
3. Unifying and explanatory world views
4. Ventilative confession
5. Faith-based social support systems
6. Rituals and sacraments
7. Belief in divine intervention/forgiveness
8. Belief in a life after death
9. Unique ethos of the pastoral crisis interventionist
10. Uniquely confidential/privileged communications[7]

George Everly notes that the individual must have a receptive state of mind and a desire or expectation for scriptural guidance and other forms of spiritual insight. He also lists the potential pitfalls of pastoral crisis intervention based on his experience:

1. Arguing or debating spiritual/theological issues with the person in acute crisis.
2. Attempting to explain theologically why a trauma occurred.

3. Preaching to or praying with the "unreceptive individual."

4. Attempting to "convert" the unreceptive individual.[8]

Traumatic events raise spiritual questions regarding injustice, unfairness, meaning, and purpose. Trauma tears at the fabric of one's faith. To develop a full understanding of the trauma story, the survivor must examine the moral questions of guilt and responsibility and reconstruct a system of belief that makes sense of the undeserved suffering.[9]

The intent of this project was to employ many of the elements listed under the umbrella of pastoral crisis intervention. Everly and others in this field readily admit the value of a spiritual dimension, but leave the details open-ended for faith-based groups and leaders to determine. The goal of this project was to flesh out those details in Woodward.

A Crisis Intervention Team

Churches want to make good use of talented and well-trained volunteers. Unfortunately, the listing of ministries that utilizes capable people rarely includes a crisis intervention team. Licensed counselors are sought out for referral purposes. A police officer is occasionally asked to assist with security during a church function. But counselors, peace officers, social workers, and paramedics are not characteristically put together on a team at church for crisis intervention.

The project intervention entailed bringing these professionals together to serve on one team. In the following section, I will describe training for team members, and other logistics. Now, ten years later, I would do some things differently, so I will also offer additional ideas that might serve a community of believers even better.

Team Formation

A congregational crisis intervention team is ideally comprised of no more than twelve qualified individuals. Professional credentials, spiritual maturity, and emotional capacity to cope with a ministry of this nature determine participation on the team. A team leader should be chosen first based on the possession of excellent organizational and interpersonal communication skills. That individual should additionally be certified in Basic Group and Individual Crisis Intervention. The International Critical Incident Stress Management Foundation (www.icisf.org) provides training and certification in these areas.

The team leader then seeks out professionals in the fields of medicine, education, and the behavioral sciences. Other potential teammates could include police officers, firefighters, and medics. The leader conducts an initial interview with prospective members in order to assess emotional maturity, willingness to work as a team member, and overall suitability to serve in a high-pressure context. In addition to those traits, the team leader must assess the prospective members' ability to maintain confidences and work within their professional limits.

A licensed professional counselor who possesses advanced CISM credentials assumes responsibility for a second interview to assess the prospective member's prior exposure to traumatic events. Past exposure to trauma could impede a person's performance on a team of this nature. The counselor then makes a final recommendation concerning each individual's ability to serve effectively. It would also be helpful to seek out an evaluation of each potential team member's spiritual maturity from respected members in a congregation.

Critical Incident Stress Management (CISM)

What is CISM? It is not a field that intersects with church life every day. CISM is a specific discipline that has evolved over the years as an effort to provide immediate emotional first-aid to those who have been traumatized by a critical incident. The following terms are unique to the field of critical incident stress management:

Critical Incident: An event that has the potential to overwhelm one's usual coping mechanisms, resulting in psychological distress and an impairment of normal adaptive functioning.

Critical Incident Stress Management: An integrated and comprehensive multicomponent program for the provision of crisis and disaster mental-health services.

Crisis Intervention: Urgent and acute emotional first aid designed to stabilize and reduce symptoms of stress.

Critical Incident Stress Debriefing:

1. A specific model developed by Jeffrey T. Mitchell and George S. Everly.
2. It is used with a homogenous group of individuals who have experienced a crisis or traumatic event.
3. It is designed to bring psychological closure to a traumatic event.
4. A specific seven-stage protocol is involved.
5. The critical incident stress debriefing is the most complex of all the critical incident stress management interventions.
6. It was originally designed to reduce stress in emergency personnel after extremely traumatic experiences.

7. The overuse of this tool in response to relatively minor events is not a proper application of the process.

8. The goals of a debriefing are as follows: mitigate the impact of the critical incident, accelerate normal recovery processes in normal people who are experiencing normal stress. Identify people within the group who might be in need of referral for additional assistance.

Critical Incident Defusing:

1. The defusing is a twenty- to forty-five-minute discussion of the crisis event that is conducted within twelve hours of the crisis.

2. It is designed to bring about a restoration of functioning.

3. It includes three phases: introduction, exploration, and information.

4. The defusing is a shortened version of the debriefing and may actually eliminate the need to do a debriefing at a later time.

5. It has some degree of structure but is less organized than a formal debriefing.

6. Well-trained peer support personnel can easily provide the defusing.

7. The goals of the defusing are as follows: a rapid reduction in the intense reactions to the traumatic event. A "normalizing" of the experience so that people can return to their routines as quickly as possible. A reestablishment of the social network of the group is prompted so that people do not isolate themselves from each other. Instead they see that their reactions are similar to each other's. In recognizing similarities in others, people are often more willing to help each other in troubled times.

The Training Experience

Individuals chosen to serve on a crisis intervention team bring their own strengths and professional expertise to the group. A shared training experience is valid for several reasons. The goals of a team with a spiritual focus need to be articulated clearly. The team members will have varying experiences with CISM. The use of those skills as a team must be emphasized. The group will function in a church context. That too may be a new experience, even for seasoned interventionists. The training curriculum involves ten sessions that have a distinct purpose and theme. They are as follows:

Session One—An Introduction to Crisis Ministry

During the first session, a fictional case study is utilized which revolves around an incident of school violence. In the fictional case, church members are directly impacted by the incident at the school. The story of the case is as follows: A troubled teenager opens fire on a group of high school students participating in a Christian devotional in the school cafeteria just before classes begin early one morning at the high school. There are six students injured and one killed. Five of the students injured and the deceased student are members of the same church of about three hundred members. Several first responders and a physician in the trauma center at the hospital are members of that same congregation. The fictional case is written with the specific intent of demonstrating all of the relationships that are endemic to both small and medium-size towns. In other words, it would not be uncommon for both a responding police officer and an emergency-room physician to be members of the same church where teenage victims from a local high school have been injured or killed. A hard copy of the case is distributed to each participant and then read orally. The primary issues in the case study are discussed, along with the implications for the affected congregation, and appropriate actions for the crisis response team.

After discussing the case study in detail, a pretraining inventory is distributed to the group. This inventory is designed to gauge their thoughts on crisis ministry before getting into the training experience in depth. The case study serves as the basis of the inventory. The questions included on the pretraining inventory are as follows:

1. What are the primary spiritual issues facing the victims involved in this case?
2. What are the primary spiritual issues that other individuals involved in the case are facing? (This would include the police officers, paramedics, and attending physicians in the emergency room.)
3. What actions should be taken on behalf of various individuals impacted by the crisis to aid them in the process of spiritual healing?
4. What can be done to assist the entire congregation in the process of spiritual healing?

It is stressed to those undergoing the training that there are no wrong answers at this point in the process.

Session Two—The Providence of God

In the intervention conducted with the Woodward congregation as a part of the project thesis, I invited Dr. Fred Aquino, professor of theology at ACU's Graduate School of Theology, to conduct a seminar that had the providence of God as its focus. Since the seminar would benefit the entire congregation, it was not offered exclusively to the crisis intervention team. At the beginning of the second training session, copies of Dr. Aquino's notes were distributed to each team member. After a summation of the seminar content, several theological matters were brought to the forefront.

The models of God's providence (Semi-Deist, Process, Openness, Molist, Calvinist, and Fatalist) were discussed at the seminar. Some level of awareness of the differing models equips interventionists to serve more effectively. Compassionate Christians must be theologically reflective in advance of a crisis situation because of the potential to do untold damage to traumatized people when theological thoughtlessness prevails. Understanding of God's providence is fundamental to ministering to people in traumatic situations. The second session concludes with a brief introduction to the use of critical incident debriefings and defusings with a spiritual orientation.

Session Three—Providing Spiritual Care in the Midst of Congregational Trauma: Part 1

Theological issues outside the realm of God's providence are the primary focus of the third session. The group discusses several thought-provoking quotations regarding the integration of faith with the reality of trauma. The case study used earlier in the training becomes the focus of the discussion in a more specific manner. Participants answer questions dealing with theologically thoughtful ways to communicate with individuals who have been impacted by trauma. The ministry of silence as a valid medium of communication is considered in this section. Such a ministry expresses itself in at least three forms:

1. Presence: Primary comfort for the griever does not come through the words of comforters but through their presence.
2. Listening: We are God's instruments of comfort, and just as God listens, so should we.
3. Action: When we act, we put ourselves in the place of seeing the world with their eyes.

Particular attention is given to the book of Job. The group examines the ministry of silence from the viewpoint of Job and analyzes the verbal shortcomings of Job's friends. The team then makes ministry applications concerning service to the traumatized, based on the erroneous conclusions and verbal attacks of Job's friends.

Secondly, several forms of prayer are considered. In particular, biblical examples of lament are appropriated for traumatic situations. Laments included in the training experience are: Psalm 13:1–6; 73:1–28; 77:1–15.

There are moments when verbal communication becomes important in the crisis intervention process. The following statements are fitting in a traumatic ministry setting:

I can't imagine how painful this must be for you; I am so sorry.
I am praying for you, and I want you to know that I love you.

The group brainstorms other fitting statements that can be conveyed when ministering in a crisis context. The team is also given a sampling of things never to say to someone in crisis:

1. This was the will of God.
2. God plucked a rose out of his garden.
3. Some good will come out of this.
4. It was for the best.
5. You need to take a hard look at your life.

Once again brainstorming ensues to determine additional statements that should never be made to someone feeling the pain of trauma and loss. This third training session is an engaging experience because it brings to light common pitfalls of communication in tense situations.

Session Four—Providing Spiritual Care in the Midst of Congregational Trauma: Part 2

The discipline of critical incident stress management is formally introduced in this portion of the training. It is imperative that team members undergo basic certification in group and individual crisis intervention offered by the International Critical Incident Stress Management Foundation prior to undergoing this training experience. This training is often hosted by law-enforcement agencies, fire departments, and hospitals. The ICISF website provides current information regarding nationwide opportunities for training. The primary purpose of this session is to discuss the use of CISM interventions by a team that has distinct religious purposes. This time is also used to assess what experiences the individual team members have had in using CISM tools either professionally or as a volunteer with another organization.

Session Five—Spiritual Defusing: Part I

This session assumes that participants are familiar with the concept of a critical incident defusing based on prior training. The group begins by discussing the important dynamics of a successful defusing. The team then considers the unique dynamics of a spiritually-focused defusing. The original case study is used as a framework to discuss defusings. Using the case, details are outlined in the specific format of a spiritual defusing.

As the case study is reviewed, the spiritual needs of those impacted by this trauma are discussed. Using role play, a spiritual defusing is acted out. One person is designated as the facilitator. Another person assists by being prepared to exit the defusing with an emotionally distraught participant if needed. A third person on the team functions primarily in a support role. That experience will take place in the following order:

1. The facilitator begins the defusing by leading prayer.
2. One of the questions to be posed in the process is: What thoughts about God or your relationship with God ran through your mind as the traumatic event unfolded?
3. The facilitator will present a list of spiritually-driven emotions such as: guilt, anger and forgiveness to the group. The question will be posed: Which of these emotions are you experiencing to larger degree in the process of your recovery?
4. Team members will take the time to stand behind individuals and pray for them before the defusing concludes.

The components therefore include but are not limited to: prayer, the use of Scripture, and the consideration of faith issues the traumatized person is facing. The session concludes with an emphasis on the need to follow up on defusings with appropriate referrals.

Session Six—Pastoral Defusing: Part 2

Next, three teenagers and one adult are used to role-play a pastoral defusing based on the case study used in the training. Each of the participants play the role of having been directly impacted by the trauma described in the case study. The trainer leads the defusing without assistance, so he can stop periodically during the process and make necessary observations.

Several compelling themes surfaced. Three of the participants described the traumatic experience in detail. The theological issues of fear and forgiveness came to the surface. One of the role players remained silent during the entire defusing. Observers immediately picked up on the danger signs of such a refusal. One of the role players was extremely emotional in her reaction to the trauma. Still another was matter-of-fact in her analysis. One person stated that the experience caused her to reevaluate her relationship with God. The session ended with a follow-up discussion. Observers shared their reactions to the experience. It appeared as if the defusing shocked team members. The role-play was a reality check, giving every person in the group an indication of what a real spiritual defusing experience would look like.

Session Seven—Pastoral Defusing: Part 3

In this session, volunteers play the roles of the professionals involved in the case study used throughout the training experience. The purpose is to make the experience as real as possible. In addition to the role-play, rules of confidentiality are discussed.

Session Eight—CISM Debriefing

Next, the training focused on the use of a critical incident stress debriefing in the aftermath of a congregational trauma or in another event where the church crisis team is deployed to serve the community. The assumption is made that team members have a basic familiarity with all CISM interventions, including a debriefing, based on previous certification training. This session is therefore devoted to role-playing a debriefing that would have a distinct spiritual dimension.

Critical incident stress debriefings conducted in a group setting have a seven-step protocol. The seven phases are as follows:

1. Introduction: Introductions are made and protocol is discussed. Issues pertaining to confidentiality are stressed.
2. Fact: Participants describe the facts of the incident from their viewpoint as a participant or an eyewitness.
3. Thought: The first thoughts of each participant in the group are explored and discussed.
4. Reaction: The most common question used during this phase is: "What was the worst part of this situation for you personally?"
5. Symptoms: The team leader begins the process of moving the group back to cognitively oriented material in this phase. This is

accomplished by asking participants to describe any cognitive, emotional, or behavioral things they may have experienced during the critical incident.

6. Teaching: The team member points out the normalcy of the symptoms they maybe experiencing.

7. Re-Entry: Issues are clarified; questions are answered; summary statements are made. The discussion reaches a closure point.[10]

The spiritual dimensions included in a formal debriefing are similar to the elements included in the defusing setting. Questions of a faith-driven nature can be posed openly. Group and individual prayer are integral components. Scripture can be shared at the beginning or as a means of concluding the activity as a group.

Session Nine—Special Issues

In the final session in the training process, emphasis is placed on the issues that a Christian crisis-response team would not be equipped to address. The team is not designed or responsible for providing counseling. Those on the team with the proper credentials may pursue that form of care individually outside the realm of the team. Otherwise, team members make appropriate referrals to professionals who specialize in meeting a particular need. Special attention is given to post-traumatic stress disorder, listing its characteristics and carefully pointing out that this list is only to be used for the purpose of awareness and not for diagnosis.

An Assessment of the Training Experience

The ministry intervention conducted with the Fifth Street Church of Christ in Woodward, Oklahoma, was instructive. The content of the fictional case study used as a basis for discussion shocked the members of the congregation who agreed to participate in the crisis-ministry training. School violence has indeed become a reality with which communities of various sizes have been forced to cope in recent years. The class members were fully aware of such events.

Discussing and evaluating the case study was disturbing to each participant but proved to be an effective way to begin the training experience. The reality of traumatic experiences for believers with whom we worship every week surfaced in the ensuing discussion. Each participant was eager to discuss intervention strategies.

As a result of the intervention stemming from the project thesis, it became evident that discussion revolving around crisis ministry in a congregational setting must be as specific as possible. If the case study had not appeared to be germane to the ministry setting in Woodward, the results would have been unsuccessful. The interest on the part of the participants would have been diminished if the scenario being discussed had seemed out of step with the realities of life in rural northwest Oklahoma. No one in the training group denied the need to address crisis ministry aggressively.

Dr. Aquino's seminar focusing on God's providence was helpful, but equally unsettling in content. Seminar attendees were surprised to discover the varying concepts regarding the nature of God's providence. If they had a model of providence worked out in their minds prior to the seminar, it was challenged significantly. Several of those participating indicated intent to reevaluate their positions regarding God's activity in the world.

Those who took part in the seminar came away with a new appreciation for the complexity of spiritual difficulties that arise when a tragic event unfolds. Aquino used the events surrounding September 11, 2001, to illustrate what people experience spiritually after a traumatic occurrence. He repeatedly posed questions regarding the presence of God. Seminar attendees were forced to come to some conclusions. The varying views of God's providence provided the necessary framework in which to carry out the conversation. I would not recommend conducting the training in critical incident stress management principles in a congregational setting without the theological foundation created by exploring God's providence in depth.

Ministry Possibilities

Future ministry stemming from this project would fall into two areas. Conducting a training experience similar to what was done in Woodward could serve as a catalyst to launch a Christian crisis-response team that could meet the needs of a given geographical area. All team participants would need to be certified by the International Critical Incident Stress Foundation or a similar organization that provides certification in this area of service.

The second area of ministry arising from this project would be ambitious but useful. If several Christians sought certification as instructors in critical incident stress management from ICISF, then they could offer that kind of training to churches, thereby taking care of the need for certification of team members. They could also offer seminars on critical incident stress management to churches. If members of a church were interested in putting together their own Christian response team, certified professionals could offer training to facilitate that goal.

I continue to be actively involved in crisis ministry. At the present time, I am serving as a volunteer chaplain for both the Texas Department of Public Safety and the Granbury Police Department. Other agencies in Hood County, including the Hood County Sheriff's Office and the Hood County Fire Marshal's office, make use of my chaplaincy services as well. I have also been fortunate to be a part of the formation of a countywide critical incident response team that is comprised of first responders, chaplains, and counselors in the area. The execution of this project reminded me of the gravity of such a role, and the need for well-trained servants who can do crisis ministry in a congregational setting.

---

1. John Knox, "Developing a Regional Christian Crisis Response Team at the Fifth Street Church of Christ, Oklahoma" (DMin thesis, ACU, 2003).

2. Donald A. Carson, *How Long, O Lord? Reflections on Suffering and Evil* (Grand Rapid: Baker, 1990), 248–51.

3. John Mark Hicks, *Yet Will I Trust Him: Understanding God in a Suffering World* (Joplin, MO: College Press, 1999), 119.

4. Karl A. Slaikeu, *Crisis Intervention: A Handbook for Practice and Research* (Boston: Allyn and Bacon, 1990), 15.

5. Charles V. Gerkin, *Crisis Experience in Modern Life: Theory and Theology in Modern Life* (Nashville: Abingdon, 1979).

6. Slaikeu, *Crisis Intervention*, 18.

7. George S. Everly, "The Role of Pastoral Care in Disasters, Terrorism, Violence, and Other Community Crises," *International Journal of Emergency Health* 2.3 (2000): 139.

8. Ibid.

9. Merle R. Jordan, "A Spiritual Perspective on Trauma and Treatment," *NCP Quarterly* 5.1 (Winter 1995): 1.

10. Jeffrey T. Mitchell and George S. Everly, *Critical Incident Stress Debriefing: An Operations Manual for CISD, Defusing, and Other Group Intervention Service* (Ellicott City, MD: Chevron Publishing, 2001), 144ff.

A Son's Memorial

JOHN SIBURT

A few years ago my mom found a poem by Edna St. Vincent Millay entitled "Dirge without Music" that she kept with her throughout our family's battle against myeloma. The poem reads:

> I am not resigned to the shutting away of loving hearts in the hard ground.
> So it is, and so it will be, for so it has been, time out of mind:
> Into the darkness they go, the wise and the lovely. Crowned
> With lilies and with laurel they go; but I am not resigned.
>
> Lovers and thinkers, into the earth with you.
> Be one with the dull, the indiscriminate dust.
> A fragment of what you felt, of what you knew,
> A formula, a phrase remains,—but the best is lost.
>
> The answers quick and keen, the honest look, the laughter, the love,—
> They are gone. They are gone to feed the roses. Elegant and curled
> Is the blossom. Fragrant is the blossom. I know. But I do not approve.
> More precious was the light in your eyes than all the roses in the world.
>
> Down, down, down into the darkness of the grave
> Gently they go, the beautiful, the tender, the kind;
> Quietly they go, the intelligent, the witty, the brave.
> I know. But I do not approve. And I am not resigned.[1]

We know Dad has died but we do not approve and we are not resigned. We do not approve of this beautiful life being cut short at age sixty-five. We are not resigned to living without his unfailing love, courageous faith, deep wisdom, and joyful smile. We fought with everything in us to give my dad more time among us, and, honestly, we are still trying to figure out how to bear what seems to us an unbearable loss.

It seemed so fitting to me that ACU lowered the school flag to half-mast in Dad's honor, because as far as I am concerned a *hero* has fallen . . . he's been my hero my entire life. Even before I could read and write, I would type "sermons" on the family typewriter and deliver them from the fireplace hearth because I wanted to be like my dad. He would take me with him when he went to preach Wednesday night sermon series in small East Texas towns outside of Tyler. We would enjoy "fine dining" at the local Dairy Queen or Braums, and I thought he was the most important man in the world.

Over the years I have had the privilege of discovering that he was not only my hero . . . he became a hero to many of you as well. In fact, that is the most often used term by you this week in comments to our family. Over and over you have told us that he was your hero. He was a hero because he showed us God's love especially when we needed it most . . . because he believed in us more than we believed in ourselves . . . because he loved us enough to tell us the truth even when it was painful to hear. My dad was a hero but he didn't have superpowers unless you consider poor eyesight, bad blood, and the ability to put your fist in your mouth "superpowers." What he possessed was a heroic belief in the good news of God's love and a willingness to let the power of God's love shine through him.

Dad truly was an "ambassador for Christ" and he allowed himself to be used by God to reconcile people to God and to one another. Many of us here today believe in a God of love and believe God might actually love us because my dad loved us so well. He gave us a glimpse of the love of God and let us know that we were full recipients of it. We believe that God must be forgiving because when we messed up the most he was the first to forgive. We believe that story about a loving father running to wrap prodigals in his arms and welcome them home. We believe God must be that kind of God because we found ourselves wrapped in the arms of Charlie Siburt who was ready to show us grace and throw us a party when we woke up and returned to our senses.

We believe God has a contagious laugh, a beaming smile, a beautiful singing voice, and deep love for babies and children because they were VIPs to my dad. And we believe God must have a fine appreciation for beautiful women because no matter how bad my dad's vision he said, "I may be blind but I can still see beautiful!" When my parents were in Hawaii, Mom said, "It's too bad you are blind, Charlie." And Dad said, "Why, so I could see that blonde in the blue bikini?" He would gloat over my mom, my wife, my sister-in-law, and his granddaughters because "he may be blind, but he can still see beautiful."

We believe all these things because my dad worked tirelessly to reveal them to us and because he allowed God to do through him what God can do through any of us . . . reconcile people to God. Dad did not have superpowers. He merely allowed himself to be used by God's power to share God's love. The power displayed in my dad's life is one that is available to us all. We too can be ministers of reconciliation. In fact, many of you here today already are, and Dad considered it a privilege to join you in the work of God.

The thing I've been wrestling with for months in anticipation of this day is how do we keep going after a hero has fallen? This seems like a big defeat. It is a huge loss. He seems irreplaceable. It is tempting to feel cheated, to feel like God has abandoned us, fallen down on the job. I have felt all of these things the past few months, but I was convicted by an experience I had last week. I was in Dad's study going through some of the cards and notes sent to him . . . there was one thanking him for a talk he gave last year at the Lifeline Chaplaincy Dinner and remembering what a powerful title he chose. In the midst of suffering with cancer, dad entitled his talk "Why Has He Been So Good to Me?" I was wrestling with a different "why" question? "Why did he have to be blind? Why did he have to get cancer? Why does he have to leave us?" And Dad asked, "Why have you been so good to me?"

Dad never felt abandoned or cheated by God. He felt blessed beyond measure, grateful for the beautiful wife and two strong sons given him by God. Grateful for the legacy that lives on in his grandkids and for the privilege of the ministry given him by God and for all the wonderful people it allowed him to serve and to love. Dad lived with joy and gratitude even in the midst of suffering, especially in the midst of suffering, and he learned from experience that the power of Christ is not displayed in the avoidance of suffering but in the faithful enduring of it.

He knew that the only way to experience the power of Easter Sunday is to walk through the darkness of Good Friday. He was like the apostle Paul in that he came to "know Christ and the power of the resurrection by sharing in Christ's suffering and becoming like him in his death." And what is amazing about my dad is that he not only found ways to be victorious over his own suffering, he volunteered to enter into ours to walk alongside us when things were at the worst. He willingly took our suffering upon him and helped us find joy and be faithful. Isn't that what an ambassador of Christ should do? Isn't that what Christ did?

Dad truly believed there was victory in Jesus and he experienced it time and time again. Dad got used to being victorious over suffering and so the final weeks of his battle with cancer were tough on him because he felt like maybe he was finally going to lose a battle. He did not like the scoreboard. But his good friend and caregiver, Dr. Vega, told him that not even myeloma could defeat him. Dr. Vega commended him on living one of the most victorious lives he had ever seen. Dr. Vega helped Dad see that even if myeloma was going to cause his death it could not rob him of a "victorious" life. So Dad prepared for one more battle and turned his sights on being victorious over death.

Our family was privileged to walk with him into the "valley of the shadow of death" and in the spirit of Psalm 23, we did so without fear because we knew God was with us and that his rod and staff would comfort us. And amazingly the shadow of death was nowhere to be found in hospice room 7103 as my dad took his last breath. It was drowned out by the bright glow, the warm light, of life and love. Dad entered into the suffering of death and claimed victory once again. He was a hero to the very end.

And so we will move forward. In the spirit of my hero, we will be victorious. We will live in the same spirit of joy and gratitude my dad displayed with the same unwavering faith in the power of God's love. We will not walk around the pain of our grief. We will walk through it and it will not defeat us. We will claim victory yet again. We will laugh. We will love. We will find joy. We will choose to be grateful. We will show grace. We will offer forgiveness. We will give encouragement. We will speak truth. We will help God redeem and restore. We will take our place as "ambassadors of Christ" like my dad. For I am convinced of what my dad believed, that nothing, not even death . . . not even the death of my hero . . . can separate us from the love of God in Christ Jesus.

---

1. Edna St. Vincent Millay, "Dirge without Music" from *Collected Poems*. Copyright 1928, © 1955 by Edna St. Vincent Millay and Norma Millay Ellis. Reprinted with the permission of The Permissions Company, Inc., on behalf of Holly Peppe, Literary Executor, The Millay Society. www.millay.org.

APPENDICES

Select Bibliography: The Writings of Charles A. Siburt Jr. (1978–2011)

Compiled by Craig Churchill and Karissa Herchenroeder[1]

Integrative Unit Project

1978 "Foundations for Youth Ministry in the Local Church." Integrative unit project, Austin Presbyterian Theological Seminary.

Books Edited

2006 *Like a Shepherd Lead Us: Guidance for the Gentle Art of Pastoring* (with David Fleer). Abilene, TX: Leafwood.

2007 *Good Shepherds: More Guidance for the Gentle Art of Pastoring* (with David Fleer) Abilene, TX: Leafwood.

Scholarly Journal Articles, Essays, and Reviews

1976 "Game of Rejecting God: Luke 7:31–35." *Restoration Quarterly* 19: 207–10.

1977 "Response by Charles Siburt." *Austin Seminary Bulletin* [Faculty Ed.] 92:8 (May): 30–34.

1981 Review of *Ministry in America*, by David S. Schuller, et al. *Papers Delivered at the First Christian Scholars Conference* (July 18): 1–11 [155–65].

1983 "Contemporary Marriage and Family Therapies: A Biblical Perspective." *Paper Delivered at the Third Christian Scholars Conference* (July 24): 1–14 [319–32].

1995 "Congregational Unity: Faith and Opinion." In *Church Unity: Stability and Flexibility in the Church*, edited by Donald Michael Kinder, 75–90. Harding University Graduate School of Religion, 1995 Preacher's Forum. Nashville, TN: Gospel Advocate.

1995 "A Response to 'And They Were Silent.'" *Christian Studies*, no. 15: 41–45.

2004 "Ministerial Compensation among Churches of Christ in the United States." (with Malcolm Coco and Tim Coburn) *Restoration Quarterly* 46: 29–50.

Surveys

2004–11 "Minister's Salary Survey." Administered annually via e-mail to ministers. Abilene Christian University, College of Biblical Studies, Siburt Institute for Church Ministry. Survey Results http://www.acu.edu/siburt-institute/resources/salarysurvey/index.html [accessed October 12, 2012].

Popular Articles

1979 "A Word Fitly Spoken." *Twentieth Century Christian* 41 (April): 26–27.

1981 "The Biggest Disease." *Twentieth Century Christian* 43 (May): 4–7.

1982 "The Fall." *Twentieth Century Christian* 44 (February): 7–9.

1983 "When to Love." *Twentieth Century Christian* 45 (July): 9–11.

1987 "Care for the Dying." *Twentieth Century Christian* 49 (August): 15–17.

1990 "Forgiven Parents." *UpReach* 12 (May–July): 4–6.

1991 "Worship—The Real World." *Gospel Advocate* 133 (February): 23.

"Choose Your Future." *UpReach* 13 (April–June): 4–7.

"Lighting the Darkness." *UpReach* 13 (October–December): 6–7.

1993 "Turned by Grace." *UpReach* 15 (July–September): 17–19.

1994 "Training Tomorrow's Ministers." *ACU Today* (Spring): 5.

2001 "Be of One Mind . . . Anyway." *Leaven* 9: 210–11.

2002 "Dealing with Negative Church Experiences." *Church and Family Magazine* (Summer): 29-30.

"Resource Guide: Bibliography Crisis Ministry." *Leaven* 10: 155.

2004 "Question and Answer: Providing Resources to Churches." *ACU Today* (Spring): 20.

2006 "Preparing for Conflict and Sustaining Peace." (with Royce Money and Joe L. Cope) *Christian Standard* 141 (September 10): 582–85.

---

1. The following student workers assisted with the research for all four appendices: Kyle Yarbrough, Dwayne Lee, Steven Brice, and John Kern.

APPENDIX B

Charles A. Siburt Jr: Primary Advisor

Compiled by Craig Churchill and Karissa Herchenroeder

Charles Siburt influenced hundreds of graduate theology students at ACU, in various programs (MS, MAR, MACM, MDiv, and DMin), through teaching, advising, counseling, examining, and mentoring. It is impractical to attempt to document the full scope of his activity in all of these areas. We can, however, illustrate something of the extent of his influence by focusing on one aspect of his work with a specific group of students: the ministers who entered the DMin Program during Charles's tenure at ACU.

From 1988 to 2012, Charles served as Director of the DMin Program at ACU. He served on more than seventy-five oral defenses for DMin candidates, and he was the major advisor for approximately fifty project theses. He served as secondary advisor on well over a dozen theses and as a reader on several more. Here follows a compilation of theses by students for whom Charles served as primary advisor.

Adcox, James M. "Christ Living Through His Church: Calling the Southwest Church of Christ to God's Vision for Christian Community." 1999.

Alexander, L. Bert. "Developing a Model for Incarnational Ministry at the Webb Chapel Church of Christ." 2009.

Bynum, David Otto. "Increasing Volunteer Participation in a Need Meeting Ministry in Rural Churches and Communities." 1994.

Camp, Daniel F. "Discerning a Vocational Theology of Marriage for the Smyrna Church of Christ." 2011.

Cartwright, Terry. "Developing a Theology of Worship for the Lakewood Church." 1991.

Cole, Paul Russell. "Equipping Church Leaders to Function as Spiritual Mentors." 1998.

Cook, Russell L. "An Initial Congregational Study in a New Ministry Setting." 1994.

Cummings, Ronald Gregory. "A Strategy for Increasing the Participation of Young Adults in the Kerrville Church of Christ." 2000.

Dykstra, Wayne Arthur. "Leadership Development in Christian Churches and Churches of Christ in Northeast Nebraska." 1999.

Edge, William Mark. "Establishing Criteria for Elder Selection at the Shiloh Road Church of Christ." 2008.

Ethington, Robert A. "Learning to Lead: Modifying Members' Psychological and Job Readiness Levels to Lead New and Existing Ministries through Situational Leadership Training." 1992.

Gore, Harold T. "Leadership Training for Initiating Ministry Teams at Fellowship Church of Christ." 1996.

Greene, Perry M. "The Initial Impact of a Small Group Bible Study Ministry on a Declining Church." 1990.

Griffith, Anna M. "Implementing an AIDS Ministry Model Inside and Outside the Congregation." 1998.

Hall, Douglas L. "A Roadmap for the Shepherds at Meadowlark Church of Christ." 2005.

Hall, John W. "Equipping Lay Leaders to Manage Pastoral Transitions at the First Baptist Church in Munday, Texas." 1999.

Hayes, Mark K. "Using the Myers-Briggs Type Indicator to Enhance Christian Community." 1993.

Henderson, Robert Mark. "Leadership and the Life of God: Distribution of Ministerial Gifts and Leadership Practices at the Quail Springs Church of Christ." 2004.

Hendrickson, Marion A. "Leadership Training to Equip and Develop Leaders for Service in the Winnie, Texas, Church of Christ." 1998.

Henry, Mark A. "A Model for Training for Outreach to Soldiers at Fort Lewis, Washington, Who Are Inactive Members of the Churches of Christ." 1996.

Hile, Pat Waters. "Oak Hills 101: New-Member Seminar Revision." 2000.

Hubbard, Robert E. "Parental Influence in Faith Formation of Their Children." 1991.

Jenkins, Jerry Austin. "Inspiring a Church to Dream." 1990.

Johnson, Stephen C. "A Narrative Model for Forming Pastoral Leaders at the Edgemere Church of Christ." 2000.

Jordan, Richard Wayne, II. "Building People and Teams for Effective Ministry at the Pitman Creek Church of Christ." 2001.

Keele, Billy Mac. "A Leadership Development Model for Volunteer Church Workers." 1994.

Knox, John. "Developing a Regional Christian Crisis Response Team at the Fifth Street Church of Christ, Woodward, Oklahoma." 2003.

Love, Mark. "Reimagining Evangelism at East County Church of Christ: Nurturing Individuals in the Art of Narrative Evangelism." 1997.

Marcho, Robert K. "The Sanderson Church of Christ: Interim Ministry with a Church in Transition." 1999.

Martin, David Forrest. "When Christians Disagree: Equipping Participants for the Promotion of Redemptive Conflict Management." 2002.

Marutzky, Gregg L. "Transforming Leadership Model for the Denver Church of Christ." 2007.

Morris, Daniel M. "Finding Our Way in Times of Conflict: A Training Seminar for Christian Conflict Management at Third and Central Church of Christ." 2001.

Neill, Jerry A. "Embracing an Informed Vision of the Maturation of the Body of Christ for the Functioning of Elders at the Meadowbrook Church." 2009.

Niestrath, Sean E. "As Those Who Have Hope: A Christian Constructive Approach to Grieving Death Losses among the Members of the East Main Church of Christ, Kalamazoo, Michigan." 2007.

Owen, Larry D. "A Model for Managing Congregation Transition during Leave-Taking by the Senior Minister." 2000.

Pape, Jack N. "A Model for Permission-Giving Leadership at the Eastside Church of Christ." 1997.

Peters, Douglas B. "Selecting Spiritual Leaders: Spiritual Discernment and the Selection of Church Leaders at the North Davis Church of Christ." 2006.

Redd, Harold R. "Leadership Training for Congregational Transition: A Case Study in an African American Church." 2000.

Sampson, David A. "Toward Renewed Theological Identity and Vision: Team Building for the Eldership and Staff of the Park Row Church of Christ." 1990.

Shotwell, Silas Howell. "Applying the Situational Leadership Model to Small Group Leaders in the Conejo Valley Church of Christ." 1990.

Torpy, Thomas James. "An Intervention to Enhance Cohesion for the Campus View Church of Christ and Her Related Campus Ministry." 1999.

Utley, Bruce. "Intergenerational Education in the Church: Assessing a Program of Family Cluster." 1991.

Vinzant, David Gene. "Building Community among Adults of Different Generations." 1997.

Walling, Aaron. "Implementing a Discernment Phase for Those Nominated in the Shepherd Selection Process at the Cinco Ranch Church of Christ." 2011.

Warren, David W. "Developing an Intentional Start-Up Strategy for a New Pastor at the First Baptist Church, Seymour, Texas." 2011.

Willingham, Randy. "Fighting for Peaceful Fighting: A Teaching Ministry Moving Church Members from Suppressing to Managing Conflict." 1995.

Young, Robert J. "Building Cohesion in Church Leadership: A Cohesion Enhancement-Empowerment-Training Model for Leadership Team Building." 1994.

Zustiak, Gary B. "An Educational Manual for the Development of a Congregational AIDS-Procedure Policy." 1994.

Charles Siburt's Career and Work as a Minister, Professor, and Consultant

Compiled by Craig Churchill and Karissa Herchenroeder

Minister

From 1971 to 1988, Charles Siburt served as a full-time minister for three churches, including thirteen years with the Glenwood Church of Christ in Tyler, Texas. Subsequent to his transition from full-time ministry into higher education, he served as interim preaching minister for two churches. The churches he served, along with dates of service, are as follows:

Minister for the Meadow-Lark Church of Christ, Fort Collins, Colorado (1971–73)

Associate Minister for the University Avenue Church of Christ, Austin, Texas (1973–75)

Preaching Minister for the Glenwood Church of Christ, Tyler, Texas (1975–88)

Interim Preaching Minister for the Broadway Church of Christ in Lubbock, Texas (May–Sept, 1989)

Interim Preaching Minister for the Highland Church of Christ in Abilene, Texas (1990–91)

In addition, and largely subsequent to, the preaching responsibilities associated with full-time ministry, Charles frequently served as a guest preacher for churches throughout the country.

These ministerial activities and emphases were consonant with Charles's educational background: "Preaching," was one of his major areas of emphasis as a doctoral student at Austin Presbyterian Theological Seminary, where he received the DMin in 1978.

Charles had an extraordinary influence on the churches he served, and his wife, Judy, was an exemplary partner in ministry. Appropriately enough, the

Herald of Truth named Charles and Judy Siburt as the "Outstanding Family Ministry Couple of the Year" at the National Family Conference in San Antonio, Texas, September 26, 1998.

Professor

Charles's role as a professor emphasized ministering to and educating ministers and church leaders (see also "Consulting," below). Charles's influence was further heightened through his service on numerous committees at ACU (forty-four by his own count). Here follows an outline of Charles's various academic assignments, roles, and responsibilities from 1986 to 2012. All assignments were with ACU unless otherwise indicated.

Academic

Position/Rank:

Adjunct Professor, 1986–88 (Teaching Area: Church Leadership)

Visiting Professor at Pepperdine University, 1987 (Teaching Area: Church Leadership)

Professor of Ministry, 1988–2012 (Teaching Areas: Ministry, Church Leadership, Pastoral Ministry Skills, Conflict Management)

Director, Doctor of Ministry Program, 1988–2012

O. L. and Irene Frazer Professor of Church Enrichment, Graduate School of Theology, 1994–2012 (see also "Committee Service," below)

Associate Dean for Ministry Programs and Services, 1998–2004, 2010–12

Vice President for Church Relations, 2004–10

Courses Taught

BIBM 607 *Introduction to Christian Ministry*

BIBM 644 *Pastoral Ministry Skills for Church Leaders*

BIBM 645 *Managing Conflict in Churches*

BIBM 701 *DMin Orientation*

BIBM 706 *Christian Leadership Development*

BIBM 725 *Project/Thesis Seminar*

Advising

DMin degree advisor for all DMin students, 1988–2012

MDiv degree advisor for all MDiv students, 1997–99

MS degree advisor for all Christian Ministry students, 1996–99

Oral Exams

Served on approximately 150 oral exams for MS, MAR, and MACM candidates

Served on more than seventy-five oral defenses for DMin candidates

Served on approximately fifty comprehensive exams for MDiv candidates

Committee Service (Select)

College:

DMin Program Committee, Chair, 1988–2012

GST Center for Church Enrichment Committee, 1990–2012; Director, 2001–12

GST Strategic Plan Committee, 2002–03

GST Academic Council, 2002–12

GST ATS Self-Study Subcommittee Chair, 2005–06

GST Partnership for Missional Churches Project, Leadership Team, 2008–09

CBS Ministers Renewal Workshop Committee, Chair, 1988–95

CBS Center for Adolescent Studies Advisory Board, 1989–98

CBS Lectures on Preaching Committee, 1989–2005

CBS Library Acquisitions, Liaison, 1991–99

CBS Academic Council, 1994–2000

CBS ACU Lectureship/Summit Committee, 1995–2012

CBS Ministers Support Network Team, Chair, 1997–2012.

CBS Ministry Partners Editorial Committee, 1998–2003

CBS Leadership Team, 1998–2012

CBS Summer Workshop Committee, 2000–2007

CBS ElderLink Forum Team, Chair, 2000–2012

CBS Small Churches Workshop Committee, Chair, 2004–07

CBS Communications and Technology Committee, 2008–12

University:

Search and Review Committee for ACU Provost, 1996

Search and Review Committee for CBS Dean, 1997

SACS Self-Study Committee on Organization and Administration, Chair, 2000–2001

Center for Conflict Resolution Advisory Group, 2001–12

Centennial Spiritual Reaffirmation Task Force, 2003–05

President's Council, 2004–08

Board of Trustees Purpose and Governance Committee, 2004–10

Editorial Committee for *ACU Today*, 2004–10

Calendar Committee, 2004–10
Crutcher and Vickie Scott Foundation Board, 2002–12; Chair, 2010–11
Presidential Search Advisory Committee, 2009

Awards:
Recipient of the CBS Outstanding Graduate Faculty Award, 1994–95.
Recipient of the ACU Faculty Senate Award for Outstanding Service to the University, April 20, 2001.

National/Professional Service:
Association for Doctor of Ministry Education (ADME), Steering Committee, 1990–93; Nominating Committee, 2001
National Board for the Center for Parish Development (CPD), Chicago, Illinois, 1995–2008
Association for Case Teaching (ACT), Search Committee for Director, Cochair, 1998–99
Christian Leaders Benefits Alliance (CLBA; providing benefits for Christian leaders within Churches of Christ), President, 2007–12

Consultant
Charles provided hundreds of presentations for churches in a variety of contexts (consultations, conferences, seminars, workshops, lectureships, retreats, and in one-on-one mentoring contacts with leaders), and he was the theme speaker or keynote lecturer at many of these venues. He provided consulting services for more than 175 congregations and their leaders. Here follows a representative list of consultation themes.
• Conflict Management and Coaching Intervention
• Church Leader Crisis Intervention
• Congregational Effectiveness Assessment (a Ministry Audit)
• Elder Selection Process Coaching
• Leadership Coaching and Team Building
• Minister Effectiveness Coaching
• Minister Growth Review Assessment and Coaching
• Minister Transition and Search Consultation
• New Minister Start-Up Consultation
• Training in Caring Ministry Skills

Awards:

K.C. Mosier Award for Outstanding Service to the Church, from Lubbock Christian University, Lubbock, Texas, March 1, 2003

Distinguished Christian Service Award, [with wife, Judy] from Pepperdine University, Pepperdine Lectures, May 2, 2007

ElderLink (2000–2012)

Compiled by Craig Churchill and Karissa Herchenroeder

Charles Siburt exercised an enormous influence on churches through his leadership and service on various committees and programs, and by his work as a consultant. The select representation of committees on which he served, and the types of consultations he provided (see Appendix C), are suggestive of that influence. Even so, such listings are of limited value: the scope of his involvement with certain programs—and the lives touched through those programs—was extraordinary. Charles's involvement with ElderLink is a case in point.[1]

Charles led the ElderLink Forum (ELF) from its formation in November 2000 until his death in 2012. The most recent, official description and purpose statement of the program is as follows:

> ElderLink is designed to equip, encourage and link those who serve as
> leaders in Churches of Christ. This means that not only elders, but also
> ministers, deacons, ministry leaders and spouses can take advantage
> of an opportunity to improve their leadership skills and experience
> much-needed spiritual refreshment.[2]

Currently, the Siburt Institute Team holds events at various times of the year at the following locations: Highland Oaks Church of Christ, Dallas, Texas; North Atlanta Church of Christ, Atlanta, Georgia; and the Georgetown Church of Christ, Georgetown, Texas.

The times, venues, and frequency of these forums changed over the years. The first ELF was held on November 4, 2000, at the Holiday Inn Select Hotel in Dallas. The most recent event was the Central Texas ElderLink Seminar held in Georgetown on April 21, 2012. At its peak in 2005–06, ElderLink met six times per year. In total, forty-five ElderLink Forums have been held at thirteen different sites, in six states, and two countries. "Brazil ElderLink" met at a retreat center in Sao Paulo, August 4–10, 2010.

Despite the changing venues for ElderLink, Charles's leadership of and participation in the program was a constant. He attended forty-one of the forty-five forums—missing only four due to illness—and directed all forty-five. In addition to leadership and planning responsibilities, Charles often led multiple sessions or provided multiple presentations.

In some ways, Charles's involvement with ElderLink serves as a microcosm for his overall ministry. The qualities of character, gifts, disciplines, and practices that enabled him to have such extraordinary influence through ELF allowed him to excel in other contexts. Among these were a remarkable capacity for leadership; exemplary people skills; the gifts of teaching, encouraging, and mentoring; and his faithfulness and constancy in serving—often through considerable adversity—over many years.

---

1. One might just as easily highlight Charles's involvement with the Ministers Support Network (MSN) to mention another example.

2. "ElderLink," Abilene Christian University, College of Biblical Studies, Siburt Institute for Church Ministry, accessed October 12, 2012, http://www.acu.edu/siburt-institute/elderlink/index.html.

CPSIA information can be obtained at www.ICGtesting.com
Printed in the USA
LVOW080724210513

334747LV00002B/4/P